HOW
TO
STEAL
A
COUNTRY

ROBIN RENWICK
WITH ILLUSTRATIONS BY ZAPIRO

HOW TO STEAL A COUNTRY

STATE CAPTURE AND HOPES FOR THE FUTURE IN SOUTH AFRICA

\Bᵇ\
Biteback Publishing

First published in Great Britain in 2018 by
Biteback Publishing Ltd
Westminster Tower
3 Albert Embankment
London SE1 7SP
Copyright © Robin Renwick 2018

ISBN 978-1-78590-361-8

10 9 8 7 6 5 4 3 2 1

A CIP catalogue record for this book is available from the British Library.

Set in Adobe Caslon Pro and Futura

Printed and bound in Great Britain by
CPI Group (UK) Ltd, Croydon CR0 4YY

For Thuli Madonsela, Pravin Gordhan and all those in the press, judiciary and civil society who combined to 'save South Africa' and its constitution under threat.

CONTENTS

CONTENTS

PREFACE

This book describes the vertiginously rapid descent of political leadership in South Africa from Mandela to Zuma, and its consequences. It may read in parts like a novel – a crime novel – for Sherlock Holmes' old adversary, Professor Moriarty, the erstwhile 'Napoleon of Crime', would have been impressed by the ingenuity, audacity and sheer scale of the looting of the public purse in South Africa and the impunity with which it has been accomplished.

Readers will find an impressive array of rogues and villains in this account, together with some authentic heroes – and heroines. But this is also an uplifting story. For though the odds appeared to be stacked against them and it looked for a while as if they could lose out decisively, those struggling for the chance of a better government in the end prevailed – by just ninety votes.

Is there something in the nature of liberation movements that causes them, once power is achieved, to morph into kleptocracies, as in Angola, Zimbabwe and South Africa under

Zuma? Or is it a function of leadership? How is it that internationally reputable companies such as KPMG, McKinsey, SAP and HSBC are so easily drawn into such a web of corruption?

Is such a process reversible? In South Africa we are about to find out.

In the last years of apartheid, it fell to me to persuade Margaret Thatcher that there could be no solution for South Africa without the ANC. Mandela, however improbably, kept urging me to join it because, he said, 'You think like us.' I told him that I thought like him, but not like a lot of his colleagues. I was fortunate also to count Oliver Tambo as a friend and, in my opinion, the ANC alone was capable of governing South Africa in the first two decades after majority rule. When the only two signed copies of the Freedom Charter came up for auction, I was glad to help buy them for the Liliesleaf Trust and the national archives, it being South Africa's version of Magna Carta. Although the movement had long since had its dark side, given the divisions of the opposition left and right, there are many who have continued to believe that the best outcome for South Africa would be for the ANC to reform itself, the question being whether it can find the capacity to do so.

Corruption has become so endemic within the ruling party, a way of life for so many of the party cadres at the centre and in the regions, that there still are many doubts on that score. Cyril Ramaphosa will have a titanic struggle to do better, but ending the spectacular looting of the state-owned enterprises, which has inflicted so much damage on the economy and the public finances, should be within his grasp.

Twenty-four years into majority rule, the black middle class is numerically stronger, and soon will have more purchasing power, than their white counterparts. The private sector still is dominated by white South Africans, who also own two thirds of the commercially cultivable land. There has been a tidal wave of affirmative action, biased towards the politically connected. The post-apartheid governments have provided low-cost houses, electricity and clean water for millions of black South Africans who had no access to them before. Social grants are being provided to almost 18 million people – one third of the population – who would be in truly desperate poverty without them, but no dent has been made in the vast army of the unemployed.

Acknowledging these major achievements is very different to accepting the party's legitimacy under the presidency of Jacob Zuma. The country has deserved better than the looting of state coffers to which it has been and currently still is subjected. For, despite all the problems from its tragic past, South Africa has succeeded in establishing a non-racial society full of remarkably determined, talented and enterprising people, offering plenty of hope for the future. They include the serried ranks of courageous independent journalists, black and white, who have proved no more able to be silenced today than they were under apartheid, and the judges, who have acted with equal courage and independence. The country contains too much talent, and too large an emerging middle class, to be turned into a banana republic.

Mandela, in my experience, was genuinely colour blind. At

his trial, he declared that he was against white domination, he also was against black domination. He wanted white South Africans to 'feel safe'. He understood that the new South Africa could not thrive without the vital contribution the white community makes to the economy.

The rhetoric from those who just, so narrowly, lost the ANC presidency, was increasingly race based. Instead of attributing the country's ills to the failure to tackle unemployment and promote economic growth, they were supposed to be the fault of 'white minority capital', whereas the only monopolies in fact are the state-owned enterprises, where the worst problems lie. While further 'transformation' certainly will now take place, it is likely to be on a more rational basis.

It is unwise to despair about the 'Beloved Country' of Alan Paton and Nelson Mandela any more than they did, in far worse circumstances. The incredibly narrow cliff-hanging victory of Cyril Ramaphosa and his succession as President will provide far greater integrity at the head of the party and of the country. His greatest difficulty is going to be in dealing with his own colleagues, half of whom, for the past nine years, have been pillars of the Zuma regime.

Yet this wafer-thin victory was of fundamental importance for the South African economy and for the constitution. For continuance of the Zuma regime was fast approaching the point at which it would have proved incompatible with a free press and judiciary, or with free elections.

So how did this extraordinary result come about? It was a famous victory for the still fiercely independent South African press, for a fearless judiciary, a formidably effective and highly motivated civil society and for the outstanding examples set by such champions of integrity as Thuli Madonsela and Pravin Gordhan, battling a fundamentally corrupt and evil system. One of those who did so most effectively, the cartoonist Zapiro, has provided the illustrations for this book. The cumulative effect of their efforts was to persuade delegates who voted for Ramaphosa that, otherwise, they would lose the next election.

So contrary to many expectations, including those at times of the present author, this grim story has become a more hopeful one. Ramaphosa was Mandela's choice to succeed him. The challenges facing him will be huge and will come more from his colleagues than from his political opponents. The jury is still out on whether the ANC will prove to be reformable. But this magnificent country once again will have a President committed to honouring the constitution he helped to negotiate.

INTRODUCTION

'I argued with someone who said that the country comes
first and I said as much as I understand that, I think
my organisation, the ANC, comes first.'

JACOB ZUMA, 7 NOVEMBER 2015

In March 2014, South Africa's Public Protector, Thuli Madonsela, addressed a packed meeting of students at Wits
University in Johannesburg. She had recently published her
report, entitled *Secure in Comfort*, on the 246 million rand
worth of 'security upgrades' at President Zuma's homestead
in the desperately poor neighbourhood of Nkandla in rural
KwaZulu-Natal.

Speaking almost in a whisper to a rapt overspilling audience
in the Senate Hall, she observed that

George Orwell tells us about a community, pretty much like
ours, but it's a community of animals. These animals were
enslaved by humans, and the humans made those animals

work very hard ... the humans ate all of the food and gave the animals very little. Over time, among the animals, leaders emerged that started to tell the animals that it's not right to be oppressed by humans ... one day the animals revolted and kicked the humans out of the farm.

When the animals started to govern their own farm, they created rules for themselves. These rules included all animals are equal, no animal should eat milk or eggs, no animal should sleep in a bed with sheets. It was going to be from each according to their ability, and to each according to his needs. After a little while everyone was happy. The humans were gone. The animals that liberated most of the other animals were the pigs. After a period of time, the pigs started to feel that we liberated you, we deserve better, and after time the pigs started to eat more than the others ... they do all of the thinking, they do all of the coordination, they liberated the animals, they deserve to be fed better. And the rules started changing, imperceptibly overnight ... It used to say all animals are equal, then suddenly, it said some are more equal than others.

* * *

When his great friend Nelson Mandela died in December 2013, Desmond Tutu was given no part in the services of remembrance for him. He was not even on the 5,000-strong guest list for the funeral, though he received a last-minute invitation following a public outcry. He was, he said, very hurt by this, though he was thrilled to be invited to preach at the memorial service in Westminster Abbey.

Archbishop Tutu knew very well why he had not been invited to do so in South Africa. Several months before, he had declared that he would not be voting for the ANC in the 2014 elections. While he had never belonged to a political party, he had wanted to support one that would be close to 'the sort of things that we would love to see. On the whole, the ANC was that. Have you noticed the tense?' He acknowledged the achievements – many more people had electricity and running water, social grants for the poor and, by this time, a huge HIV programme. But he could not accept the self-enrichment, corruption, abuse of power and failure to tackle inequality.

In February 2016 he declared (hyperbolically) that the Zuma government was worse than that under apartheid 'because at least you were expecting it with apartheid'. They had been expecting a government that was sensitive to the constitution. Tutu declared that 'one of the big problems is that the ANC reckons that the freedom we have is due to them' and that others who campaigned against apartheid did not matter. 'Mr Zuma,' he added, 'you and your government don't represent me … You are behaving in a way that is totally at variance with the things for which we stood.' He reminded the ruling party that the Nationalists too had enjoyed a large majority; the ANC 'had better watch out!'

Tutu's differences with the ANC had started long before. No one had done more than he had to support the cause of liberation in the townships. But he was appalled by and did what he could to prevent the killing of 'collaborators' by necklacing (hanging a burning tyre around their necks). A great admirer of the older generation of ANC leaders – Sisulu, Tambo, Kathrada and others, who had sacrificed so much for the cause – he was less impressed by the power-hungry cadres who appeared the moment 'liberation' had been achieved.

It was his initiative to set up the Truth and Reconciliation Commission, which had to listen to the appalling litany of crimes and murders by the apartheid regime, but he found the ANC extremely reluctant to acknowledge any misdeeds of their own, including the arbitrary execution of supposed dissidents at the infamous Quatro camp in Angola. The ANC were furious that the report highlighted these abuses, along with the misdeeds of Winnie Mandela, and by the statement that its armed wing, Umkhonto we Sizwe (MK), had ended up killing more civilians than agents of the regime. Thabo Mbeki denounced 'scurrilous attempts to criminalise the liberation struggle'.

The ANC's attempts to get this part of the report suppressed caused Tutu to denounce the 'abuse of power', warning that 'yesterday's oppressed can quite easily become today's oppressors'. But Mandela intervened to insist that everyone must move on and accept the conclusions of the Commission.

Tutu thereafter was strongly critical of the failure of the Mbeki government to condemn the behaviour of the Mugabe regime in Zimbabwe. In 2008 he said that Mugabe should stand down or be removed by force for 'destroying a beautiful country'. He accused the government of kowtowing to China when it refused to issue a visa to his friend, the Dalai Lama, who was invited to attend the Archbishop's eightieth birthday celebrations. By then, his disillusionment with the ANC in government was complete.

* * *

Along with Archbishop Tutu, the other most popular and admired figure in South Africa is the former Public Protector, Thuli Madonsela. Having grown up in Soweto and attended Evelyn Baring High School in Swaziland, she joined in student protests and was detained for three months in Diepkloof prison. She graduated in law from the University of Swaziland and Wits University,[1] and became an ordinary member of the Pretoria branch of the ANC. She believed, however, that holding political office would not be her 'best contribution as a human being', declining nomination as an ANC MP. As a member of the team who drafted the new constitution, she said of Mandela: 'We will always admire him for gladly submitting his administration to the checks and balances such as the courts and institutions supporting democracy when its actions came into question.'

Madonsela served as a member of the South African Law Reform Commission, before being appointed Public Protector by President Zuma, with all-party support in the National Assembly, in 2009. Zuma declared that she would carry out her work 'without fear or favour'. In 2012 she investigated 'kickbacks' received by the then ANC Youth League leader, Julius Malema, from an engineering contractor.

Her report on the 'security upgrades' to Zuma's homestead at Nkandla (*Secure in Comfort*), published in March 2014, began by quoting the former US Supreme Court Justice Louis Brandeis: 'If the government becomes a lawbreaker, it breeds contempt for the law; it invites every man to become a law unto himself.'

Madonsela concluded that Zuma had benefited unduly from the 246 million rand spent on Nkandla. Among other features of the palatial upgrade was the construction of a large swimming pool, subsequently described as a 'fire pool', a chicken run and an amphitheatre. Her report produced a violent reaction from Gwede Mantashe and Lindiwe Sisulu for the ANC, with Mantashe denouncing it as a 'political' report, followed up by attacks from other leading members of the ANC.

In August 2014 Zuma, who initially had claimed that his family were paying for the upgrades, responded with a submission to Parliament in response to her report. Madonsela replied that this had not answered the questions she had raised. Mantashe and his deputy, Jessie Duarte, said that the ANC wanted her to 'behave correctly', not to abuse her powers, and stop being 'populist'. She subsequently was accused of 'behaving like a counterrevolutionary' and being a CIA spy.

Parliament failed completely in its duty to act on her report. No proper parliamentary inquiry was ever held. Instead, a series of ANC ministers and spokesmen perjured themselves in testifying that Zuma had no case to answer, only for them to be left high and dry when, alarmed at the prospect of an imminent further judgment from the Constitutional Court,

Zuma executed a U-turn, offering to repay the costs of the upgrades deemed to have benefited him personally, to the embarrassment of all the acolytes continuing to insist that he had done nothing wrong.

On 31 March 2016, in a televised ceremony, the full bench of the Constitutional Court, clad in their judicial robes, led by the Chief Justice Mogoeng Mogoeng, delivered a unanimous verdict that the President had acted in violation of the constitution in failing to comply with the Public Protector's judgment that he must pay back the money spent on non-security features of the upgrades to his homestead at Nkandla, such as the swimming pool. Parliament also was criticised by the Court for having failed to uphold the constitution, the ANC members of it having backed Zuma to the hilt in his assertions that he had no case to answer. There could have been no more striking demonstration of the fundamental incompatibility of the Zuma regime and the rule of law.

Having tried and failed to vilify Madonsela, Zuma was obliged to apologise and promise to pay the money back. Demands that the President should resign or be recalled by the ANC for having been found guilty of violating the constitution were dismissed as having no chance of succeeding by Zwelinzima Vavi, former Secretary General of the trade union federation, because, he contended, 'Jacob Zuma is an embodiment of the ANC today'. The Youth and Women's Leagues immediately came out in support of the President, as did the Secretary General, Gwede Mantashe, who declared that, Zuma having apologised, it would be wrong to take any action against him. It was left to the older generation of Robben Islanders led by Ahmed Kathrada, along with Trevor Manuel, to call for his resignation. In the impeachment vote in Parliament, all 243 ANC MPs present supported the absurd proposition that the President had done nothing wrong.

This response, confirming Vavi's analysis, not only betrayed the prior ideals of the ANC, but did nothing to restore public confidence in them or undo the huge amount of damage their unconditional support for Zuma had inflicted on them. Those who did emerge with honour in this affair were Thuli Madonsela and the judges of the Constitutional Court, while South Africa was left to contemplate how it could possibly afford three more years of Jacob Zuma as President.

The doubts as to whether it could do so were further reinforced with the publication in October 2016 of Madonsela's final report, *State of Capture*, setting out in detail the relationships between the President and his family, the Gupta family and the role they appeared to be playing in seeking to remove the Finance Minister and others in the South African Treasury who were an obstacle to their commercial ambitions.

CHAPTER I

FROM MANDELA TO MBEKI

On 10 May 1994 Nelson Mandela was sworn in as the first democratically elected President of South Africa in the presence of his counterparts from around the world, amid scenes of great emotion. The relatively peaceful end to the apartheid regime was hailed as a near miracle around the world and by many in South Africa. It took two Nobel Prize winners, not just one, to steer the country away from the abyss into which it was heading. The apartheid laws had all been repealed not by Mandela, but by F. W. de Klerk who, despite the misgivings of many of his supporters, had shown the political courage and wisdom to take the actions necessary to break the cycle of ever greater political violence and conjure away the spectre of civil war.

In retrospect, it may seem the obvious thing to have done, but when on 2 February 1990 he announced the unbanning of the ANC, the forthcoming release of Mandela and his intention to achieve a negotiated solution, hardly anyone had expected him to do so. Having got to know F. W. de Klerk well over the previous two years, I became convinced that this very conservative but fundamentally decent man would end up surprising us all. De Klerk rang me at midnight before making his speech. 'You can tell your Prime Minister,' he said, 'that she will not be disappointed.' 'We could have held out for another twenty years,' some of his supporters protested, to which de Klerk's reply was 'And what would we have done then?' There are many South Africans, black and white, who would have ended up being killed in further senseless violence but for F. W. de Klerk.

But it was Mandela who, thereafter, became the most admired leader on the planet, and utterly deservedly so, given the magnanimity he displayed towards those who had imprisoned him for twenty-seven years, his lack of bitterness, determination to embrace his former enemies, genuine colour blindness and insistence that the new South Africa should be *inclusive* and not subject to division on racial lines. This did not mean any lack of determination to redress the injustices of the past or to engineer a redistribution of wealth.

On his release from prison, his first act was to read out what the *Financial Times* correspondent described as a 'speech from hell', written for him by the ANC and strongly influenced by Winnie Mandela.[2] But next morning, in the garden of Archbishop Tutu, the world heard the real Mandela declare that he wanted the whites, who were going to have to hand over power, to 'feel safe', believing as he did that the country could not succeed without them.

Having invited Mandela to his first meal in a Johannesburg restaurant after twenty-seven years in jail, I saw him greet every one of the business executives lunching there as if they were long-lost friends, even though, as he well knew, half of them had voted to keep him in prison. When in April 1993, at a crucial moment in the transition to democracy, the ANC's military leader, Chris Hani, was assassinated on the orders of a white extremist, creating a serious risk of racial violence, Mandela took to the airwaves to say that a white neighbour, at risk to herself, forthwith had given the police the licence plate number of the murderer, so as to bring him to justice.

This he followed by inviting General Constand Viljoen, leader of the Afrikaner 'bitter enders' and at the time threatening a coup, to a discussion over tea, with Mandela, naturally, serving the tea himself. The General was disarmed, as most of Mandela's adversaries tended to be, abandoning plans for an insurrection. There followed Mandela's adoption of the Springbok rugby captain, Francois Pienaar, whose team consisted of fourteen white South Africans and one black. When, at the June 1995 Rugby World Cup Final in Johannesburg, Mandela walked out on to the field wearing Pienaar's Springbok jersey, there was not a dry eye among the tens of thousands of Afrikaners present in the stadium.

But the Mandela I knew was no saint. He was, in fact, the craftiest political operator I ever encountered, having met quite a few. His opponents constantly were kept off balance by his tendency at least to pretend to see their point of view. Knowing very well that many in his party had an agenda far more radical than his own, he never hesitated to read out hardline speeches written by his colleagues, while invariably seeking compromise himself. Having founded the military wing of the ANC (MK) as the only way of getting the attention of the regime, he never believed that it would be feasible to defeat them in battle. They could only be defeated politically.

As his great friend Archbishop Tutu observed, this diamond had just one flaw, which was to put his faith in colleagues who did not always deserve his confidence. This led him for years to pretend that the violence affecting South Africa had nothing to do with the ANC, but was entirely the responsibility of their rivals in the Inkatha Freedom Party (IFP) and 'third force' elements supported by sections of the security forces, which were indeed contributing to the mayhem. While the IFP's Chief Buthelezi had refused to negotiate with the government so long as Mandela remained in jail, once he was released, at the behest of ANC militants in Natal, Mandela declined to meet him for a year. This, Mandela confessed to me afterwards, was a mistake. Only once they met did joint efforts begin to be made to reduce ANC/Inkatha violence in Natal.

He did not, in private, really believe in ANC innocence himself. On one occasion, I showed him a photograph of young thugs necklacing a Zulu hostel dweller. 'But these are not our people,' he said. I pointed to the ANC T-shirts they were wearing. Not until shortly before his election as President did he declare publicly that the ANC were just as responsible as others. The great man quite frequently, and deliberately, at least in public, was in denial about the misdeeds of some of his colleagues, whatever he thought of them privately. When I arranged for him to take a holiday in KaNgwane with his and my friend Enos Mabuza, he was bombarded by messages from his wife, heavily involved with violent township youth ('Come back, Baba. We are at war').

Concerned to retain the support of 'the youth', Mandela asked me to help persuade the government to release the young activist Peter Mokaba, only for Mokaba then to make a speech about 'One bullet, one Boer'. When I remonstrated with him about this, Mandela told me, with a straight face, 'The young man must have been misquoted!' He knew perfectly well that this was not the case and Mokaba, I was told by others, got a severe dressing-down. It subsequently was the jackal-like Mokaba who led the attack on Mandela at the last meeting he ever attended of the ANC politburo (see page 24).

Each time he told me that his wife, then standing trial, was innocent of any involvement in the case of Stompie Moeketsi, murdered by her 'football team', I would remain silent, only for him then to say that it was his fault anyway, having abandoned her for twenty-seven years. It was not her other misdeeds that caused him to break with Winnie, but the discovery of her infidelity.

As Mandela said to me, for a leader who loses the support of his followers, it remains only for him to write his memoirs. His loyalty to his party and determination to retain the support of all sections of it, including especially the youth wing, could lead him to defend the indefensible, as he did in March 1994 just six weeks before the elections, when guards at Shell House, the ANC headquarters in Johannesburg, opened fire on Inkatha demonstrators, killing nineteen of them. He even claimed that he had given the order to defend the building and to 'kill, if necessary', though in fact the order to shoot was given in panic by the head of security there. The Nugent Commission of Inquiry rejected ANC claims that Inkatha had been responsible, declaring that the shooting had been unjustified.

In his book *Knowing Mandela*, John Carlin paints a portrait of the real Mandela, at least as wily as he was saintly, insisting on both counts on the inclusion of verses from the Afrikaner anthem *Die Stem* in the new national anthem and that the rugby team should go on calling themselves the Springboks.

Following repeated clashes between Zulu hostel dwellers and ANC youth in Katlehong, addressing an extremely militant ANC crowd, demanding weapons and no peace, Mandela told them that they too were responsible for the violence. 'You must ask a member of Inkatha, why are we fighting?' When this produced an uproar: 'Listen to me! Listen to me! I am your leader! Do you want me to go on leading you?' until the crowd were subdued.[3]

The least ideological of politicians, Mandela actually had been classified briefly as a member of the South African Communist Party by virtue of his leadership of MK, but all those imprisoned with him on Robben Island knew that he was an African nationalist, whose one absolute guiding principle was one person, one vote. While on the Island, there were some fiery exchanges between Mandela and Govan Mbeki, father of Thabo, in response to Mbeki senior's hardline communist views.

In a series of meetings with him after his release Mandela from time to time would urge me to join the ANC – a curious proposition to make to Thatcher's envoy. It was, he claimed, a broad church, 'and you think like us'. The ANC to him was not a party, but a movement. He told his friend George Bizos that, when he died, he would seek among the Elysian fields to join the local branch of the ANC.

When I raised with him the commitment in the Freedom Charter to public ownership of the banks and mines, Mandela said with a smile, 'It was fashionable then!' (when he was about to go to jail), adding, 'And we got these ideas from you!' I said that they had ceased to be fashionable, even in the Soviet Union.

While the rest of the ANC, even after his release, wanted to continue fighting with Margaret Thatcher about sanctions, Mandela knew from his great friend, the anti-apartheid campaigner Helen Suzman, who had secured for the Robben Islanders many improvements in their conditions of imprisonment, and from me – as I was permitted to reply to a letter he had written to me from jail – the efforts Thatcher had been making to help get him released. Whatever the rest of the movement thought, Mandela told me, he was determined to 'get her on my side'. Conducting a hilarious rehearsal for his meeting with her, I told him that we would support him on 'one person, one vote', but 'You must stop all this nonsense about nationalising the banks and the mines.'

I asked Thatcher to give him time to tell her his story. 'You mean I mustn't interrupt him?' she said. And she didn't, in – a record for her – nearly an hour. For she was just as impressed as others by the extraordinary dignity and lack of bitterness of her visitor. As the meeting went on for ever, the journalists outside started to chant 'Free Nelson Mandela'. On emerging, he declared: 'She IS an enemy of apartheid.' But not before she had told him to 'stop all this nonsense about nationalising the banks and the mines', provoking a grin from him to me.

He was an even greater success with the Queen, who he took to calling Elizabeth – not a form of address permitted to anyone else on the planet, save the Duke of Edinburgh.

As for his personal style, his most effective and acerbic critic in Parliament was the leader of the Democratic Party, Tony Leon. The party had a proud history in the efforts its forebear, the Progressive Federal Party (PFP), had made in opposing every aspect of apartheid, but had been wiped out in the 1994 elections, emerging with just 1.7 per cent of the votes. When Mandela said that he was fed up being attacked by the representative of a Mickey Mouse party, Leon replied that he was fed up with Mandela's 'Goofy economics'. While in intensive care after being struck down by a heart attack, Leon heard a voice behind the curtain say: 'Hello, Mickey Mouse, this is Goofy,' as Mandela visited him in hospital.[4]

Meeting Mandela on his return from a visit to Libya, I told him as politely as I could that it was not a good idea to have described Gaddafi as a 'great supporter of human rights', only to be interrupted by Helen Suzman. 'How could you be so silly, Nelson!' she exclaimed.

He never held these exchanges against her. As, to the fury of his colleagues, she lambasted the ANC government for its misdemeanours, just as she had their predecessors, he wrote her a letter to say that he was beginning to feel sorry for her former opponents in the National Party.[5]

A few months before the 1994 elections Mandela asked me to arrange a dinner at the British embassy in Washington, at which he could appeal to investors to return to South Africa.

Discarding at my request the usual dreadful speech written for him by the ANC, Mandela announced that he intended to invite Buthelezi to join the new government, and Derek Keys, who was serving under F. W. de Klerk, to stay on as Finance Minister. When I pointed out to him that several of the businessmen travelling with him had been pillars of the old regime, Mandela laughed and said: 'But I need them now.'

Mandela told Helen Suzman that he did not want his party to win more than two thirds of the vote, as he did not want there to be any temptation to try to change the constitution. Before becoming President, he had cultivated the friendship of the two most distinguished business leaders in South Africa: Harry Oppenheimer and Anton Rupert. They and others also helped to persuade him that nationalisation was not going to be the answer to South Africa's problems, but economic policy was a subject he left firmly to his deputy, Thabo Mbeki. That applied to the conduct of the government in general, with Thabo acting as de facto Prime Minister, while Mandela contented himself with presiding and, to worldwide applause, playing his iconic role in the political stratosphere. Mbeki found this frustrating. Mandela, said Mbeki, paid no attention to the actual business of government, so he had to. Mbeki resented 'Mandela exceptionalism'.

Mandela in his inauguration speech had added himself the words in Afrikaans, 'Let's forget the past. What's done is done.' This was not the philosophy of Mbeki, who felt that Mandela was earning media applause as a 'good native'.

The body language between the two was never very good and

in 2003 Mbeki, now President, arriving late for a dinner attended also by Mandela, was upset to receive a stinging public rebuke. One legacy of Mandela's years of iron discipline as a prisoner was a fetish about punctuality. Every meeting with him was expected to start to the minute on time. Robert Mugabe, arriving two hours late for a Southern African summit presided over by Mandela, was subjected to a tirade by him about his discourtesy.

To help break a deadlock in the negotiations for a new constitution, and to guard against militant right-wing resistance to the new regime, it was Joe Slovo, head of the South African Communist Party (SACP), who had proposed that the first post-apartheid government should be required to be a 'government of national unity'. The government that took office following the 1994 elections, therefore, under the terms of the interim constitution, was a coalition including the ANC, the National Party (which, under de Klerk, had won 20 per cent of the votes) and the IFP, which had won in KwaZulu-Natal.

The ANC refused to contemplate any form of further power-sharing in the final constitution, adopted in 1996, though Buthelezi served in the government until 2004.

In response to public criticism by de Klerk of the ANC's position on various issues, Mandela launched a tirade against him in a Cabinet meeting in January 1995, causing de Klerk to consider withdrawing from the government there and then, only to find next day Mandela 'his usual charming self'. There followed, on the subject of violence in Natal, an exchange of letters ending with Mandela, in reply to the man who had freed him from jail, denouncing the legacy of 'the inhumane system of apartheid, of which you were one of the architects'. These and subsequent attempts to denigrate de Klerk reflected ANC concerns about his popularity, including with many non-whites. Yet when he attended Mandela's funeral celebration in Soweto in December 2013, de Klerk was applauded by the huge crowd in the stadium, while Jacob Zuma was booed by it.

Following the adoption of the final constitution, de Klerk concluded that it no longer served any purpose to continue serving in government. Some of his colleagues disagreed, founding the New National Party (NNP), aligned with the ANC. A year later, de Klerk withdrew from party politics, establishing a foundation to help protect the constitution.

Annoyed to hear from his biographer, Anthony Sampson, and others that Mandela had started saying that he had preferred dealing with P. W. Botha, I asked to see him in the President's office in Cape Town. I recalled that in that office I had argued unsuccessfully with Botha for his release, and – more successfully – for some of his supporters' lives, in particular those of the Sharpeville Six. But for de Klerk, he might still be in jail. Mandela laughed, telling his assistant, 'The ambassador is right,' and that he should make some peace offering to de Klerk.

*   *   *

Though nearly everyone wanted him to serve a second term as President, Mandela was not to be persuaded. He wanted to set an example to others in Africa by relinquishing power long before he had to. Thabo Mbeki was not Mandela's chosen successor. While admiring his competence, he had reservations about Mbeki's personality and would have preferred as his successor Cyril Ramaphosa, who had led the National Union of Mineworkers and negotiated the new constitution for the ANC.

With his father in jail, Thabo Mbeki, after a period of student activism that earned him six weeks in detention, had been despatched into exile at the age of twenty. It took him nearly thirty years to be able to return to South Africa. Regarded from the outset as ANC royalty and shown great kindness by Oliver and Adelaide Tambo, after studying at Sussex University, he was fast-tracked as the youngest and smartest member of the future party leadership. As, thanks to his intelligence and Tambo's patronage, he progressed rapidly upwards within the party's ranks, he had to guard himself against its own jealousies and internal conspiracies. It was never an easy apprenticeship and nor did he ever enjoy much popularity with the rank and file.

Mbeki never believed in the ANC mantra of a seizure of power, subscribed to, among others, by his greatest potential rival, Chris Hani. He understood that the apartheid state was far too powerful for that to be a realistic option. Instead, as he told me, what he believed in was seduction.

Having given up the leadership of his party to do so, in 1987 Van Zyl Slabbert led a group mainly of Afrikaners to a meeting with Mbeki at Dakar in Senegal. He did so at risk to his freedom and even life. In the British embassy, we were sufficiently concerned about what might happen to Slabbert and his colleagues to be among those meeting them at the airport on their return. As we warned Van Zyl, given the existence of P. W. Botha's death squads, he was a potential target for assassination. Slabbert, Willi Esterhuyse and Alex Boraine – described as 'useful idiots' by P. W. Botha – had been deeply impressed by Mbeki's intelligence, reasonableness and readiness to compromise. The pipe-smoking Mbeki, often clad at the time in a tweed jacket, was very reassuring to his new-found Afrikaner friends.

In one very important respect, however, they were to feel that they had been misled. This was the impression given by Mbeki that the ANC were ready to be inclusive in their approach to governing South Africa, which proved not to be the case. Slabbert especially felt badly disillusioned by this – with Helen Suzman, who had a better understanding of the Manichaean nature of the ANC, asking him: 'Well, what did you expect?'

When it came to Mandela's succession, the ANC exiles had been ruthless about sidelining the internal resistance, led by the United Democratic Front (UDF), which had done as much or more to bring down apartheid as the exiles had. The party apparatus were adamant that Mbeki must be the successor, as were the alliance partners, the South African Communist Party (SACP) and the Congress of South African Trade Unions (Cosatu). So Mbeki was appointed Deputy President and duly was anointed as Mandela's successor at the ANC conference in 1997, to the bitter disappointment of Ramaphosa. Rejecting Mandela's offer to make him Foreign Minister, his reaction to being outmanoeuvred by Mbeki was to opt out of politics and concentrate on developing his business career. Mandela reacted philosophically to this, telling his and Ramaphosa's friend Johann Rupert that it could be no bad thing for the 'young man' to go off and make some money, so that he could act without fear or favour when he returned to government, as Mandela hoped and believed he would.

At the conference, Mandela, very uncharacteristically, made a four-hour speech, largely written for him by Mbeki. He denounced corruption to, ironically, the cheers of the delegates and included a rant against the press and non-governmental organisations which had dared to be critical of the government. But he also delivered a warning, not appreciated by Mbeki, that a leader who was elected unopposed could be tempted to surround himself with yes-men and -women, whereas he had a special responsibility to listen to others and to govern inclusively. Mbeki's clumsy response was to say, when asked how he could step into Mandela's shoes, that he would not dream of doing so, as Mandela wore such ugly shoes. He also made an attempted joke about Mandela carrying his briefcase.

It would be a mistake to imagine that the Mandela years were not marked by signs of trouble to come. Hopes that the South African Broadcasting Corporation might enjoy a measure of independence, rather than acting as a mouthpiece of the government, were shortlived. The country was afflicted by a tidal wave of violent crime. Mandela himself was not above launching attacks on the press, though no one doubted his genuine commitment to press freedom, in contrast to the attitude of some of his colleagues. It also was, at any rate nominally, on his watch that the ANC government became embroiled in the first of its major scandals, the arms deal, characterised by the extremely shady dealings chronicled by Andrew Feinstein, at the time an ANC MP, in his book *After the Party*.[6]

CHAPTER II

THE TROUBLE WITH THABO

Thabo Mbeki's major contribution to post-apartheid South Africa was his successful management of the economy which, during his term of office, grew at a rate of 4.5 per cent per annum and was marked by the development of a rapidly expanding black middle class. South Africa in this period attracted the bulk of foreign direct investment in Africa. These results were achieved on the basis of orthodox economic policies, with an emphasis on fiscal discipline, which were criticised from the left and by the trade unions, but delivered impressive results. To reassure the extremely nervous financial markets, in June 1996, the market-friendly Growth, Employment and Redistribution policy (GEAR) had been put forward by Mbeki and Trevor Manuel, with little consultation with the unions and Mbeki allegedly declaring 'Call me a Thatcherite'.

An integral part of this programme was the policy of Black Economic Empowerment (BEE), facilitating a transfer of wealth which benefited mainly the expanding black middle class, and particularly the political elements within it.

Employment equity schemes favouring the advancement of black professionals led to some over-promotions but made a major contribution to the emergence of a self-confident new professional class. The policy was less successful in addressing the problem of mass unemployment, which remained stubbornly high at over 25 per cent of the workforce, or the lack of basic skills among the vast army of unemployed.

The South African government was well served by a first-rate Finance Minister, Trevor Manuel, and Treasury team, and impressive leadership of the Reserve Bank, but Mbeki himself was the key factor in ensuring that the policies set were implemented and adhered to. Whatever the negatives about his presidency, this was a huge service he rendered to post-apartheid South Africa and a period in which it proved possible to achieve both growth and redistribution, at any rate to the rapidly expanding black middle class.

Unfortunately, the negatives were quite a few. The country suffered from one of the highest violent crime rates in the world. The struggle against apartheid had left plenty of weapons in the townships and people who knew how to use them. The extremes of wealth and poverty self-evidently were a major contributing factor. According to external studies, a differentiating factor about crime in South Africa was the very high degree of violence associated with it. Highly organised criminal gangs engaged in a systematic campaign of carjackings in the urban areas. The transformation of the police from the grim white-led force it had been into a black-led and officered force inevitably was accompanied by disruption. Black policemen living in the townships frequently came under pressure from the 'tsotsis' (gangsters) also living there. In many cases where arrests were made, there were failures in achieving successful prosecutions as the papers were mislaid or incomplete and the prosecuting system crumbled under the sheer weight of criminal activity taking place. Johannesburg had claimed the title of murder capital of the world. South Africa also was leading the world in violence against women, mainly rape.

This tidal wave of crime affected the black population worse than the white community, but the outcry from white South Africans and the 'white' press infuriated Mbeki. In 2004 he launched an attack on commentators who argued that violent crime was out of control, calling them white racists who wanted the country to fail. Some journalists, he contended, depicted black people as 'barbaric savages' who liked to rape and kill. One campaigner, who had herself been raped, was accused of 'saying our cultures, traditions and religions as Africans inherently make every African man a potential rapist'. In 2007, the *African Peer Review* reported that South Africa had the world's second highest murder rate – with Mbeki still arguing that fears of violent crime were exaggerated, reflecting a 'populist' view.

Tony Leon, leader of the opposition Democratic Alliance, dismayed many of his colleagues by suggesting re-establishment of the death penalty. Mbeki came close to suggesting that whites who were so negative should leave the country, and indeed, among the several hundred thousand white South Africans who have left since 1994, the main contributing cause declared by them has been violent crime, followed by a perceived lack of opportunities due to affirmative action.

Mbeki's denialism was the more surprising and unnecessary as the government was trying to do more to cope with the problem, and the murder rate did fall significantly for a time. The denialism did not survive his departure, with the South African government ever since accepting that violent crime is a major problem that has to be confronted, with one Zuma minister, Susan Shabangu, famously or infamously urging the police to 'shoot the bastards'. The murder rate, which at one stage had fallen to just over thirty a day, currently is back up to nearly fifty a day and South Africa remains near the top of the list for violence against women as well.

* * *

When the Mandela government took over in 1994, a powerful lobby within it led by the Defence Minister, Joe Modise, argued for a large and expensive programme to modernise South Africa's defences. The main focus was on the air force and navy, which had been debilitated by sanctions.

The Cabinet committee to decide on the procurement of new weapons and equipment was chaired by the de facto Prime Minister, Thabo Mbeki, without whose advocacy it would not have happened. For the navy, the decision was taken to buy new fast corvettes and, bizarrely, three new submarines, even though there manifestly was no external threat to South Africa. No member of the South African government at the time was able to explain to me why the country needed submarines. The ships were bought from Germany, with the French armaments company, Thomson-CSF (now Thales), providing the weapons systems for the corvettes.

When it came to the air force, the decision, heavily influenced by Modise, against all expert advice, was to buy Gripen fighters from Sweden and Hawk trainer aircraft from British Aerospace, even though the Hawks were more expensive and arguably less capable than the Italian Aeromacchi. When the Gripen/Hawk decision was announced, the Secretary for Defence, General Pierre Steyn, resigned in protest. The Gripens were suited to conventional combat rather than peacekeeping operations. The total estimated cost of the programme was close to 50 billion rand, at a time when the rand stood at six to the dollar.

Crucial to the presentation of this immensely expensive programme, amid South Africa's other more pressing needs, was the contention that the country would benefit from huge offsetting investments from the companies profiting from these contracts. To a large degree, the offsetting investments were never forthcoming, with the government subsequently revealing that the armaments companies would face only very limited penalties for failing to meet these undertakings.

The Auditor General had identified the arms deal as 'high risk' from an audit point of view. In September 1999 the Pan Africanist Congress MP, Patricia de Lille, presented in Parliament a private document by 'concerned' ANC MPs about possible corruption in relation to the deal.

An inquiry by the Auditor General and other government investigating agencies was heavily sanitised before it was released. But it revealed that the head of procurement at the Ministry of Defence, Chippy Shaik, had been actively involved in the meeting that decided the award of the information management system for the corvettes to African Defence Systems (ADS), despite his brother Schabir's major shareholding in Nkobi Holdings, the partner for this purpose of ADS and Thomson-CSF. The tender had been awarded to ADS despite a lower bid from another contractor, which Shaik had inflated by adding a 'risk factor'.

The Defence Minister, Joe Modise, who had insisted on favouring British Aerospace, by this time had acquired interests in a company designed to benefit from their industrial development programme. His close associate, the ANC-connected fixer Fana Hlongwane, was acknowledged to have received multimillion-dollar payments as an intermediary for British Aerospace. The defence was that he was 'simply paid for services rendered'.

Mbeki responded furiously to allegations that the initial inquiry was a cover-up, in what by now had become familiar terms. Behind these claims, he declared, was the 'racist conviction that Africans, who now govern the country, are mutually prone to corruption, venality and mismanagement ... that Africans and black people generally are corrupt'. He demanded 'an end to the insulting lie that we, as Africans, we are less than human'.

A far more damning original version of the Auditor General's report eventually found its way into the public domain. Chippy Shaik had claimed that his brother's company, ADS, had no connection with Thomson when the contract was awarded to ADS. In reality, Thomson had bought a 50 per cent stake in ADS.

With the case now being pursued by the Scorpions, the special investigating agency established by Mandela and Mbeki and led by Bulelani Ngcuka, in 2002 the *Mail and Guardian* alleged that Deputy President Jacob Zuma had solicited a payment of 500,000 rand from Thomson-CSF. Shaik was then charged with fraud. Ngcuka said that there was a prima facie case of corruption against the Deputy President. In 2003 *City Press* printed allegations that Ngcuka had been an apartheid-era spy. These were found by the Hefer Commission to have originated with Moe Shaik, brother of Schabir and Chippy Shaik, who had been involved with Zuma in underground operations of the ANC, and with the ANC veteran, Mac Maharaj. The allegations proved to be baseless, but Ngcuka resigned.

In May 2005 Judge Hilary Squires found Schabir Shaik guilty of corruptly trying to influence the decisions of the Deputy President. The judgment showed that between his return from exile in 1995 and 2002 Shaik had 'loaned' Zuma 1.2 million rand. In September 1999 he allegedly met a Thomson executive, Alain Thetard, to request a payment for Zuma. In March 2000 Shaik, Thetard and Zuma met in Durban. According to Squires' judgment, Thomson agreed to pay Zuma 500,000 rand a year in return for his protection against any inquiry into the dealings of Thomson-CSF. Schabir Shaik was sentenced to fifteen years in prison and lost his appeals, but served only a short period in jail before being released on controversial medical grounds.

*　*　*

As he showed in periodic outbursts as President, unlike Mandela, who regarded the white community, despite the horrors of apartheid, as having a vital role to play in the future of the country, Mbeki was hypersensitive to criticism in general, but especially if it came from white South Africans, many of whom he regarded as his intellectual inferiors. This was the more surprising as, ever since his days at Sussex University, he had been the darling of European liberal intellectuals whom he had helped to convince of the ANC's non-racialism.

It was this not even latent suspicion of and hostility to white certainties that led to his tragic denialism about Aids. Mbeki, surfing the internet in support of his prejudices, and fastening on to the ideas of dissident 'experts', convinced himself that HIV did not cause Aids. He declared that no one actually died of Aids, that the categorisation of the problem was related to racist attitudes about Africans and to the determination of Western pharmaceutical companies to oblige African governments to purchase unaffordable treatments.

Mbeki, who at this stage was appearing to see virtually everything in racial terms, believed that Aids orthodoxy was being used to portray a 'depraved people' as 'perishing from self-inflicted disease'. The real causes, according to him, were deprivation and poverty. These theories were loyally supported by his hopeless Health Minister, Manto Tshabalala-Msimang. His government's refusal to supply anti-retroviral drugs to pregnant women to prevent transmission of the disease to their children resulted in many tens of thousands of avoidable deaths.

In April 2000, Mbeki had caused consternation to Western leaders by writing to Bill Clinton, Tony Blair and others about a 'scientific view against which dissent is prohibited', causing them to worry that their highly intelligent counterpart had gone slightly mad.

Mbeki continued to resent the large shadow cast by his predecessor. Mandela was finding his advice entirely unwelcome to his successor. He told me that he could get through to any head of government in the world except his own, who would not take his phone calls.

In July, Mandela appealed for an end to disputes about the science and that 'we proceed to address the needs and concerns of those who are suffering and dying'. In September 2000, Mandela declared that HIV definitely caused Aids. In the same month, Mbeki told the ANC parliamentary party that nonsense was being reported about Uganda's success against Aids. Vaccines caused other diseases. 'If we say HIV = Aids, that means = drugs ... The CIA has got involved ... US companies wanted it to be a virus'. This bizarre statement was greeted with cries of 'Viva Thabo, Viva'.

The Health Minister rejected an offer from Germany to provide anti-retroviral drugs free of charge. In November 2001, after his attempts to meet Mbeki on the subject had been rebuffed, Mandela called publicly on Mbeki and his wife, Zanele, who Mandela knew to be just as concerned as he was, to assume personally leadership of the campaign against Aids.

Mandela made attempts for several months to see Mbeki about Aids, but kept being put off. He then attended a meeting of the ANC politburo, the National Executive Committee, to deal with the issue, but Mbeki was conspicuously absent. Mandela joked that he must have been 'too busy' to attend. Mandela argued that they were giving the impression that they did not care about the victims of Aids and that they must supply anti-retrovirals to pregnant women as a start.

This was followed by a further meeting of the National Executive Committee in March 2002, to which Mandela was summoned. In the meeting, Mbeki's acolytes were encouraged by the presidency to attack Mandela. One after another did so, in the words of one of those present, 'like a pack of dogs'. Mandela was told that he was retired, should not have spoken publicly and was heckled and jeered at. A furious Mandela never attended another leadership meeting of the ANC.

At this point the South African courts ordered the government to make anti-retrovirals available to pregnant women. Yet in 2003 Mbeki still was saying that he did not know anyone who had died of Aids or suffering from HIV. This was despite the fact that many ANC MPs were taking the anti-retroviral drugs denied to others. Mbeki's spokesman, Parks Mankahlana, died of Aids, as did the head of the ANC youth league, Peter Mokaba, who had led the attacks on Mandela at the ANC leadership meeting in March 2002. Mandela declared that one of his sons had died of Aids, as did Buthelezi. None of this affected Mbeki's denialism, with a document circulated by him claiming that Mankahlana had died from the anti-retrovirals he was taking, not from Aids.

Tutu's successor, Archbishop Ndungane, declared the government's inaction on Aids to be a world disgrace as serious as apartheid. The Health Minister was reappointed after the 2004 election, even though she was an alcoholic in need of a liver transplant. In 2008 the *New York Times* estimated that, because of Mbeki's Aids denialism, 350,000 people had died. Mbeki's successors did not have his hang-ups about Aids. Today South Africa has a massive, well-conducted anti-Aids programme under the present Health Minister, Aaron Motsoaledi.

In the months before the 1995 Commonwealth heads of government conference in New Zealand, Nelson Mandela was extremely concerned about the fate of the Nigerian writer, Ken Saro-Wiwa, sentenced to death by the notoriously corrupt and autocratic Abacha government in Nigeria. The world, he said, expected a response from him, but he was persuaded to leave this problem to Mbeki, who was confident that he could solve it quietly through his contacts in Lagos. At the outset of the Commonwealth conference, Mandela was furious to discover that Saro-Wiwa had been executed. Cyril Ramaphosa, at the time still Secretary General of the ANC, called on the Commonwealth to expel Nigeria forthwith. In Wellington, Mandela declared that he would lead the move to suspend Nigeria from the Commonwealth, with Mbeki still feeling that this was hasty and ill-considered.

* * *

Nelson Mandela, as he told me on more than one occasion, could not stand Robert Mugabe, who he regarded as totally uninterested in the welfare of his people and responsible for most of their suffering. He was in the habit of referring to him derisively as 'Comrade Bob'. Asked when he was no longer President what should be done about Mugabe, Mandela said that he should be removed. When asked how, he replied 'If necessary, take up arms!' This earned him a rebuke from the Mbeki government, intent on pursuing 'quiet diplomacy'.

Having declared that Africa was about to undergo a Renaissance and having agreed with other countries on the New Partnership for Africa's Development (NEPAD), extolling the virtues of true democracy for the continent, Mbeki was confronted with the problem of Zimbabwe. In 2000, infuriated by defeat in a referendum to increase the already large powers of the presidency, orchestrated by the opposition Movement for Democratic Change (MDC), Mugabe unleashed bands of 'war veterans', in reality young thugs paid by the Central Intelligence Organisation, to drive white farmers off their land, causing a catastrophic fall in food production.

In April 2002, Mbeki believed that he had persuaded Mugabe to call off the land invasions in return for Britain renewing funding for land reform, only for Mugabe to renege on this. In August, Mugabe and Mbeki made a joint announcement that the 'war veterans' were being recalled, only for Mugabe again to renege on this supposed agreement.

In rigged elections in Zimbabwe in 2002, to general amazement, the South African observer mission, on instructions from the presidency, declared that 'they should be considered legitimate', with the rest of the world united in condemning the outcome. Mbeki also had sent two South African judges, Sisi Khampepe and Dikgang Moseneke, to observe the elections. Their report was kept secret until the *Mail and Guardian* forced its publication in 2014. It stated that the elections could not be considered free and fair and documented over 100 murders, mostly committed against supporters of the opposition Movement for Democratic Change.

Mbeki, on two subsequent occasions, including before the even more blatantly rigged 2008 elections, told me that he had persuaded Mugabe to retire. I said that if this was so, he would deserve the Nobel Peace Prize, but that, knowing Mugabe as I did, I did not for one moment believe that he would ever willingly stand down so long as there was a breath left in his body. Mbeki must have known this too. His whitewash of the 2008 elections was described by *The Economist* as 'unconscionable'.

Following the 2008 election, Mbeki devoted his efforts to shoehorning the MDC into a coalition on Mugabe's terms, which did achieve some improvement in the economy, thanks to the MDC Finance Minister, Tendai Biti, who abolished the country's by now worthless currency, but neutered the opposition as a political force.

The failure of South Africa to stand up for human rights in Zimbabwe was denounced by the ANC veteran Tokyo Sexwale, given the extent to which those who had struggled against apartheid had depended on external support. The cost of inaction included the effects on the South African economy of 4 million refugees arriving from Zimbabwe.

Mbeki from the outset had appeared prejudiced against the Movement for Democratic Change and its leader, the former trade unionist Morgan Tsvangirai.

When Zuma took over from Mbeki, there were hopes that he might be tougher with Mugabe, but these were soon disappointed. A dinner I was asked to arrange for Zuma in London, shortly before he became President, coincided with a refusal by shipworkers in Durban to unload a consignment of arms for Zimbabwe. Zuma had his own connection to the opposition in Zimbabwe, as one of his and Dlamini-Zuma's daughters was married to the son of Welshman Ncube, at the time prominent in the MDC, and we all drank a toast to the shipworkers. But once in office, as expected, the Zuma government continued to pursue a complaisant attitude towards Mugabe.

The opposition in Zimbabwe were well aware that they would never be allowed to win an election. But Mugabe's efforts to ensure that he was succeeded by his wife, Grace, ended by bringing about his downfall. Following an attempt to poison her principal rival, Emmerson Mnangagwa, who was dismissed by Mugabe as Vice-President, the Zimbabwe army chiefs, who had served with Mnangagwa in the bush war, revolted in his favour and forced the resignation of Mugabe, after thirty-seven years in power in Zimbabwe.

A friend in one of the most senior positions in the ANC had confirmed to me at the time why we were wasting our time urging the South African government to be more robust in its dealings with Mugabe. Mugabe was applauded from time to time by crowds in South Africa precisely because he had seized the land back from the whites, whatever the consequences. The opposition was led by the head of the trade unions in Zimbabwe. The ANC had worries that the same might happen closer to home. Above all, the ANC were determined that the liberation movement must not lose power. That would create an extremely dangerous precedent.

Mbeki's extraordinary and totally unnecessary denialism about Aids was far more damaging to his legacy than Zimbabwe, overshadowing his considerable achievements as President. For, in retrospect, his tenure has looked like something of a golden era for South Africa in which, thanks to economic policies guided by him, the country achieved rates of economic growth well in excess of the increase in the population and which saw a rapid expansion of the black middle class, in contrast to the lost decade the country has endured under his successor.

While Mbeki's macroeconomic policies were successful in promoting economic growth, it was on his watch and not that of Zuma that the country ran out of power. The government had failed to invest in new capacity for the power utility Eskom. Electricity prices were held artificially low as the government sought to deliver power to millions of households that had never enjoyed it before, and they were successful in doing so, though frequently not in securing payment for it. Under incompetent, over-promoted senior management, the company had run down stocks at the power stations in favour of 'just in time' delivery.

As a deliberate policy, Eskom had become highly dependent on supplies from new black-majority-owned mining groups who could not always deliver on time. At the end of 2007, when deliveries stalled, so did the power stations, plunging the country into several years of 'load shedding', otherwise known as power cuts.[7]

Power supplies to the mines and industrial enterprises had to be rationed. Power cuts knocking out the traffic lights in Johannesburg created chaos in the city and the impression that South Africa, with by far the most advanced economy in the region, was heading rapidly in the direction of some of its least successful neighbours.

In the longer term the situation was retrieved by a $3.75 billion loan from the World Bank to build two massive new power stations in the next several years, while sharp electricity price increases affected demand. To the annoyance of Robert Zoellick, head of the World Bank, the US and Britain voted against the loans because the new plants would be coal-fired. As Zoellick pointed out, the alternative would have been to leave South Africa short of power for the foreseeable future.

The new plants took years longer to build than scheduled. Hitachi gained valuable contracts through an association with the ANC's investment vehicle, Chancellor House, but there were difficulties with its performance. Power cuts did not end until 2016 as the new Medupi power plant came on stream, aided by weak demand from the depressed economy. The South African economy, which grew at 5 per cent in 2007, has never looked like reaching that level of growth since. The costs to the economy from this avoidable disaster have been incalculable.

CHAPTER III

THE DOWNFALL OF MBEKI

Having grown up amid the infighting within the ANC in exile and seen off the challenges to his pole position from, first, Chris Hani, and then Cyril Ramaphosa, Mbeki was paranoid about possible further challenges to him, as were his intelligence and security ministers and his closest adviser, Essop Pahad. In 2001 the country was astonished to be told by the Minister of Safety and Security, Steve Tshwete, that a plot had been uncovered whereby Cyril Ramaphosa and the former Premiers of Gauteng and Mpumulanga, Tokyo Sexwale and Mathews Phosa, were planning to oust Mbeki. No shred of evidence was produced for this and Tshwete ended up having to apologise. From Mbeki's point of view, however, the 'plot' had served its purpose as, like Ramaphosa, Sexwale and Phosa thereafter had to concentrate on their business interests, though they remained members of the ANC's National Executive Committee. This episode was to come back to haunt Mbeki a few years later.

In the 2004 elections, albeit with a lower turnout, the ANC

won its highest share of the vote at 69.4 per cent, thereby exceeding the two thirds majority required to amend the constitution, though Mbeki, to his credit, showed no wish to do so. The civil service by this time had been 'transformed'. The Treasury and Reserve Bank remained islands of competence and high performance amid a sea of mediocrity elsewhere in the increasingly bloated bureaucracy, attributable to the 'deployment' of party cadres to fill posts for which frequently they were underqualified.

The ANC doctrine that party loyalists must be 'deployed' to posts at all levels and in all government services – central, regional and local – and wherever else the government has been able to influence such appointments has been hugely rewarding for the party cadres, fostering the idea of the party as a career path or, as Desmond Tutu put it, a gravy train ('They stopped the gravy train just long enough to get on it themselves'). It also, self-evidently, is incompatible with the efficient delivery of public services. The appointment of unqualified people has been particularly lethal in relation to the state-owned enterprises. The effects have been dramatically worse under Zuma, but the doctrine of deployment was fully developed under Mbeki.

Mbeki also presided over a huge expansion of the national, regional and municipal bureaucracies, which then accelerated further under Zuma, resulting in the number of public-sector employees today being estimated at 3 million. The vast majority of these jobs went to ANC supporters. As the public sector is far more highly unionised, they were able to achieve annual pay settlements well in advance of inflation, with average pay nearly 50 per cent higher in the public than in the private sector, imposing a huge burden on the public finances.

Corruption in the ANC, unfortunately, did not have to wait for Jacob Zuma. It was under Mbeki, in 2005, that Kgalema Motlanthe, Secretary General of the ANC, reported that 'this rot is across the board ... almost every government project is conceived because it offers opportunities for certain people to make money'. When, at this time, I expressed concern to a senior member of the ANC about corruption, I was told that there was a worse problem than corruption. When I asked what this was, I was told: 'Competence.'

*   *   *

In July 2005, two weeks after the Squires judgment sentencing Schabir Shaik and incriminating Zuma, Mbeki informed Parliament that he was 'releasing' Jacob Zuma from his position as Deputy President of the country while court cases proceeded. Zuma, however, remained Deputy President of the ANC.

According to his biographer, Mark Gevisser, Mbeki was worried that Zuma and his backers had no respect for the law, would revive ethnic (Zulu/Xhosa) divisions, and that his leftist associates would damage the economy and lead the country towards 'another post-colonial kleptocracy'.[8]

In August 2005 the Scorpions investigative team seized a large haul of documents from Zuma and Thomson, but there was a long delay before bringing any case against him. Zuma had no intention of taking his dismissal as Deputy President lying down. The period was used by him and his allies to organise opposition within the ANC to the remote and, it was felt, autocratic Mbeki, with the ANC Youth League and Julius Malema, the South African Communist Party and the Congress of South African Trade Unions all supporting the much more gregarious and approachable, and supposedly more left-wing, Jacob Zuma, against the President, one of whose weaknesses was to rely on a small tightknit group of advisers, led by his closest associate, best man and companion from their days together at Sussex University, Essop Pahad. Pahad saw himself as the President's enforcer, making himself cordially detested in that role.

The constitution provided that Mbeki could serve only two terms as President of South Africa, but he had made clear his intention to seek re-election as President of the ANC at the party conference in December 2007, eighteen months before the expiry of his term as President of the country. Given the dominant relationship of the party to the government, this clearly was liable to have resulted in a de facto Thabo third term. Mbeki, furthermore, had appointed Phumzile Mlambo-Ngcuka, wife of the head of the Scorpions, to be Deputy President, despite her lack of support in the party. The pro-Zuma campaign morphed rapidly into what became his candidacy to take over the presidency of the party from Mbeki.

In December 2005, Zuma was charged with the rape of the daughter of a deceased family friend. Amid turbulent scenes organised by his supporters, led by Julius Malema and members of the ANC Youth League threatening to 'kill for Zuma' outside the court in Johannesburg, Zuma sang what had become his anthem – *Umshini Wami* ('Bring me my machine gun'). He argued that the sex had been consensual: he had been encouraged by the short skirt the woman was wearing.

Zuma, who nominally headed the ANC Aids Council, acknowledged that he had not taken any precautions, despite knowing that the woman was HIV positive, though he said he had taken a shower afterwards 'to cut the risk of contracting HIV'. (Ever since, the cartoonist Zapiro has never failed to portray Zuma without a shower above his head). He also argued that it was unbecoming for a Zulu male not to respond to such an invitation. In May 2006, to the jubilation of Zuma's supporters, the court judged that the sex had been consensual. They believed that the case had been a set-up, especially as the woman had spoken to Mbeki's intelligence chief, Ronnie Kasrils, also a friend of her family, shortly after the incident.[9]

Zuma could rely on overwhelming support from KwaZulu-Natal, which had resented Xhosa domination of the ANC leadership and where Zuma supporters in the supposedly non-tribal ANC were proclaiming Zuma to be a '100 per cent Zulu boy'. He also was able to exploit the antagonism of the trade union federation Cosatu, the South African Communist Party (SACP) and the ANC Youth League to Mbeki's stringent economic policies, carefully cultivating his relations with them while Mbeki engaged in world tourism or presided in splendid isolation in Pretoria. Neither Mbeki nor his advisers understood that they were facing a populist revolt within the

ANC. Zuma supporters did not regard the charges against him as anything more than a peccadillo.

So blind were the President and his advisers to this ground-swell of revolt within the party that they left for the ANC National Conference in December 2007 in Polokwane convinced that they would prevail. On arrival there, the President suffered the humiliation of being jeered on the podium, and a sea of banners supporting Zuma. Mbeki's bid for a third term as President of the ANC was decisively defeated, leaving him ashen-faced on the podium. Zuma, an absolute natural in addressing any crowd, led his supporters in a victory song and dance. For some this was seen as a victory for democracy. For others, such as the ANC veteran Pallo Jordan, the Zuma ascendancy was a sign that the ANC had become 'just another grubby political party'. Zapiro published a memorable cartoon, describing the takeover of the party by the 'Pirates of Polokwane'.

Ironically, one of those defeated on the Mbeki slate at the Polokwane conference was his candidate to be Deputy President – Zuma's ex-wife, Nkosazana Dlamini-Zuma! She was defeated by the ANC Secretary General, Kgalema Motlanthe.

* * *

What now lay between Jacob Zuma and becoming President was the risk of a criminal conviction that, if it led to a sentence of imprisonment for more than a year, would have disqualified him from serving as President. By the time the corruption case against him came to be heard, it was after Zuma had defeated

Mbeki for the party leadership at Polokwane. In rejecting Schabir Shaik's appeal, the Constitutional Court had declared it to be accepted for their proceedings that 'Mr Shaik did pay bribes to Mr Zuma to promote Mr Shaik's business interests' and that, in attending meetings with Thomson-CSF, 'Mr Zuma did, as a matter of fact, promote Mr Shaik's interests'. Payments of over 4 million rand were made by Mr Shaik to Zuma and his family, with Shaik also soliciting payments to him from Thomson-CSF.

Yet in September 2008, after the ANC Conference in Polokwane had enthroned Zuma as President of the party, the Natal judge Chris Nicholson ruled that the National Prosecuting Authority had erred in not granting Zuma the right to be heard before reinstating the charges against him (a judgment struck down in damning terms by the Supreme Court of Appeal, declaring that 'the judge had taken his eye off the ball'). He contended that there had been political meddling in the case by Mbeki and the Minister of Justice and that the timing of the indictment after Mbeki's defeat at Polokwane was 'most unfortunate'. Judge Nicholson's highly contested judgment sufficed to save Jacob Zuma from being disqualified from becoming President of South Africa.

* * *

As Mbeki, still President of the country though no longer of the ANC, made clear his intention to appeal the Nicholson judgment, a meeting of the National Executive Committee of the ANC was convened on 19 September 2008. The former

Premier of Gauteng and Robben Islander, Tokyo Sexwale, led the demand for Mbeki's removal. He recalled the false allegations against him, Ramaphosa and Mathews Phosa in 2001, that they had been conspiring against Mbeki, as a ploy to force them out of politics. He reminded the delegates of Mbeki's disgraceful treatment of Mandela, in arranging for him to be heckled and jeered at in a meeting of the ANC leadership because of their disagreement about Aids.

After several hours of debate, Mathews Phosa called for a vote, the outcome of which was to 'recall' Mbeki from his position as President, for which he had been mandated on behalf of the ANC. It was left to his deputy, Kgalema Motlanthe, to inform Mbeki of this decision, which he knew there was no point in contesting. Motlanthe succeeded Mbeki as President of the country up to the 2009 elections, after which Zuma would take over.

Though no one doubted that he was keeping the position warm for Zuma, Motlanthe served as President with dignity and competence, leaving many wishing that he could have stayed on. Displaying many of the virtues of the older generation of ANC leaders, he was admired within the ANC as being the opposite of self-seeking and outside it as someone who sought to put the interests of the country first. When Jacob Zuma became President after the 2009 elections, Motlanthe reverted to the role of deputy. As Zuma did not really seek to run the government, except for the security agencies, Motlanthe did his best to coordinate the activities of other ministries, only to find his efforts countermanded periodically by associates of Zuma.

CHAPTER IV

JACOB ZUMA

Following Zuma's takeover of the party in December 2007, a number of ANC leaders, including a former chairman of the party and UDF leader, Mosiuoa 'Terror' Lekota, formed a breakaway party called the Congress of the People, COPE. In the 2009 elections, despite COPE, which immediately was riven by disputes over its leadership, and the displacement of Mbeki by the apparently corrupt Jacob Zuma, the ANC won the elections with 66 per cent of the vote (down from nearly 70 per cent in 2004), with Zuma taking over from Motlanthe as President.

* * *

Jacob Zuma was born at Nkandla in rural KwaZulu-Natal. His father was a policeman, who died soon after the birth of his son; his mother was a domestic worker. He had no formal education, becoming a herd boy when he was twelve. He joined the ANC in his teens, the military wing, Umkhonto we Sizwe

(MK), when he was twenty, and the South African Communist Party in the following year. His life thereafter was devoted to the struggle against apartheid. From 1963 he was imprisoned for ten years on Robben Island. Unlike other leading figures in the ANC, he showed little interest in furthering his rudimentary education while on the island, though he did organise a chess club. He was best known for playing in and refereeing the football matches.

On his release, however, he became the key organiser of the underground resistance in Natal, operating mainly from Swaziland and Mozambique. In that capacity, he formed a close partnership with Thabo Mbeki, senior to him in the ANC hierarchy. Arrested with Mbeki in Swaziland, they narrowly avoided being deported back to South Africa. Mbeki vetoed as too dangerous a plan to send Zuma back into Natal. Zuma was far more directly involved in the armed resistance than Mbeki but, contrary to his theme song, *Umshini Wami*, there is no evidence of Zuma ever having been engaged in combat, any more than there was for almost any other of the ANC leaders, except for Chris Hani (whose combat experience was in Zimbabwe). Zuma did, however, become the indispensable deputy to Mbeki, as they rose up the ANC hierarchy together. He also became head of intelligence for the military wing. This is the world he feels most at home in to this day, having never lost the habits of conspiracy and reliance on often questionable intelligence sources he learned in exile.

As he was Mbeki's deputy, I had numerous dealings with Jacob Zuma, including before his return from exile. In all my experience of him at the time, he played an entirely positive role in the transition to democracy in South Africa. He was as committed as Mbeki to a negotiated outcome. As the leading Zulu in the exile hierarchy, he also understood far better than his colleagues, including Mbeki, that Buthelezi and Inkatha had deep roots in Natal. They could not simply be crushed. There was going to have to be a negotiation with them. Zuma, who had started by helping to supply the ANC in KwaZulu-Natal with weapons to fight Inkatha, ended up playing a positive role in working for a reduction of violence in the province. He had a more realistic assessment of the situation there than either Mandela or Mbeki, both of whom were surprised when Inkatha won the 1994 elections in Natal.

So how did this archetypical 'struggle' figure of simple tastes turn into the polar opposite he has become today? After he became President, Zuma reminded me one day ('Because you were there') of the circumstances in which the ANC leaders returned from Lusaka in 1990. 'When we came back, we had nothing,' he observed. 'No money, no office, no car, no secretary, no place to stay.' Every one of them, including Mbeki, and Mandela himself, had to rely on the generosity of business friends to help them. For Zuma, these were the Shaik brothers, with whom he had been associated in the underground in Natal.

A first concern was with the education of his children, which they promised to arrange, thereafter his living arrangements, which were financed by them. As one set of favours led to another, he ended up in court, for good reason, still believing that he had done little more than others had done.

But Zuma had an ever increasing household, running eventually to six wives (currently four) and around twenty children. A KPMG report about him for the Scorpions in 2006, eventually published in the *Mail and Guardian*, revealed extreme financial recklessness, as he blithely incurred large debts, opening numerous bank accounts, frequently in deficit, relying on interest-free 'loans', which were never going to be repaid, mainly from the Shaik brothers, but also from other Durban businessmen, including Vivian Reddy and some more dubious figures, to keep his head above water.[10] The banks were not going to foreclose on so prominent a political figure.

In 2005, following Zuma's suspension as Deputy President by Thabo Mbeki, Nelson Mandela, aware of Zuma's financial troubles, loaned him 1 million rand. Mandela had always liked Zuma, who he felt to be 'inclusive' (in contrast to Mbeki), but became very disillusioned by him. The last picture of them together shows a grinning Zuma forcing himself on a frail and very ill-at-ease Mandela.

Meanwhile, as Deputy President, Zuma's relationship with Mbeki had changed fundamentally. The control-obsessed Mbeki gave him little to do. Zuma, in the words of one of his colleagues, 'does not read', and never seemed to have done so before Cabinet meetings. Mbeki did not believe that his uneducated deputy was up to the task of being President one day. His obsession with plots against him led him to take a step that definitively burned his bridges with his hitherto loyal deputy, when Mbeki insisted that Zuma must declare that he had no ambition to succeed him as President, which Zuma reluctantly agreed to do.

A gregarious, polygamous teetotaller, Jacob Zuma, whenever he wishes, can be exceptionally good company. He is extremely fond of his cheerful and attractive daughters. But his second wife, Kate Mantsho, mother of Duduzane, committed suicide, describing her life with him as twenty-four years of hell.

Polygamy may not always have worked well for him. In June 2014 Zuma suffered a mysterious and painful illness, for which he sought treatment in Moscow. The Security Minister David Mahlobo evicted one of his wives, Nompumelelo Ntuli-Zuma, from the Nkandla residence, on suspicion of having tried to poison him, which she strongly denied. She has never been charged, though the National Prosecuting Authority still has not decided to close the case.

Despite his lack of any formal education, I never found Jacob Zuma lacking in intelligence. On the contrary, he generally turned out to be a good deal shrewder than many of his more sophisticated colleagues. Starting with Mbeki, his opponents consistently have underestimated Zuma. He has been described as more brazen, wily and brutal than any of them bargained for, repeatedly challenging his critics to try to overthrow him, which few of them had the courage to attempt.[11]

As they prepared to return to South Africa, Mbeki and Zuma both concluded that membership of the South African Communist Party had become more of a handicap than the advantage it had been when the comrades controlled many of the workings of the ANC. Both withdrew from the SACP so thoroughly as to bury memories of their membership. Zuma regards himself as a socialist, and has always been a populist, but with no ideological moorings. Issues such as nationalisation were of no real interest to him.

As for his political modus operandi, Zuma's middle name, Gedleyihlekisa, is generally understood as meaning in Zulu 'He who smiles while planning to do you harm'. The middle name was not given to him at birth, but was attributed to him in his teenage years. Zuma contends that this only applies to people conspiring against him, but the fact that this is believed, in his home province, to be an accurate portrayal, of itself tells a story about him.

The opposition leader, Helen Zille, who kept calling for his impeachment, nevertheless would find Zuma ('this charming man') welcoming and friendly whenever she met him. As she was due to attend a first Cabinet meeting with the regional Premiers, Zuma telephoned her to say that she would be the only opposition person there. She was not to worry: she would be very welcome.

At the next meeting, he invited her to dance. Ignoring her protest about lack of dancing skills, he said, 'I will lead you,' and, as she clung on desperately, 'Relax. I will steer you!' which he proceeded to do around the dance floor, to the astonishment of his Cabinet. Asked where he had learned ballroom dancing, he confessed that in his youth he had enrolled at the Arthur Murray School of Dancing in Durban. He even commiserated with her recently about her treatment at the hands of her party (see Chapter XVI). His warmth and friendliness made her feel bad about attacking him, which she would have ceased to do – had he not been bent on undermining the constitution.[12]

To this day, anyone meeting Jacob Zuma will find him affable, friendly, full of jokes and apparently willing not just to listen, but to agree with much of what is being said to him. The phenomenon was familiar to Shakespeare: 'One may smile, and smile, and be a villain' (*Hamlet*, Act I, Scene v). This joviality has masked a ruthless determination to stay on top of the pile in the ANC and to use the security agencies, which he sees as the real basis of his power, to damage his critics or opponents, with no holds barred. His visitor also will find that his apparent agreement often is feigned, and even more often, indeed almost always, is not followed by any corresponding action at all.

Presenting to him one day the empowerment plans for South African Breweries, designed to benefit 60,000 employees and suppliers of the company, rather than a few politically connected businessmen, he enthusiastically agreed that this should set a pattern for broad-based economic empowerment for the future. It soon transpired that we had been wasting our breath. On another occasion, when I warned against appointing a protégé of his to a key post for which he was unqualified (being both incompetent and corrupt), he actually held up the appointment – only to make it eighteen months later.

On the campaign trail, Zuma is a charismatic figure, in contrast to Mbeki, whose lectures about policy left mass audiences cold, while Zuma lists the benefits of the ANC before, typically, breaking into *Umshini Wami* and other songs, accompanied by energetic dancing, to the enjoyment of the crowd. Also unlike Mbeki, he is very much at home in the rural areas, having done much to bolster the position of the traditional chiefs, many of whom are now paid by the government and provided core elements of his support. In office, he has more than once dismissed criticism of him as coming from urban 'clever blacks'.

His international counterparts have found Zuma not at all difficult or intransigent in meetings with them, though his foreign policy orientation, in harmony with that of his party, is firmly pro-Russian and pro-Chinese, there being no danger of criticism about corruption of any kind from them. His reputation, however, has inflicted real damage on South Africa, with major Western leaders, representing South Africa's largest investors, not at all anxious to meet him. A planned visit by him to London for a BRICS (Brazil, Russia, India, China and South Africa) group meeting had to be cancelled as the Prime Minister, David Cameron, declined to meet him, pleading prior engagements. Following an adverse court judgment over the failure to take action during his visit to South Africa against President Bashir of Sudan, accused of war crimes, South Africa withdrew from the International Criminal Court in The Hague. Any pretensions South Africa may have had to moral authority in world counsels have long since been dispelled.

When Jacob Zuma was reported to have agreed to be bribed by the French company Thales in the context of the arms deal, the investigator in charge of the case expressed to me at the time surprise that Zuma had sold himself for so little (500,000 rand). It did not take long for him to discover his true market worth and to display the characteristic inability of the 'big man' in Africa to distinguish between the public and the private purse. Although he had available splendid official residences in

Pretoria and Cape Town and excellent conference facilities in Durban, the Department of Public Works were encouraged to spend vast sums upgrading his homestead at Nkandla. Mandela paid for his own homestead at Qunu and Mbeki's roots perforce had been mainly abroad.

As the costs sky-rocketed to 246 million rand the Nkandla upgrade became a major scandal, looked into by the Public Protector, Thuli Madonsela. Following the unanimous ruling against him by the Constitutional Court, Zuma benefited from a rather benign Treasury ruling that only 7.8 million rand needed to be paid back. Ironically, despite Zuma's largesse, Nkandla remains a stronghold of Buthelezi's Inkatha party.

CHAPTER V

ZUMA TAKES OVER

Once installed as President after the elections in May 2009, Zuma appointed as Finance Minister his former comrade in arms in the resistance to apartheid in Natal, Pravin Gordhan. Gordhan was well known in the financial community, having served very successfully as head of the South African Revenue Service (SARS). SARS was one of the best run and most respected agencies of the South African government, with a reputation for integrity and efficiency, and tax receipts improved impressively during Gordhan's tenure.

Zuma appointed loyalists in most portfolios. While ministers like Aaron Motsoaledi in the Health Ministry and Naledi Pandor performed very competently, most of the others did not. It soon transpired that Zuma was not much interested in the day-to-day running of the government, with his deputy, Kgalema Motlanthe, trying to fill the gap. Zuma's overriding interest was in the security and intelligence 'cluster' of ministries controlling the army, the police and the intelligence agencies. Ultra-loyalists from KwaZulu-Natal were appointed to key positions in these areas, many of whom proved both thuggish and incompetent. One of those especially close to the new President was Richard Mdluli, who was particularly feared as the suspected organiser of all the intercepts of Zuma's colleagues' phone calls. Among other crimes, including charges of fraud, Mdluli was suspected of the murder of his girlfriend's husband. An elaborate system of espionage was set up covering all ANC MPs as well as the opposition.

Zuma was unlucky in his timing, as South Africa suffered from the world economic crisis and the attendant fall in commodity prices. But supervision of the banks by the South African Reserve Bank was far more effective than in many other countries. Pravin Gordhan soon established as impressive a reputation as his predecessor, Trevor Manuel, as Finance Minister. There was no longer any denialism about the wave of violent crime, which continued to affect black South Africans even more severely than whites. The Zuma association in the early part of this period remained closer with the Shaik brothers than with the soon to become legendary Guptas. While corruption was widespread, with Gordhan at the Treasury, Zuma's first term was not marked by scandals on anything like the scale the country has been experiencing since.[13]

But halfway through that term there came an episode South Africans had thought never to witness again, as the country paid the price of Zuma's choices in the leadership of the police.

* * *

On 16 August 2012 South African police opened fire on a demonstration by striking miners at Marikana in the platinum mining area of South Africa, killing thirty-four people, in the single most lethal use of force against civilians since the Sharpeville massacre in 1960.

The incident was triggered by a wildcat strike against the platinum mining company Lonmin called by rock drillers demanding better pay and conditions, with the strikers rebelling also against the established union, the National Union of Mineworkers (NUM). The conflict was extremely violent before Marikana, with several NUM members killed by strikers determined to prevent them reporting for work. Shortly before the shooting, two police officers and two security guards were killed. The relatively new and far more radical Association of Mineworkers and Construction Union (AMCU) backed the strikers against the NUM.

According to the BBC, eyewitness reports confirmed that the shooting took place after a group of demonstrators, some holding spears, clubs and machetes, rushed towards a line of police officers. One or two shots also were believed to have been fired at the police. The shooting by the police in return, however, clearly was both uncontrolled and beyond all reason, with many of the strikers shot in the back and several apparently hunted down in acts of revenge by the police for the deaths of their comrades. A powerfully emotive film, *Miners Shot Down*, was made about the tragedy.

A commission of inquiry was appointed, headed by a former Supreme Court judge, Ian Farlam. The recently appointed Police

Commissioner, Riah Phiyega, who had no prior police experience, was adamant that the shootings had been in self-defence.

One of the directors of Lonmin and their black-empowerment partner was Cyril Ramaphosa, former head of the National Mineworkers Union. The Farlam Commission's report concluded that Ramaphosa, as a director and major shareholder of Lonmin, had not acted improperly in requesting an increased police presence, because of the violence, nor did he contribute to the massacre, as his opponents alleged. The crisis had originated as a result of the strikers 'enforcing the strike by violence and intimidation'. Ramaphosa had described the violent strike as 'dastardly criminal' and requested the government to take 'concomitant action' to end the violence. The decision to disperse and disarm the strikers was taken by the police hierarchy.

The report questioned the competence of Commissioner Phiyega and the regional commander. The police had failed to use sufficient non-lethal force. The officers who opened fire did fear for their lives, but seventeen people were killed thereafter in questionable circumstances and the operation should have been stopped before this happened. In November 2015, Commissioner Phiyega was suspended for having been obstructive and less than straightforward in her evidence to the inquiry.

* * *

In the run-up to the ANC national conference in Mangaung in 2012, it was assumed that Kgalema Motlanthe would continue as Deputy President, with every chance thereafter of succeeding Zuma as President. But Motlanthe, who felt that the ideals of the party were going to be compromised, was no longer prepared to serve with Zuma. Instead he declared that, for the health of the party, there needed to be a choice for the leadership and that he would contest it. To the disappointment of his supporters, however, Motlanthe declined to campaign for the leadership, still less to make any promises to or deals with other leaders who might have supported him.

The result at Mangaung, therefore, was a foregone conclusion, as the KwaZulu-Natal representation by now had by far the largest contingent of delegates within the ANC and Zuma had co-opted the Premiers of Mpumalanga, North West Province and the Free State (the so-called Premier League), leaving only Gauteng supporting Motlanthe and the Eastern Cape divided. In the circumstances, it was surprising that Motlanthe won as many votes as he did – a quarter of the total. It was already known that the government had paid 246 million rand for the upgrades to Zuma's residence in Nkandla. ANC members knew what they were voting for – power and patronage versus a greater emphasis on principle.

The Motlanthe candidature, however, posed the problem of finding a new deputy for Zuma who could help to limit any damage at Mangaung – a problem solved by Zuma nominating Cyril Ramaphosa to be Deputy President of the party and the country. Since being sidelined by Mbeki, Ramaphosa, with his vast array of connections, had succeeded in building a very successful business empire. The Shanduka Group, which he founded and controlled, has major investments in mining, financial services and telecommunications. He became chairman of the financial company Bidvest, of the major mobile telephone group MTN, and the paper and forestry group Mondi and a director of SABMiller and of Lonmin, where he bought out the previous empowerment partners.

The business community were reassured, probably more than they should have been, as Ramaphosa clearly felt and told his associates that he 'would have to keep his head down'. Also, very obviously, he was going to have to mend fences with the left wing of the party, who especially held against him his support for Lonmin against the striking workers at Marikana.

As Deputy President, Ramaphosa made valiant efforts to help contain the fallout from the disastrous management and corruption of the state-owned companies and to support the Treasury and the Reserve Bank in their efforts to avoid the country being downgraded to junk bond status. He had limited contact with many of his former associates and the speeches he made in his new incarnation were forcefully about the need to press ahead with 'transformation', with South African businesses in future to be managed and owned by black South Africans ('and those who don't like this, tough for you!').

*   *   *

Julius Malema, head of the ANC Youth League from 2008 until his suspension in 2011, had led non-stop pro-Zuma demonstrations throughout Zuma's struggle with Mbeki and had been described by Zuma as a future leader of the ANC. But thereafter he had proved a troublesome ally. On a visit to Zimbabwe in 2010 he described Mugabe's opponents as creatures of imperialists and called for Zimbabwe-style land seizures in South Africa. On his return, Malema attacked the Zimbabwean opposition party, the Movement for Democratic Change, for having an office in the upmarket Johannesburg suburb, Sandton. When the BBC correspondent pointed out that Malema himself lived in Sandton, Malema became very threatening. The ANC and Zuma personally criticised him for this and when, in response, he compared Zuma unfavourably to Thabo Mbeki, Malema faced disciplinary charges from the ANC, including for singing 'Shoot the Boer' at political rallies. He apologised, but was warned that he would face suspension for reoffending.

Malema, whose financial resources and lifestyle at the time were difficult to explain otherwise, was believed to have enriched himself from 'tenderpreneurship' activities in Limpopo and faced racketeering and corruption charges. The South African Revenue Service claimed large amounts in unpaid taxes from him, though he eventually settled with them and this did not hamper his political career. He proceeded to campaign energetically for nationalisation of the mines. He also proclaimed ambitions to overthrow the government of Botswana. Some of his supporters also declared that South Africa was for blacks only.

In August 2011 Malema was summoned to a fresh disciplinary hearing. In November he was suspended by the ANC for five years, a decision upheld on appeal in 2012, in a hearing chaired by Cyril Ramaphosa, when he was expelled from the party.

Malema's response, in June 2013, was to launch his own political party, the Economic Freedom Fighters (EFF). He is an accomplished and charismatic political operator, with many characteristics in common with Zuma. Clad in overalls and wearing their signature red berets, his supporters made an impact in the 2014 elections, exploiting their well-founded accusations of corruption against the Zuma-led ANC and appealing to the masses of 'have nothings' who he sees as his core supporters. They made life well-nigh impossible for Zuma in Parliament with their chants of 'Pay back the money' whenever he appeared there. In 2015 there ensued a scandal in Parliament, when the security chiefs signal-jammed reporters' mobile phones while the EFF members were hauled out of the chamber.

In 2016 Malema caused an uproar, and was threatened with a charge of treason, by declaring that if the regime resorted to violence, then Zuma would have to be removed 'at the barrel of a gun'. Later in the year, he caused another furore by suggesting that the whites did not need to be slaughtered 'just yet'.

CHAPTER VI

ENTER THE GUPTAS

On the morning of 30 April 2013 a civil airliner from the Indian company Jet Airways landed at the South African National Defence Force's Waterkloof air force base on the edge of Pretoria. The airliner was carrying the Gupta brothers' guests for the wedding of their niece, Vega Gupta. They were greeted by Atul Gupta and whisked away by helicopter or in blue-light motorcades to the festivities in Sun City.

Radio reports about the use of an air force base for this purpose caused an immediate storm of protest and a denial by the Defence Department that permission had been given by them for the landing, but the Department of International Relations apparently had done so. The party spokesman, Jackson Mthembu, demanded an explanation on behalf of the ANC.

The incredibly lavish wedding ceremonies, lasting four days, were estimated to have cost tens of millions of rand. The Justice Minister, Jeff Radebe, announced that the government was investigating this serious security breach. Five officials were suspended.

It transpired that the member for agriculture of the Free State executive council and close Gupta associate Mosebenzi Zwane had invited his counterpart in Uttar Pradesh to attend the wedding – after earlier attempts to get permission to land at Waterkloof had been turned down by the Defence Department. The press reported that the Guptas approached the International Relations Department on the grounds that Indian ministers would be attending. In fact no ministers from the Indian government attended, though five or six provincial ministers did.

The government report censured the head of protocol in the International Relations Department, Ambassador Bruce Koloane, and Lieutenant Colonel Christine Anderson of the Waterkloof air force base. Koloane was reported to have told the political adviser in the Defence Department on 2 April that 'he was under pressure from Number One' to find a place for the Guptas' guests to land and, separately, that the Transport Minister had been instructed by the President to assist the Gupta family. Anderson also believed that this was the wish of Number One. The presidency flatly denied that Zuma had given any instructions to Koloane, who proceeded to act as the chosen fall guy. After forgoing two weeks' salary, his 'punishment' was to be appointed ambassador to the Netherlands.

Jacob Zuma was to have been guest of honour at the wedding, but decided at the last minute not to attend, given the media storm over the use of the air base.

The episode propelled the Gupta brothers into the headlines in South Africa, from which they have rarely been absent since. While the Waterkloof saga put them well and truly on the map, elements of the South African Security Agency including, ironically, Moe Shaik, the brother of Shabir Shaik, had been worried about their influence on the President and Cabinet ministers since 2011 as, by this stage, was the *Mail and Guardian*.

The reaction of Vavi, General Secretary of Cosatu, to their use of the air base was to declare that

> We face the nightmare future of a South Africa up for auction to the highest bidder, a society in which no one will be able to do business with the state without going through corrupt gatekeepers who … unless they are stopped may systematically use their power to control large areas of the economy.

The Guptas, he declared, were running a shadow government – a phrase that has stuck with them ever since.

At the time, their use of the air base was seen as an embarrassment for them. They were felt to have been too blatant in demonstrating their influence over the government. This kind of judgement was based on a serious misunderstanding of their modus operandi. For their entire business model henceforth was based on demonstrating *urbi et orbi* the full extent of the influence they exerted at every level of government, from the President down. In the face of several flat refusals from the Defence Department, they had proved able to get their way, on the basis of their proximity to Number One.

* * *

The Gupta brothers ever since have pointed out that they have never been convicted or even charged in South Africa with any crime. The South African press and their numerous critics have contended that this is because, following the capture by President Zuma of the main prosecuting authorities (see Chapter VIII), they have never been investigated. In particular, the President avoided appointing the independent judicial commission of inquiry into their activities called for by the Public Protector Thuli Madonsela in her *State of Capture* report in October 2016.

Leaving aside the issue of criminality, which can only be decided by the South African courts, what follows is the truly extraordinary story of the rise of this Indian family to a point at which they were universally acknowledged to be the leading power broker/dealers of what the Public Affairs Research Institute in their *Betrayal of the Promise* report described as the 'shadow state' in South Africa.[14] How on earth did they attain this position? And what sort of profits have they made from it? And who from?

It is not difficult to demonstrate that these have amounted to many billions and potentially tens of billions of rand, that these enormous sums have come from the state-owned enterprises, which have been well and truly 'captured', and those trying to do business with them, and therefore very largely have come from the public purse. According to the latest rough estimates, the amounts received by Gupta-related entities from public coffers – in particular from the Free State government, the Industrial Development Corporation, Transnet, Eskom and Denel – are due to reach at least 15–20 billion rand – so well over a billion US dollars. The Guptas may contend that these estimates are exaggerated, and if they will open the accounts of the thirty or so companies involved, it will be possible to print a correction. The net worth of Atul Gupta was estimated by Wikipedia at US$773 million in 2016, all of it accumulated since his arrival in South Africa. The former Finance Minister Pravin Gordhan estimates the overall cost of state capture at over 200 billion rand.

Self-evidently, these results could not have been achieved without the wholehearted support of Number One, whose alter egos they set out to become, of Cabinet ministers, senior officials and the executives and boards of the state-owned enterprises. If the brothers ever were to be convicted of wrong-doing, an awful lot of people would find themselves in the dock with them.

*   *   *

So how did three brothers of Indian origin, largely unknown in their own country, get themselves into a position to make such a mark on the history of South Africa?

Ajay, Atul and Rajesh (known as Tony) Gupta grew up in Saharanpur in the landlocked and relatively backward Indian province of Uttar Pradesh. Corruption has been a hallmark of its politics for many decades.

In 1993 Atul Gupta, then aged twenty-three, was despatched by his father to seek his fortune in South Africa. He concentrated on developing a computer and information technology business, initially called Correct Marketing. The name then was changed to Sahara Computers, giving the impression that it was somehow related to the much larger and better known Indian Sahara group, though there was no connection between them. By 1999 the company had achieved an impressive turnover (127 million rand). The family at this stage had developed a very successful business model based on low-cost computer assembly. Rajesh arrived in 1997 and, after frequent business visits, Ajay permanently moved to South Africa in 2003.

Zuma became Deputy President under Mbeki in 2004. The Guptas established a relationship with Mbeki's closest confidant, Essop Pahad, but they were unable to establish any meaningful relationship with Mbeki himself. They did, however, boast from an early stage of a close relationship with Jacob Zuma. Like the Shaik brothers, they appear to have started by paying for Zuma's children's education. Ajay Gupta was reported to have told a business associate that if Zuma one day became President, their ship would come in.[15]

In 2001 the Gauteng government had announced a 500 million rand programme to bring schools online. Sahara Computers was given one of the six primary contracts, alongside far better known names such as Dell and Hewlett Packard. The programme turned out to be an expensive failure, from which however Sahara earned over 60 million rand and went on to win other significant schools contracts, despite issues with their performance. In 2003

Jacob Zuma's son, Duduzane, aged twenty-one at the time, was given a job by the Guptas with Sahara Systems.

From 2004 the Guptas started sponsoring South African cricket on the basis that the Newlands ground in Cape Town and two other notable grounds would have the name Sahara attached to them. The South African cricket captain, Graeme Smith, and other prominent cricketers became 'brand ambassadors' for Sahara. In 2005 the South African cricket team interrupted their Indian tour to appear in the Guptas' home town of Saharanpur. The Guptas became suppliers of IT products and services to Cricket South Africa and then to South African rugby. In March 2012 the Guptas secured naming rights for their new newspaper *New Age* to a limited-over cricket match between India and South Africa in Johannesburg. President Zuma was summoned to attend the match and both the South African and Indian teams attended a reception at the vast compound the Guptas had acquired in the most expensive area of Johannesburg, Saxonwold.

Following Zuma's election as ANC President at the Polokwane conference, Duduzane Zuma and (briefly) his twin sister, Duduzile, were appointed directors in a number of Gupta companies. Duduzane was regularly reported to be asked to intervene to pressurise officials and ministers who were not being responsive to the Guptas' commercial demands. He also on many occasions was supplied with the CVs of people seeking key government appointments. Jacob Zuma attended several functions hosted by the Guptas in this period before he became President of the country in May 2009.

HEADING FOR A PREDATOR STATE

In 2009, the year of Zuma's inauguration as President, the Guptas became involved in their first major scandal. The Sishen Iron Ore Company was owned 78.6 per cent by Kumba Iron Ore, a subsidiary of Anglo American, and 21.4 per cent by the steel maker ArcelorMittal. ArcelorMittal failed to apply for new order mining rights on the due date of 30 April 2009. Kumba/Sishen applied for them instead.

It then transpired, however, that a brand new shell company called Imperial Crown Trading (ICT), with the connivance of the Department of Mineral Resources, had bid for them as well. The two bids were supposed to have been received on the same day, 4 May. In December the Department ruled in favour of ICT, despite its lack of any capacity or track record, because, supposedly, it had better empowerment credentials. This was regarded, in the international mining industry, as akin to highway robbery.

While Sishen appealed against the Department's ruling, in March 2010 a shell company, Pragat Investments, under Jagdish Parekh, CEO of JIC Mining Services, controlled by the Guptas and Duduzane Zuma, acquired 50 per cent of ICT, though Ajay Gupta claimed that this had nothing to do with them.

Kumba appealed to the Hawks – the independent investigative wing of the South African police service – with evidence of fraud in the ICT application, including allegedly copying details of Sishen's own application with the help of the Minerals Department's officials, forging signatures from a drilling company and fabricating geological reports. Although certified by the Department as having been received on 4 May 2009, the signature on the document was dated 5 May and supporting documents followed on the 8th and 9th. Applications for mining rights were supposed to be dealt with by the Department on a first come, first served basis.

On 10 August, in an effort to preserve their rights, ArcelorMittal announced that it would buy ICT for 800 million rand, with the Gupta companies and Duduzane Zuma providing the black economic empowerment element of the transaction.

In response to questions as to how Indian entrepreneurs were able to benefit from a BEE transaction, the head of the empowerment consortium explained that the Guptas had brokered the agreement between ICT and ArcelorMittal. This was confirmed by ArcelorMittal, who said that they had been discussing it with the Guptas and Parekh since April 2010 (a point at which the Guptas were denying any involvement).

It was this scandal that caused Zwelinzima Vavi, General Secretary of Cosatu, to read the writing on the wall much earlier than others. In August 2010 he declared:

We are headed for a predator state where a powerful, corrupt and demagogic elite of political hyenas are increasingly using the state to get rich. We have to intervene now to prevent South Africa from becoming a state where corruption is the norm and *no business can be done with government without first paying a corrupt gate-keeper.*

The Minister of Mineral Resources, Susan Shabangu, dismissed Sishen's appeal, confirming the award of the prospecting rights to ICT. Shabangu was a regular visitor to the Guptas at Saxonwold and a guest at the Gupta wedding in 2013. Shabangu and the Director General of the Minerals Department, Sandile Nogxina, were attending meetings with the Guptas in this period and also were reported to have attended a meeting with Jacob Zuma and the Guptas at Zuma's official residence. In January 2011 Nogxina informed Sishen that their application for the mining rights had been rejected.

The board of Anglo American came under huge political pressure to find a compromise solution, which would have entailed accommodating ICT, but the government were told that Anglo intended to uphold its legal rights.

The Hawks were continuing their inquiries and the state prosecutor, Glynnis Breytenbach, also was involved. ICT accused her of working with their opponents, an allegation rejected in a disciplinary hearing. Realising, however, that she had no future in the National Prosecuting Authority, she subsequently left and joined the opposition Democratic Alliance.

In May 2011 ArcelorMittal changed sides, announcing that it was joining Sishen in its case against ICT and the Department of Mineral Resources, heralding withdrawal from their empowerment deal with Duduzane Zuma and the Guptas. In December 2011 Judge Raymond Zondo of the North Gauteng High Court ruled that the rights had been improperly awarded to ICT, a judgment upheld by the Appeal Court and then by the Constitutional Court.

This was the first highly controversial venture in which the Guptas and Duduzane Zuma, with the help of the Department of Mineral Resources, stood to benefit to the extent of several hundred million rand. The failure did not deter them, as similar tactics later were employed with the assistance of an even more compliant Minerals Minister in their forced acquisition of the Optimum mine from Glencore. Neither the minister, Susan Shabangu, nor the Director General, Sandile Nogxina, suffered any consequences from the ICT fiasco and the court judgments against them.

DAIRY FARMING

The Guptas meanwhile had established the Estina dairy farm project in the Free State, with the support of the Premier and close Zuma ally, Ace Magashule, and especially of the member for agriculture on the Free State executive council (MEC), Mosebenzi Zwane. The investment by the Guptas followed what was to become a familiar pattern: hardly any of their own money was put at risk. The company controlled by the Guptas, who had no relevant farming experience, was awarded a large farming area, rent-free, near Zwane's home town of Vrede. As with nearly all their investments, their own very modest contribution was dwarfed by the investment by the Free State government. The project never looked like succeeding. By the time it was wound up in June 2014, the Free State government was reported to have committed 220 million rand, mostly transferred to Gupta-related companies with no involvement in farming. Thirty million rand of the proceeds was used to finance the cost of the 2014 Gupta wedding at Sun City, despite a junior KPMG auditor questioning how this could be described as a business expense.

GOING NUCLEAR

The Guptas had acquired a taste for mining, given the preferential treatment they no doubt hoped to continue to enjoy from the Department. Their next and, ultimately, even more ambitious venture was in uranium. In May 2010 it was announced that for $37.3 million they had acquired the mothballed Dominion uranium mine in the North West Province from a company called Uranium One. Atul Gupta and Duduzane Zuma became directors of what was now Shiva Uranium. The state-owned Industrial Development Corporation (IDC) loaned the Guptas' Oakbay company 250 million of the 270 million rand they needed to buy Dominion. The Guptas were unable to repay the loan when it fell due in 2013. By February 2014 the obligation to the IDC, including interest, had swollen to a much larger sum.

When the Guptas listed Oakbay Resources and Energy on the Johannesburg Stock Exchange in December 2014 the IDC, incredibly, agreed to convert 257 million rand of the loan into a mere 3.6 per cent of Oakbay. Oakbay listed at 10.08 rand per share, giving it a nominal value of 8 billion rand – forty-eight times its full-year revenue – though its auditors' (KPMG's) valuation was less than half of that. It subsequently transpired that the Guptas had influenced the listing price by lending a million US dollars to a company (UEC) in Singapore, which was instructed to buy shares at 10.5 rand each on the day before the listing.[16] This would have caused all those concerned to be disqualified as directors, had such price manipulation occurred on the London Stock Exchange.

Oakbay delisted in 2017, with the IDC stake now worth little or nothing. The IDC belatedly is now trying to recover the 287.5 million rand it claims to be owed by the Guptas on the grounds of alleged fraud and misrepresentation by Oakbay, citing also in support of their claim the apparent fraud involved in the Estina dairy farm project in the Free State.

When the Guptas bought the Dominion mine, there was surprise in the industry that they had done so, as the uranium price remained in the doldrums and it had been a notoriously unprofitable operation. It soon became very clear that this was a bet on Zuma committing South Africa to what the Treasury regarded as an unaffordable nuclear programme to be built, notwithstanding the absence of any formal tender process, by Russia's Rosatom.

The Americans and British reportedly asked their South African contacts if the Guptas could be relied upon to ensure that any uranium produced from the Dominion mine did not go to undesirable destinations. Meanwhile the South African State Security Agency had noted the closeness of the Guptas to the President and their boasting about close ties with several

Cabinet ministers, including the then Public Enterprises Minister Malusi Gigaba, Nkosazana Dlamini-Zuma, Tokyo Sexwale and Susan Shabangu. During Zuma's state visit to India in June 2010, to the businessmen accompanying the President, the Guptas appeared to be largely in charge of the programme, even though they were not very well known in India.

On 18 September 2011 *City Press* reported that the Guptas' activities were being monitored for 'alleged influence on top government officials and politicians'. Apparently on Zuma's behalf, the State Security Minister Siyabonga Cwele ordered the monitoring of the Guptas' activities to cease. This was resisted among others by Moe Shaik, at the time head of foreign intelligence. Moe Shaik and his two senior counterparts were forced out of the agency late in 2011; he was given instead a post with the Development Bank. One of the three, Gibson Njenje, confirmed that they had been monitoring the Guptas. Moe Shaik, five years later, also went public about this.

PRAISE SINGING

In July 2010, to help consolidate their influence on the government, and expecting to benefit from government block orders and advertising, the Guptas launched their newspaper *New Age*. It was made unashamedly clear from the outset that this would be a pro-government publication, intended to emphasise positive news. As the paper commenced publication, the editorial staff resigned. From the first edition, the paper was full of government advertising, praise for Zuma and hostility to his critics within the ANC.

Zuma attended a celebratory dinner in Durban to heap praise on *New Age*. The replacement editor objected to insinuations that 'the paper was the family's gift to President Zuma, ostensibly in return for certain favours'. Despite its very modest circulation, government departments and state-owned companies like Transnet and Telkom, successively under Brian Molefe, gave it huge advertising contracts. The government spokesman, Themba Maseko, was later to testify that he was told by Zuma to 'help the Guptas'. Ajay Gupta allegedly told him: 'Tell departments to give you money. If they refuse, we will deal with them ... We will summon ministers here.' According to Maseko, when he resisted, he was told by Ajay Gupta: 'I will talk to your seniors in government and you will be sorted out.' Maseko was then summoned by the Minister in the Presidency, Collins Chabane, who said that he had been instructed by the President to fire or 're-deploy' him. He was transferred to the Department of Public Service. The Guptas responded with strenuous denials.[17]

In October 2015 the Finance Minister, Nhlanhla Nene, revealed that the near bankrupt South African Airways under Zuma's close friend Dudu Myeni had spent 9 million rand on several million copies of *New Age*.

New Age breakfast business briefings were broadcast free by the national broadcaster, SABC, attracting 37 million rand in sponsorships from Telkom, Eskom and Transnet. In 2014 the then acting CEO of Eskom, Collin Matjila, committed to spend a further 43 million rand sponsoring the briefings, overriding the objections of the company's audit and risk committee.

In 2013 the Guptas launched their TV news channel, Africa News Network 7 or ANN7, with Duduzane Zuma as the black empowerment partner. President Zuma visited the studios before it went on air. An Indian editor who resigned spilled the beans about the total lack of editorial independence and close ties to Zuma.

CHAPTER VII

'POWER, AUTHORITY AND AUDACITY'

In November 2010 the inconveniently incorruptible struggle veteran Barbara Hogan was unceremoniously removed as Minister of Public Enterprises, to be replaced by the former head of the ANC Youth League, Malusi Gigaba. Barbara Hogan subsequently revealed that she had been asked by the Guptas to get South African Airways to hand over the Mumbai route to the Indian airline, Jet Airways, in which they had an interest. The chairman of the South African Airways board, Cheryl Carolus, also had been lobbied to give up the Mumbai route.

An ANC MP, Vytjie Mentor, alleged that in October 2010 she was summoned, she thought, to a meeting with the President. Instead she was escorted to a meeting with Ajay Gupta in Saxonwold, with Zuma elsewhere in the building, to be asked to help transfer the Mumbai route away from SAA. She claimed she was told that 'You could be Minister of Public Enterprises in a week's time' when the President removed Barbara Hogan. The Guptas denied this.

Mentor added in her subsequent statement to the police that she had concluded that 'the Gupta family, the son of the President and some ministers, as well as the President to a certain extent, all have a corrupt relationship that gives unfair advantage to the Gupta family and their associates at the expense of the state'.[18]

The route was not transferred at the time. But Jet Airways was given a licence also to operate on it, rendering it less profitable for SAA. Cheryl Carolus, with six other members of the SAA board, resigned 'to protect her reputation' after what she described as a breakdown in relations with Gigaba. In January 2015 Gigaba appointed Zuma's close friend, Dudu Myeni, as chairperson of SAA, despite her total lack of knowledge of the industry. In early 2015 SAA withdrew from the Johannesburg–Mumbai route on the grounds that it was no longer profitable.

CAPTURING TRANSNET

In December 2010 the *New Age* newspaper announced that it had it on good authority that Brian Molefe would be appointed CEO of one of the country's two principal utilities, the massive transport infrastructure company, Transnet – an appointment duly made by Gigaba in February 2011. Jürgen Schrempp, the former head of Daimler Chrysler, left the Transnet board, uneasy at the direction in which things were heading. The capable but very political Molefe had started off on very shaky ground with Zuma, as he was well known to have been an extremely close acolyte of Mbeki. The Guptas were believed to have played a key role in rehabilitating him with Zuma.

In December 2010, Gigaba appointed a Gupta associate, Iqbal Sharma, to the Transnet board. The intention originally was to make Sharma chairman of Transnet, but his links to the family were felt to be too close.[19] Instead he was made chairman of the committee on procurement. In 2010/11, Transnet and Eskom between them accounted for 150 billion rand expenditure on procurement. As described in *Betrayal of the Promise*, a series of new Gupta-friendly appointments were made by Gigaba to the Eskom board.[20]

Confident of their support from Number One and from Gigaba, the Guptas made forceful attempts to win for their client, China South Rail, the new locomotives order from the Passenger Rail Authority of South Africa (PRASA). The CEO of PRASA, Lucky Montana, reported to his then chairman, Sfiso Buthelezi (later deputy Finance Minister), that he had attended numerous meetings with the Guptas, Duduzane Zuma and the Transport Minister, Ben Martins. He had taken issue with the representative of the Gupta family over what he considered to be attempts on their part to extort money from the bidders. He was 'taken aback and continue to be surprised that the representative of the said family finds such power, authority and audacity'. Montana claimed that, summoned to a meeting with Duduzane Zuma, he had 'blasted' Duduzane for the attempts to divert business to him and his partners from PRASA, including threatening to restructure the PRASA board.[21] Their efforts in that regard failed, as this locomotives order went to the French.

The Guptas more than made up for this disappointment in their campaign vis-à-vis their main target, Transnet. With Brian Molefe installed as CEO, his key assistant at Transnet was Anoj Singh, who was promoted to Chief Financial Officer (CFO) in 2012. An apparently well-researched article in the *Daily Maverick* listed 30 billion rand in crane, train and other Transnet contracts from which Gupta-related companies stood to gain around 5.6 billion rand, much of this as rewards for helping various companies secure key contracts.[22] These 'facilitation' payments frequently were channelled through two shelf companies, Homix and JJ Trading. In this period, Singh made several visits to Dubai which, he contended, were not paid for by the Guptas. The Guptaleaks (Chapter XIV) appear to tell a different story.

In 2012 Transnet announced a 300 billion rand modernisation programme. Two years later, massive contracts for the supply of new locomotives were awarded to four consortia, one of which was the Gupta-sponsored China South Rail. Sharma, who oversaw the tender process, in the course of it became involved with VR Laser Services, controlled by Rajesh Gupta, Salim Essa and Duduzane Zuma.

In July 2015 the Minister of Public Enterprises, Lynne Brown, appointed Daniel Mantsha, who at one point had been struck off the roll as an attorney, as chairman of the board of the state-owned armaments manufacturer, Denel. The Guptaleaks revealed that Mantsha had his municipal bills paid by the Guptas, travelled with them on their private plane to India, was hosted by them in Dubai and sent them confidential business information. In January 2016 the acting CEO of Denel, Zwelakhe Ntshepe, announced a joint venture with the Guptas' VR Laser (financed by funds from the Estina farm project), to market Denel products in Asia. This was opposed by the Treasury under Pravin Gordhan, who could not see what value VR Laser could possibly add, and was abandoned in 2017, having proved to be of no value at all.

The China Rail contract was just the beginning of the Guptas' campaign to capture business from Transnet. McKinsey were hired to advise the company, but had to have an empowerment partner, Regiments, under Eric Wood. Anoj Singh oversaw the drastic limitation of McKinsey's role and the extraordinary ballooning of fees to Regiments, which in turn made payments to Homix.

The Guptas tried to buy Regiments, but instead Wood was persuaded to merge it into the Gupta consultancy Trillian, led by the Guptas' closest associate, Salim Essa, which earned huge sums from Transnet for no very obvious services. The treasurer of Transnet, Mathane Makgatho, resigned, telling her staff: 'I came here with my integrity and I will leave with my integrity intact.' Regiments' fee was reported to have been increased to 265.5 million rand, with no clear motivation. Trillian was paid 93.5 million rand for helping with a bond issue that could have been arranged by any of the lead banks or by Transnet's own treasury.

Apart from these very large sums earned directly from Transnet, the Guptaleaks revealed that Salim Essa signed an agreement with China South Rail under which a vehicle called Tequesta, for its 'advisory services', would receive 21 per cent of the value of China South Rail's sale of locomotives to Transnet. The investigative journalism team at amaBunghane estimated the value of this 'reward' to the Guptas for having helped to ensure that China South Rail won the locomotive contract at 5.3 billion rand.[23] The contract stated that CSR *would not require any proof of delivery of the above services since it is understood that the project would not have materialised without the active efforts of Tequesta...*' This arrangement enabled huge profits to be extracted from Transnet's purchase of locomotives without their ever having to pass through South Africa.

In 2017 the former anti-apartheid campaigner Peter Hain told the British Parliament and the UK Financial Conduct Authority that HSBC bank were reported to have been involved in processing payments for Gupta companies outside South Africa, despite warnings from HSBC staff in South Africa about dealing with them. HSBC stated that it had sought to close all the Gupta-related accounts it could identify from 2014.

The telecom company Neotel, which had large contracts with Transnet, was found to be paying a 'success fee' to the Gupta-linked shell company Homix. By 2015 these payments had increased to 100 million rand. According to amaBhungane, another four companies contracted to Transnet made payments to Homix totalling 90 million rand. Homix meanwhile made a payment of 190 million rand to a shell company called Bapu Trading and 51 million rand to two Gupta-linked companies in Hong Kong. Regiments, having won 800 million rand in contracts from Transnet, paid Homix 84.3 million rand, apparently as commission for the business won from Transnet. According to an affidavit by a founding director of Regiments, Litha Nyhonyha, the company also channelled via an entity called Techpro a payment of 17 million rand to *New Age*, in return for no services at all.

In November 2017 the current CEO of Transnet, Siyabonga Gama, launched a court case seeking to invalidate the award of a further major contract to the Gupta-linked German information technology company, T-Systems, which, he contended, for the past five years had been benefiting from an excessively lucrative contract with Transnet despite a 200 million rand per annum lower bid by Robert Gumede's Gijima Holdings. It was alleged that the contract's value had been inflated in size by the Gupta associate Salim Essa acting as an intermediary and Anoj Singh approving its extension without a tender.

* * *

The mighty South African utility Eskom, still today one of the largest electricity generators in the world, in its heyday had supplied power to the whole of southern Africa. When in 2009 the incompetent then CEO of Eskom ousted his competent chairman, Bobby Godsell, I was asked by the Zuma first-term presidency what corrective action could be taken. I and others recommended the replacement of the CEO by the highly respected Eskom executive, Brian Dames, and the recruitment of a CFO who would carry conviction with investors.

Once Malusi Gigaba became Minister for Public Enterprises, both decided to leave, as did the Treasurer, Caroline Henry. For Gigaba proceeded to appoint several Gupta associates – Ben Ngubane, Mark Pamensky, Kuben Moodley and others – to the Eskom board.[24]

In April 2015 Brian Molefe was appointed acting CEO of Eskom, even though he was still CEO of Transnet, until he transferred formally to Eskom in September. Anoj Singh accompanied him from Transnet to become CFO of Eskom, with a familiar pattern soon being established there. The stage was now set for the most spectacular and ambitious of the Gupta coups, described in Thuli Madonsela's *State of Capture* report. This was to secure the forced sale by Glencore of the huge Optimum coal mine with, furthermore, the entire transaction financed for them by Eskom.

CHAPTER VIII

ZUMA UNFETTERED

Notwithstanding Marikana, the problems with service delivery and very slow growth in employment, the ANC under Zuma comfortably won the 2014 elections with 62 per cent of the vote. The Democratic Alliance advanced to 22 per cent and the new Economic Freedom Fighters party, led by Julius Malema, won around 6 per cent. A pattern was emerging of solid continuing ANC support in the rural areas, bolstered by Zuma's cultivation of the traditional leaders, many of whom are now paid by the government, plus an inclination anyway to vote for the ruling party, and increasing questioning of ANC rule in the major urban areas of Nelson Mandela Bay (around Port Elizabeth), Gauteng (Johannesburg) and Tshwane (Pretoria).

In early 2015 Jacob Zuma celebrated his election victory by staging a coup d'état, decapitating the three main investigative and prosecuting agencies deemed to be threatening some of his close associates. The purpose was to turn them from investigative agencies into agencies designed to thwart investigations. This was the transformative period of the Zuma presidency, in which he succeeded in near fatally subverting the constitution without actually having to change any of it. It turned out to be not just a clear signal of his intent but an extraordinarily effective way of preventing any investigation or thwarting of the massive looting of the state-owned enterprises that since then has ensued.

In 2007 the ANC government already had disbanded the most effective of these agencies, the Scorpions, set up ten years before on the initiative of Mandela, who wanted an agency to combat organised crime, and Thabo Mbeki, replacing them with the Hawks. The Scorpions had led the investigation into Schabir Shaik, and Jacob Zuma's connections with him. The South African Constitutional Court ruled that the reorganisation was 'constitutionally invalid' as the Hawks were deemed by them to be insufficiently independent of government.

The Hawks, however, now also were deemed to be too troublesome. The respected head of the Hawks, a former Robben Islander, General Anwa Dramat, was dismissed and replaced by General Ntlemeza. The Independent Police Commissioner, Robert McBride, protested at Dramat's removal, only to be suspended at the same time, despite the fact that Dramat and McBride both were ANC veterans.

In what became a familiar pattern of deceit, stories were planted in the Johannesburg *Sunday Times* by agents of Crime Intelligence, headlined 'Sent back to die!' suggesting that Dramat was responsible for the rendition of three Zimbabweans to the police in Zimbabwe.

Dramat declared that the charges were a smokescreen. What he had done was to ask for case dockets involving very influential people to be centralised under one investigating arm 'and this has clearly caused massive resentment against me'. The charges were dismissed, but this sufficed to help get rid of Dramat and of General Sibiya, head of the Hawks in Gauteng. Dramat declared that his offence had been that of refusing to compromise his principles or the position to which he had been appointed.[25]

Ntlemeza was appointed to head the country's premier anti-corruption and crime-fighting unit despite having been condemned by the North Gauteng High Court in the case concerning the suspension of General Sibiya as 'biased and dishonest' and lacking in 'integrity and honour'. Throughout his tenure at the head of the country's primary investigative agency, he lived up to this reputation, quickly destroying his own fragile credibility by stating that a Hawks investigation into South African Airways did not extend to the activities of its chairperson, President Zuma's friend, Dudu Myeni.

The National Prosecuting Authority already had been emasculated as its first head, Bulelani Ngcuka, had led the investigation of Jacob Zuma. Falsely accused of having been an apartheid-era spy, he was replaced by another ANC veteran, Vusi Pikoli. Pikoli led the investigation into the Police Commissioner and key Mbeki ally, Jackie Selebi, who also, improbably, had been elected as president of Interpol, despite being notoriously corrupt. As he insisted on pursuing the case against Selebi, Mbeki asked Pikoli to resign. Pikoli, who naively believed that he was simply doing his job, refused, whereupon he was suspended by Mbeki and not reinstated even though a parliamentary inquiry concluded in his favour.[26] Selebi, an associate of and paid by a convicted drugs smuggler, subsequently was convicted on charges of corruption in 2010.

He was replaced by a Zuma associate from KwaZulu-Natal, Bheki Cele, who in turn was fired for blatant corruption in 2012, though this did not prevent him being appointed a deputy minister. He was succeeded by the first woman Police Commissioner, Riah Phiyega, who had no prior police experience. She in turn was suspended in 2015 for her role in the shooting of striking miners at Marikana.

Worse was to come for the National Prosecuting Authority, which, self-evidently, is supposed to be at the epicentre of the fight against corruption and crime, but has never fulfilled that role under Zuma. In 2009 he appointed Menzi Simelane as the head of the authority, despite the fact that, as director general in the Justice Department, he had been censured by the parliamentary inquiry for his efforts to get rid of Vusi Pikoli, only for the courts then to uphold the Democratic Alliance's case against Simelane as not fit to head the agency.

The Zuma ultra-loyalist Nomgcobo Jiba, for whom Zuma reportedly had expunged the criminal record of her husband, was appointed as acting National Director of Public Prosecutions. No less appropriate choice could possibly have been made as, in pursuit of revenge for his role in imprisoning her husband (for embezzling a trust fund), Jiba had the well-known prosecutor, Gerrie Nel, arrested, only for the case against him to collapse forthwith, with allegations of perjury against Jiba. A similar vendetta was pursued aginst Glynnis Breytenbach.

From 2013 the new head of the authority, Mxolosi Nxasana,

made repeated efforts to charge with perjury and fire Jiba. Zuma removed Nxasana instead, claiming that he had resigned. Nxasana responded that the President's version was false: he had in fact been fired.

Jiba had fallen out with other members of the agency as a result of her refusal to continue investigations against the senior intelligence officer closest to the President, Richard Mdluli, who had been arrested on charges of corruption, intimidation and on suspicion of connection with the murder of the husband of his girlfriend, who was murdered while being escorted by the police to the scene of a prior attempt on his life!

Her next target was the head of the Hawks in KwaZulu-Natal, General Johan Booysen. As Booysen put it, 'For twenty-eight years I had a faultless career and won various national and international awards', until he started investigating Thoshan Panday, a businessman with strong police and Zuma connections who allegedly offered him a 2 million rand bribe. Edward Zuma, Jacob's son, complained that the investigation was affecting his dividends from Panday. The 'investigative' reporters of the Johannesburg *Sunday Times* ran a story entitled 'Shoot to Kill: Inside a South African Police Death Squad', alleging that Booysen had been running a police death squad in the Cato Manor area of KwaZulu-Natal, used by Jiba to charge him, only for the case to be thrown out in court with a damning judgment against Jiba.[27]

Attempts were made to withdraw the charges against Richard Mdluli, but Freedom under Law got them reinstated through a court order in 2012. Throughout his suspension, this shadowy figure continued to receive his salary for the past six years, plus a bonus, while still exerting enough influence to help get rid of some of those pursuing him, including Anwa Dramat. For her failure to pursue the case against Mdluli, Jiba ended up being struck off the roll of advocates in South Africa by the Pretoria High Court, with the judges declaring that they could not believe that she and her co-accused 'would stoop so low for the protection and defence' of Richard Mdluli.

In June 2015 Shaun Abrahams was appointed as head of the National Prosecuting Authority, in which capacity his main activity proved to be to appeal to the courts against any reinstatement of the numerous charges of corruption against the President, while trying to bring self-evidently false charges against Pravin Gordhan following his reinstatement as Finance Minister. He also withdrew the charge of perjury against Jiba relating to her prosecution of Booysen.

Thuli Madonsela said of these appointments that Zuma had captured and repurposed agencies such as the National Prosecuting Authority, the Hawks, the State Security Agency and the South African Revenue Service *seemingly to protect him, his family, the Guptas and other associates*.[28]

Throughout his first term, Zuma had relied on his former comrade in arms in the resistance in Natal, Pravin Gordhan, as his Finance Minister. While Gordhan was admired and respected by his counterparts around the world, Zuma Cabinet appointees chafed at his (tight) control of expenditure. Even more resented were the stricter controls he established, following many scandals, over allowances for ANC MPs and his campaign against ministers purchasing luxury cars (one of the worst offenders having been the head of the South African Communist Party, Blade Nzimande). He also had been showing increasing concern at the numerous cases of malfeasance in the state-owned enterprises. Following Zuma's election victory in 2014, Gordhan was replaced as Finance Minister by his deputy, Nhlanhla Nene, and relegated to the task of supervising local government.

TWO ECONOMIC POLICIES
ARE BETTER THAN ONE

Under Mbeki there never had been any doubt where the ultimate responsibility for economic policy lay. But Zuma has never displayed much interest in policy. Nominally the government claimed continuing adherence to the National Development Plan devised by Trevor Manuel, but with only the Treasury and the Reserve Bank really committed to it.

A key appointment by Zuma was that of Rob Davies as Minister of Trade and Industry. A member of the South African Communist Party, with a much stronger ideological commitment than others, Davies has some admirable qualities, as the Department has been notably free of corruption on his watch and he has an impressive record on trade policy. But he has an ineradicable belief in the vital importance and virtues of state control. One US ambassador described dealing with him as akin to stepping back in a time warp to East Germany in the 1960s. An obvious problem with his belief in state control is that it would require what Trevor Manuel described as a 'capable state', which clearly does not exist in South Africa (or in many other countries).

Davies's most important and seriously damaging initiative was to engineer the cancellation of the investment treaties with South Africa's major trading partners. Signed to help promote investment in South Africa, he objected to the constraints on the goverment's freedom of action imposed by the fact that disputes could be submitted to international arbitration. Instead, investors must be satisfied with protection from the South African courts, under whatever legislation the government enacts. The European Commision, representing the UK, Germany, France, Italy and other European investors, were not amused, warning that the cancellation of the treaties would deter investment in South Africa. The US Chamber of Commerce was even more scathing about the cancellations in terms of the effect on US investment.

These reactions might have given others pause, given that US companies are thought to employ over 200,000 people in South Africa, while the European Union accounts for three quarters of all foreign direct investment, with Russia and China lagging far behind. These concerns appeared to be borne out as investment from the US and Europe dropped off sharply by 2016.

The cancellation of the treaties intended to attract investment was totally contrary to the aims of the National Development Plan. The most senior ANC figure engaged in economic policy observed to me wearily: 'We have decided that two economic policies are better than one.'

Before the Gupta-friendly minister Zwane inflicted his own damage on investment in the South African mining industry,

Davies insisted in the new planned minerals legislation that any mineral could be designated as 'strategic', with the state then able to determine whether and the terms on which it could be sold. This was accompanied by an insistence on beneficiation (processing minerals into manufactured goods), even though the Reserve Bank Governor questioned whether the country had the electricity capacity to engage in large-scale industrial beneficiation.

The Minister for Economic Development, Ebrahim Patel, joined the unions in opposing (unsuccessfully) the acquisition of a South African retailer by Walmart. Patel, however, since then has been active in encouraging the Industrial Development Corporation to sue the Guptas' Oakbay for the loans and interest lost in financing the purchase of Uranium One.

With investors worried also about the influence of the Gupta family and the evidence of large-scale corrupton around the state-owned enterprises, their interest was further dampened by statements from the President and others about the need for 'radical economic transformation', including the confiscation of land without compensation.

HOW TO CAPTURE A TAX AUTHORITY

In November 2014 Zuma appointed a close acolyte and family friend, Tom Moyane, to head the hitherto independent and highly regarded South African Revenue Service (SARS), which had been led for ten years by Pravin Gordhan before he became Finance Minister. The investigative unit under Pravin Gordhan's chief lieutenant – the very effective acting commissioner of SARS, head of enforcement and ANC veteran Ivan Pillay – had made themselves unpopular by starting to investigate some highly questionable businessmen closely associated with the President and members of his family, including Edward Zuma.

Two weeks after Moyane took over, the security services employed their usual tactic of planting a series of articles in the Johannesburg *Sunday Times*. Headlined 'SARS bugged Zuma', these suggested that the investigative unit was corrupt and out of control. This was followed by 'Taxman's rogue unit ran brothel!' A key investigator, Johann van Loggerenberg, was targeted and suspended. The story then was used by Moyane to suspend Ivan Pillay. Printing these fake news stories in due course was to cost the journalists responsible their jobs. The new editor of the *Sunday Times*, Bongani Siqoko, apologised for the 'rogue unit' stories.

The unit previously had helped Zuma to settle his tax arrears. Van Loggerenberg had investigated the links between Edward Zuma and the tobacco smuggling industry. Zuma's nephew, Khulubuse, and close business friend, Robert Huang, also were in the firing line. SARS had made themselves unpopular by insisting on the payment of import duty on a large consignment of ANC T-shirts imported by Huang before the 2014 elections. Huang previously had spent time in prison for involvement in a murder.

Early in 2014 Ivan Pillay had had the courage to go to see his former struggle comrade Zuma himself. It must have been a fascinating conversation. Pillay will have been very deferential to his President and former commander in the military wing of the ANC. He would, no doubt, have talked about Zuma's own tax affairs, but also must have warned him about the near criminal business associations of members of his family. Zuma is said to have responded non-committally, with questions such as 'Are you sure about that?' A subsequent affidavit from Pillay confirmed that he had raised with the President the campaign underway by members of the State Security Agency to try to discredit him and SARS and the involvement of some of their agents in the tobacco smuggling industry.[29]

Following the 2014 elections, Moyane was appointed to ensure that SARS steered clear of the President and his family's associates. Within months following the ousting of Pillay and Van Loggerenberg, Moyane had got rid of nearly all Pravin Gordhan's trusted investigators, prompting a mass exodus of competent people from SARS, contributing to a serious (50 billion rand) fall-off in tax revenues.[30]

Moyane's newly appointed deputy, Jonas Makwakwa, put in charge of tax collection from exceptionally wealthy South Africans, was suspended, together with his girlfriend who he appointed as his adviser, when large cash payments were reported to have been paid into his account via ATMs. Following what was said to be an investigation by the law firm Hogan Lovells, he was reinstated. But Hogan Lovells turned out not to have looked into any possible criminal activity as, they declared, that was a matter for the National Prosecuting Authority. Pravin Gordhan described this as a disgrace.

The changes in the investigative agencies were orchestrated on Zuma's behalf by the Minister of State Security, David Mahlobo, and the Minister of Police, Nathi Nhleko. Nhleko's girlfriend mysteriously was allocated contracts worth 30 million rand from the police budget with no normal tender process. It was Mahlobo who declared in 2015 that the state security agencies were investigating whether the Public Protector, Thuli Madonsela, Julius Malema and the President of the militant mining union AMCU were CIA agents.

The former head of the Hawks, Anwa Dramat, the former SARS acting commissioner, Ivan Pillay, and the ousted Independent Police Commissioner, Robert McBride, had been highly regarded within the party. McBride had earned intense odium for the bombing of a bar in Durban in the apartheid era, in which three white women were killed. But to Zuma's dismay, as the Independent Police Commissioner, he had proved himself to be – independent. Though not as drastically as its mentors in the Communist Party of the Soviet Union, the ANC had started to eat its own children, and in some cases its elders. The three accused vowed to bring to light 'the true reason for the abuse of state resources', stating that 'corruption is the biggest threat to our constitutional democracy'. Comrades who had fought together in the same trenches were now at each others' throats to protect corrupt activities.

* * *

In the near term, pending the benefits hoped for from the nuclear programme, the acquisition of the Dominion uranium mine had turned out to be a bad investment for the Guptas, though not at their expense, as the acquisition was 90 per cent financed by the

250 million rand loan from the state-owned Industrial Development Corporation (IDC). Because of the low grades and high cost of production at Uranium One, this investment had no chance of being profitable without a preferential contract to supply a large new South African nuclear programme, however unaffordable that might be. But the new Finance Minister, Nene, was proving just as firm an opponent of the project as Pravin Gordhan. Nene and Treasury officials also were concerned about the contracts being awarded by Transnet to Regiments, then Trillian, leading Eric Wood, who went on to become CEO at Trillian, reportedly to assure his colleagues that Nene would be removed.

In November 2013, after a series of meetings between Putin and Zuma, who had been visiting Moscow in part for medical treatment, the Russian nuclear energy company, Rosatom, signed a framework agreement with the South African Nuclear Energy Corporation envisaging the acquisition of 9,600 megawatts of nuclear power from Russia. An announcement to this effect was made in September 2014.

* * *

The Guptas, meanwhile, kept flaunting their influence by summoning ministers to meetings at their huge family compound at Saxonwold, including to events organised by the Zuma-supporting *New Age* newspaper, plus lavish entertainment for the politically connected. They increasingly were alleged to have, and to boast about having, foreknowledge of ministerial appointments. The Energy Minister, appointed to this key post despite her controversial performance as Fisheries Minister, placed millions of rand of advertising with *New Age*.

HOW TO STEAL A MINE

A key supplier to the electricity utility Eskom was the huge Optimum coal mine, owned by the international mining and trading company Glencore. Optimum had been supplying Eskom with coal at a price fixed in 1993, under which it was losing 100 million rand a month. Optimum had applied to Eskom to renegotiate the contract at a viable price. But by 2015 the Eskom board had been packed with Gupta associates and Brian Molefe had been appointed by Minister Gigaba as CEO of Eskom. Molefe refused to renegotiate the contract. A fine of 2.17 billion rand was imposed on Optimum for allegedly supplying low-quality coal.

According to Ngoako Ramatlhodi, the Minister of Mineral Resources, he was pressurised by Molefe and the Eskom chairman Ben Ngubane to suspend Glencore's mining licences. The country was still suffering from power cuts and he was astonished at the scale of the fine. He refused, saying, 'I am not going to shut the mines.'[31]

In September 2015, Ramatlhodi was abruptly transferred from his post to be replaced by the Gupta-connected Mosebenzi Zwane, who had written the letter of invitation which the Guptas used to try to justify their use of the Waterkloof air base. As the member of the Free State executive council responsible for agriculture, it was Zwane who had overseen the

Guptas' Estina dairy project, proceeds from which were used to finance the spectacularly extravagant wedding.

It was at this point that one of the most respected figures in the ANC told me grimly that 'the Guptas are now running this country'. I found it still at this stage hard to believe him, but Ramatlhodi had made clear that his abrupt removal from the Minerals Department had been because he would not cooperate with the family in staging by far their most ambitious and audacious coup to date.

Following his appointment as Minister of Mineral Resources, Zwane made clear that he intended to enforce what his predecessor Ramathlodi had described as the 'insanely large' 2.17 billion rand fine designed to persuade Glencore to sell Optimum. At this stage KPMG appeared to say that they had a client offering to buy the mine.

Zwane flew to Switzerland to persuade Ivan Glasenberg, CEO of Glencore, that he had no option but to sell to the Guptas. An international mining company of the size and industry standing of Glencore would never have given way to the Guptas. As far as they were concerned, they were being held to ransom by the sovereign.

Tegeta Exploration and Resources, controlled by the Guptas and Duduzane Zuma, bought Optimum in December 2015 for 2.15 billion rand, a few days after Zwane's visit to Switzerland. Glencore executives, who did not wish to be quoted, claimed that the company had been forced to sell. Tegeta would in consequence be supplying nearly 5 per cent of Eskom's nearly 120 million tons of coal. The fine was now supposed to be paid by the Guptas, but given their influence with the Minerals Department and its minister, there was never any doubt that they would be able to get it effectively rescinded.

As the purchase of Optimum was being finalised, Tegeta was awarded a new tender to supply the Arnot power station. This was used as justification for Eskom to grant Tegeta a 'pre-payment' of 586 million rand, which was the amount needed to close the gap in the payment for Optimum caused by the South African banks declining to lend further to the Guptas. The pre-payment was authorised at a special late-night meeting of the Eskom tender committee, chaired by Brian Molefe, on 11 April 2016. As Optimum by then was in business rescue, the administrators complained that these funds should have been delivered to Optimum, which did not receive them. A draft Treasury report in April 2017 concluded that the payment should be considered a loan, as none of the funds were used to produce more coal.

Eskom senior management by this time were awarding hugely profitable contracts to the Gupta consultancy Trillian and refusing to disclose the amounts. Business with Eskom had been captured even more comprehensively than with Transnet.

The Guptas continued selectively to invest in ANC figures who could be useful to them. Within weeks of the appointment of Collen Maine as head of the ANC Youth League, *City Press* were reporting that they had helped him to buy a 5 million rand house. Maine in turn has offered unconditional support for Zuma come what may, including threats that 'there will be blood' if the President's state of the union speech was disrupted. Not surprisingly, he has been equally vocal in support of the Guptas.

CHAPTER IX

A GOVERNMENT AT WAR WITH ITSELF

In May 2014, at the beginning of Zuma's second term, Pravin Gordhan had been replaced as Finance Minister by his deputy, Nhlanhla Nene, and given a less prominent and very difficult portfolio supervising the barely solvent municipalities.

As Finance Minister, Nene too earned respect for his attempts to maintain financial discipline at a time when South Africa increasingly was at risk of being downgraded to sub-investment grade by the principal international rating agencies. Nene and senior officials in the Treasury, led by the Director General, Lungisa Fuzile, also had started taking an increasingly close interest in 'consultancy' and other payments being made by the major state-owned enterprises to Gupta-related enterprises.

Nene supervised and approved a plan for the barely solvent South African Airways to purchase several Airbus aircraft, with Airbus agreeing to extinguish serious financial claims it could have made on SAA. But the chairperson of SAA, Dudu

Myeni, was also chair of the Jacob Zuma Trust and extremely close to the President. To general amazement, Myeni wrote to Airbus that 'SAA has decided to do this transaction differently, by engaging an African leasing company to engage directly with you,' causing the Chief Financial Officer of SAA to resign. Airbus rejected this and indicated that they would pursue their financial claims against SAA.

Nene especially had fallen foul of the President and the Gupta family by dragging his feet over the South Africa/Russia nuclear agreement negotiated by Zuma with Putin in Moscow. In 2015 Nene, attending with Zuma a BRICS summit in Moscow, was presented by the Russians with a letter guaranteeing financing of the nuclear project, which he refused to sign.

'THE AXE HAS FALLEN'

On 9 December 2015 the South African Cabinet approved the proposed nuclear reactor procurement despite a paper submitted by Nene on behalf of the Treasury contending that the programme was unaffordable. Zuma thereupon astonished the financial markets immediately after the meeting by announcing Nene's dismissal and his replacement by the virtually unknown ANC MP David 'Des' van Rooyen. During his tenure as mayor of Merafong in 2009, residents chased Van Rooyen out of the township and burned down his house. He was at the time and ever since has been closely associated with the Guptas.

His appointment triggered a dramatic fall in the value of the rand.

The Director General of the Treasury, Lungisa Fuzile, was told by Nene that 'the axe has fallen'. He then was telephoned by a member of the ANC's National Executive Committee, who said: 'I suppose you're going to get a Gupta minister now … Look at what happened at the Department of Natural Resources. The Guptas decide who they want as minister. Then they send along advisers.'[32]

On the following day, two Van Rooyen 'advisers', Mohamed Bobat and Ian Whitley, arrived at the National Treasury. Whitley is the son-in-law of the ANC Deputy Secretary General, Jessie Duarte, who, according to the Ramaphosa campaign for the ANC presidency, has multiple connections with the Guptas. Bobat was involved in the Regiments consultancy, which morphed into Trillian. Van Rooyen turned out to have been in constant contact with the Guptas in the days immediately preceding his appointment as Finance Minister.

The Treasury, to their amazement, were told that his two associates had the power to authorise expenditure on behalf of the new minister. Bobat started issuing instructions to the Treasury team. Fuzile and the senior staff at the National Treasury threatened to resign.

With the South African currency in free fall, the heads of the South African banks and the leading black South African entrepreneur (and brother-in-law of Cyril Ramaphosa), Patrice Motsepe, held an emergency meeting with Zweli Mkhize, treasurer general of the ANC, and Jeff Radebe, Minister in the Presidency, on Sunday 13 December. They warned of the likelihood of South Africa losing its investment grade status, thereby increasing the borrowing costs for all South African entities, and of dire consequences for the currency when the markets opened on Monday. With Ramaphosa, Mkhize and Radebe went to see Zuma, who found himself pressured into replacing Van Rooyen after just four days and reinstating Pravin Gordhan as Finance Minister, which stabilised the markets.

On his return to the Finance Ministry, Gordhan declared that some officials treated state enterprises 'as if it is a personal toy from which you extract money when you feel like it'. He ordered SAA to proceed with the Airbus contract as approved by the Treasury.

*　　*　　*

At the end of 2016, the government was reported to have sold almost the entirety of the country's strategic oil reserve at the extraordinarily low price of $29 per barrel – a steep discount to the already depressed market price. The sale was said to have been authorised by the Energy Minister, Tina Joemat-Pettersson, without Treasury approval. The minister initially denied that anything more than a 'rotation' had taken place. In 2017 her successor, Mmamoloko Kubayi, announced an investigation into who had approved the sale.

ROGUES AND VILLAINS

It was clear that Pravin Gordhan had been forced upon the President, whose associates immediately set about undermining him. Gordhan was obliged to threaten to resign before delivering his budget speech in February 2016 as he received a menacing letter from the Zuma-appointed head of the Hawks investigative team, General Ntlemeza, demanding immediate answers about the supposedly 'rogue' investigative unit he had established when head of the SARS. Gordhan said that this was meant to intimidate and distract him from the work he was doing on the budget. He attacked 'a group of people that are not interested in the economic stability of this country', but in undermining institutions and destroying reputations. The Treasury staff were told by him that he was determined to uphold the values of Nelson Mandela.

The new head of SARS, Tom Moyane, had enlisted the help of KPMG and paid them 23 million rand to support the case against Gordhan over the supposedly rogue investigative unit. This KPMG proceeded to do in a report that turned out to be a scissored and pasted version of a document by Moyane's legal adviser, including typos and spelling mistakes. Gordhan's response was: 'I thought forensic people were supposed to come up with facts. What does this say about the reputation of KPMG?'

The ANC Secretary General, Gwede Mantashe, denounced publicly the Hawks attack on Gordhan, with Trevor Manuel calling for Tom Moyane, appointed by Zuma as the new head of SARS, to be dismissed. Gordhan said that 'If you see me sitting here in October, then I have political support and if not...' This did not stop Gordhan receiving a further threatening letter from the Hawks, causing Gordhan to say that 'the Hawks *and those who instruct them* have no regard for the economic and social welfare of millions'. He added that these interventions were 'meant to intimidate and distract us'.

This was the point at which the deputy Finance Minister, Mcebisi Jonas, revealed that he had been offered Nene's post as Finance Minister by the Guptas, provided he agreed to support the nuclear programme and remove the Director General and three other named Treasury officials who were opposed to it. He rejected the offer which, he said, 'makes a mockery of our hard-won democracy'. The Guptas denied that the meeting had ever taken place.

The ANC MP Vytjie Mentor had gone public with her claim that, in a meeting with the Guptas in Saxonwold, with Zuma present elsewhere in the house at the time, she was offered the Ministry of Public Enterprises in lieu of Barbara Hogan, if she would agree to hand the SAA route to Mumbai over to the Guptas. Barbara Hogan declared that she had rejected previous pressure by the Guptas to hand the route over to Jet Airways, in which they were investors.

As a result of the statement by Mcebisi Jonas, described by the ANC veteran and Minister of Tourism, Derek Hanekom, as a person of unimpeachable integrity, an emergency meeting of the ANC's National Executive Committee was held on 19/20 March 2016. A joint letter from the Mandela, Tambo and Kathrada Foundations urged the ANC to 'take urgent corrective actions'.

'ALL OF US HAVE SKELETONS'

The meeting expressed 'full confidence in our President', but agreed that the Secretary General, Gwede Mantashe, and other senior officials should look into the allegations being made about the Guptas. Demands by Zuma supporters that Jonas should be removed from his post were rejected by Mantashe, who said that people should not be disciplined for 'doing the honourable thing … and saying there is a problem here'. The head of the ANC Women's League, Bathabile Dlamini, declared that *'All of us there in the NEC have skeletons and we don't want to take out all skeletons because all hell will break loose'*. Mantashe criticised her for being 'ill-disciplined'. Her remarks, unfortunately, were the clearest explanation for the ANC's unwavering support of a leader who manifestly was inflicting serious damage on the party.

Mantashe, who had declared that 'we are in danger of turning into a mafia state', said that the ANC would be meeting the Guptas to discuss the allegations against them and that, if necessary, they would be 'confronted', adding that the NEC expressed its 'utmost disgust at the arrogance, disrespect and reckless journalism' in the *New Age* and the Gupta news channel. He announced that he would be conducting the ANC's inquiry into the relationship with the Guptas, only for this non-investigation to be abandoned within weeks, ostensibly because only the former government spokesman was prepared to testify in writing against them.

While the NEC was meeting, on Sunday 20 March 2016 an armed, apartheid-style military raid was carried out on the offices of the respected independent Helen Suzman Foundation. The security guard was handcuffed to a railing, while agents seized computers and documents in exactly the same fashion as in the days of P. W. Botha. The Foundation's 'crime' was to have successfully challenged in the courts a number of arbitrary and unconstitutional actions by the government, including challenging, in the end successfully, the appointment of General Ntlemeza as head of the Hawks despite the damning judicial findings against him, dismissed by the Police Minister as merely 'opinions'. The Independent Police Commissioner, Robert McBride, suspended by the government for being too independent, declared that a section of the Hawks was operating like the Gestapo.

In December 2015, while Minister Zwane was helping them to acquire the Optimum mine, the Absa bank, linked to Barclays, decided to close the Guptas' bank accounts. The three other major South African banks (First National, Nedbank and Standard Bank) followed suit in April, when KPMG also, belatedly, severed relations with them.

A TEMPORARY PANIC

This caused a temporary major panic in the family, who talked of giving up their directorships and exiting to Dubai. Their reported attempt to export a suitcase full of diamonds via the Oppenheimer-owned Fireblade VIP terminal at O. R. Tambo International Airport having failed, Fireblade subsequently found their licence application to continue operating a terminal for private jets being held up by the Minister for Home Affairs, Malusi Gigaba, who initially agreed, but then reversed his decision apparently following pressure from the Gupta-connected chairman of Denel, which owned the building housing the terminal. Fireblade contended that the licence was being blocked by pressure from the Guptas. In October 2017 the courts ruled that the licence must be granted and should not have been withheld.

But the family, if they ever really thought of leaving, very soon were back. On 28 April the South African Cabinet declared its support for the Guptas on the Orwellian grounds that the decision of the South African banks to sever their connection with them could deter future investors in South Africa, according to Jeff Radebe, Minister in the Presidency.

This, coming from a government which had done little to promote investment and much to deter it, was the exact reverse of the truth, as one of the major disincentives to investing in South Africa was the conviction on the part of foreign investors that the Guptas had such close relationships with the President and the government that there was no level playing field in terms of investment opportunities. The presidency appointed a ministerial committee including the Guptas' friend Zwane to work out how to help the Guptas to restore their banking facilities.

Gordhan refused to intervene with the banks, subsequently revealing in an affidavit that the Treasury had been concerned about the huge sums being transferred out of South Africa by the twenty-eight Gupta companies. The Banking Association of South Africa declared that the banks had to comply with the Financial Intelligence Centre Act and anti-money-laundering regulations. In June, the CEO of Oakbay, Nazeem Howa, made the mistake of revealing a letter from Standard Bank referring to the South African, US and British anti-money-laundering legislation and stating that, following enhanced due diligence on Oakbay, they had decided to terminate the relationship.

In June the Johannesburg *Sunday Times* reported that the South African Reserve Bank had approached the Bank of Baroda about offshore transfers by the Guptas. The Treasury under Gordhan were asking questions about the 1.3 billion rand rehabilitation fund taken over by the Guptas when they acquired Optimum which, they feared, had been transferred offshore via the Bank of Baroda. The fund, including the interest earned on it, was supposed to be ring-fenced and to be used only for rehabilitation.

INCONVENIENT INQUIRIES

From the moment of his return to the Treasury, Pravin Gordhan and his officials had been taking a close interest in what they regarded as the suspiciously favourable supply agreements between Eskom and the Guptas' coal mining company Tegeta.

Once the new Eskom board had been installed by Malusi Gigaba, Tegeta, co-owned with Duduzane Zuma, had been able to secure an extremely favourable ten-year 400 million rand per annum contract to supply coal from their Brakfontein mine. The Treasury wanted to know how a ten-year contract had been awarded when the company did not yet have a water licence, the mining licence was due to expire in 2020, there had been no tender process and crucial quality tests had not been conducted on the coal to be supplied. A PriceWaterhouseCoopers report to this effect had not been passed on to them. Eskom experts in earlier tests had regarded coal from Brakfontein as too problematic in quality to be relied upon. The two leading coal quality control experts in Eskom were reported to have been suspended.

The Treasury declared publicly in August 2016 that Eskom was withholding information from them about the contracts with Tegeta. Eskom previously had suspended supplies of coal from Brakfontein because of quality issues, only for the suspension to be lifted within days, allegedly following the intervention of the head of generation, Matshela Koko. The Treasury were recommending a forensic audit to determine why Eskom was giving preferential treatment to Tegeta. As a draft Treasury report to this effect was about to be issued to Parliament in April 2017, the Guptas tried unsuccessfully to apply for an injunction preventing its release.

As Gordhan attempted to sort out the problems at the barely solvent South African Airways, which would have entailed replacing Myeni and most of the board, this was countered by a visit by Zuma to SAA, expressing confidence in them.

The state-run oil company, PetroSA, also was beset by continuous scandals. The 14.5 billion rand loss it made in 2015 was attributed to board and management incompetence, as the company embarked on a failed gas exploration project with totally inadequate preparation.[33]

This was followed by the Johannesburg *Sunday Times* reporting that the Hawks were recommending that Gordhan and his subordinates in the South African Revenue Service should be charged with 'espionage'. The intention, it was claimed, was to replace him as Finance Minister and possibly also to prosecute his predecessor as Finance Minister and Zuma critic, Trevor Manuel, thereby threatening two of the most respected political figures in South Africa (and outside it). The presidency said that no decision had yet been taken to prosecute Gordhan, but Zuma continued to lament publicly that he had been prevented from nominating the 'well-qualified' Des van Rooyen as Finance Minister. Having to backtrack on this showed where 'the real power' in the country lay. 'I found no one around me,' Zuma declared.

Pravin Gordhan observed that he could not believe that he was being investigated and could be charged for something of which he was totally innocent.

Through forty-five years of activism, I have worked for the advancement of the ANC, our constitution and our democratic government. I would never have thought that individuals within the very agencies of this government would now conspire to intimidate me ... I appeal to all South Africans to support the National Treasury staff, who have diligently, honestly and skilfully served the national interest. They are recognised world-wide for their professionalism and competence. Millions of people will pay the price if this subversion of democracy is left unconstrained and unchallenged.

As the South African Communist Party denounced him and rallied to the support of Gordhan, General Ntlemeza, the severely compromised head of the Hawks, had to go into reverse, declaring that Gordhan would not be arrested 'at this stage'. The tripartite alliance was under strain, with the SACP increasingly critical of the corruption of the regime and the 'recklessly brazen' actions of the Gupta family.

The Minerals Minister, Mosebenzi Zwane, meanwhile, was continuing to say that the banks would be called to account for having severed ties with the Guptas. 'We are government, banks must realise that.' On 1 September he declared that the Cabinet was recommending to the President that he should establish a judicial inquiry, review the Financial Intelligence Centre Act and the Prevention of Corrupt Practices Act and consider setting up a state bank. The UK-based public relations firm Bell Pottinger, who were advising the Guptas, had trailed these recommendations before they were made by Zwane. The statement was disavowed by the presidency as having been made by Zwane in his personal capacity. The ANC spokesman described it as having brought the government into disrepute.

The head of the National Prosecuting Authority by this stage had become known as Shaun 'the Sheep' Abrahams. In an attempt to counter this impression, in October he boldly declared that 'the days of disrespecting the NPA are over'. The days of not holding senior government officials to account also were over. There would be a major new prosecution – of Pravin Gordhan over Ivan Pillay's pension! This was supposed to be for fraud in relation to Pillay's pension settlement with SARS, a case that appeared from the outset without foundation, as it turned out to be.

With an application by him to the North Gauteng High Court seeking a judgment that he had no power to help the Guptas vis-à-vis the banks, Gordhan attached a document listing around seventy 'suspicious' transactions from the Guptas' accounts notified by the Financial Intelligence Centre, totalling 6.8 billion rand.

CHAPTER X

AN ELECTORAL SHOCK

By 2015, the ANC leadership at Luthuli House in Johannesburg were panicking about the state of the party in the Eastern Cape, the more so as this had been a key theatre of resistance to apartheid and also the heartland from which most of the prior Xhosa leadership of the ANC had come. The regional administration, including that of the health service, was one of the worst in South Africa, contrasting with the far more efficient and less corrupt Democratic Alliance administration in the Western Cape. The DA had been making serious inroads into ANC support in the urban areas and the universities.

HOW TO STEAL A CITY

To counter this disturbing trend, the ANC drafted in Danny Jordaan, successful organiser of the South African bid for the 2010 FIFA World Cup, to take over as the mayor of the crucial Nelson Mandela Bay conglomeration around Port Elizabeth,

though Jordaan was himself being accused of having authorised a US$10 million payment via the Caribbean representative
Jack Warner to help win the bid for South Africa. As both the
municipal and regional authorities were well known to be both
faction-ridden and exceptionally corrupt, a senior ANC official
and life-long supporter, Crispian Olver, was asked by Pravin
Gordhan to help sort out the mess.

His efforts to do so, ending in fears for his safety and utter
disillusionment, are described in graphic detail in his remarkable book *How to Steal A City*.[34] He found the local administration to be inextricably involved in massive frauds involving
housing and the future transport system and engaged in fero-
cious internal turf battles over the right to allocate contracts
and benefit from them. Only very blurred lines appeared to
exist between many officials and the often questionable businessmen benefiting from their largesse. As in other provinces,
the businessmen closest to the tender processes and most
likely to contribute to party funds frequently were criminal
syndicates, rather than representative of the broader business
community.

When Olver was asked to raise money to fight the municipal elections, he found funds promised to the party often to
be syphoned off before reaching it and that it was in practice
impossible to raise money without paybacks to the businessmen
offering it, compromising his own integrity. He did manage to
get rid of some corrupt officials, but as his efforts aroused fierce
local antagonism, he found himelf without effective support.
When the ANC lost control of Nelson Mandela Bay, he wrote a

brutally honest assessment of why, including the negative effect of 'brand Zuma', which found its way into *City Press*, terminating his relationship with the current leadership of the ANC.

He describes his story of Nelson Mandela Bay as a textbook case of state capture 'and what has become a national disease'. What started out as political interference in the appointments of officials morphed into something more sinister as syndicates grafted themselves onto the relationship between the ANC and the municipality, becoming bankers to the dominant political faction. Many other municipalities, though not quite to the same degree, had become vehicles of wholesale looting, the root problem being the erosion of the separation between the ANC and state institutions.

* * *

The municipal elections held on 3 August 2016 were viewed by the press and the opposition parties as tantamount to a referendum on the performance of the ANC, in particular their failure to make any impression on the problem of high unemployment, endemic corruption – as evidenced by Nkandla and the relationship with the Guptas – and poor service delivery. Gwede Mantashe diagnosed the urban middle class as a 'soft spot'. The opposition parties historically had fared better in municipal than in national elections against the ANC.

In response, the ANC reportedly spent 1 billion rand on the elections and based its campaign against the Democratic Alliance on the proposition that they alone represented the interests of the black majority, with the DA fronting for and representing the interests of the white minority. The new DA leader, Mmusi Maimane, nevertheless made a generally positive impression in the campaign.

The results came as an unpleasant shock to the ANC. Their share of the vote fell from 62 to 54 per cent of the votes cast, with that of the DA rising to 27 per cent and the EFF to 8 per cent. The DA defeated the ANC by 47 to 41 per cent in Nelson Mandela Bay, enabling them to lead a coalition government there, with Athol Trollip taking over from Danny Jordaan as mayor. In the Zuma heartland of KwaZulu-Natal, Inkatha staged a comeback, winning 1.8 million votes in rural Zululand, and retaining control of Zuma's home district of Nkandla.

The DA also emerged as the largest party in Tshwane, the conglomeration around Pretoria, giving it the right to seek to form the administration. The ANC share of the vote fell by fourteen points to 45 per cent in Johannesburg, with the DA winning 38 per cent and the EFF 11 per cent of the votes cast. The DA, meanwhile, further strengthened its stranglehold on Cape Town and the Western Cape. Maimane said that the outcome had shown that the ANC could no longer rule 'with impunity'.

These results caused consternation within the ANC. Ramaphosa responded by saying that the party needed to show that it was listening to the electorate. Kgalema Motlanthe said that the ANC would die if it did not get back in touch with ordinary people. Although Zuma had proved to be a massive electoral handicap, when the National Executive Committee of the party met after the elections, it accepted 'collective responsibility' and the Secretary General, Mantashe, declared that no one had suggested that Zuma should stand down.

Despite these huge setbacks for the ruling party, the DA fell short of the 30 per cent share of the vote it had hoped to achieve and the EFF, with virtually no financial backing, also fell a long way short of its ambition to double its share of the vote. The ANC vote held up better with the electorate outside the main urban areas.

AN UNLIKELY ALLIANCE

Julius Malema and the EFF refused any cooperation with the ANC – which Malema described as 'corrupt to the core' – unless they dumped Zuma. Having denounced the DA as the mouthpiece of white capital, nevertheless he concluded that they were 'the better devil'. As a result the DA was able to take over in Tshwane, with EFF support.

Despite their antipathy to the DA leader in Johannesburg, the businessman Herman Mashaba, the EFF enabled the DA also to form an administration there, resulting in the DA winning control of four of the five major metropolitan centres, with the ANC retaining control only in Durban. The loss of prestige and patronage for the ANC has been severe. The reaction of Gwede Mantashe was to denounce these coalitions as 'colonial schemes'.

Within the ANC, the stage was now set for the battle to succeed Zuma as President of the ANC at the party's conference in December 2017. The chances of Zuma being able to carry on as President of the party, as earlier he was thinking of trying to do, had finally been extinguished. But Zuma and his supporters had shown their determination to try to ensure that he continued as President until 2019 – though the country and his party could ill afford it – and that in December 2017 he should be succeeded as ANC President by his ex-wife, Nkosazana Dlamini-Zuma, vis-à-vis the other main contender, Cyril Ramaphosa, in the hope and expectation that she would then help to neutralise pursuit of the corruption charges against him.

CHAPTER XI

GORDHAN VERSUS ZUPTA

The election result was greeted briefly by a strengthening of the rand, for it was felt to mean that it would now be harder for the President to get rid of the highly respected Finance Minister, Pravin Gordhan, thereby affording South Africa a respite from the danger of being downgraded to junk bond status.

A DISTASTEFUL CAMPAIGN

To general astonishment and the dismay of the South African business community, the elections were followed immediately by a clash between what many by now had come to regard as the reputable and disreputable elements of the ANC. Pravin Gordhan and the former senior officers of the South African Revenue Service were summoned by the head of the Hawks, General Ntlemeza, to make a statement in relation to the Hawks' investigation into their setting up the supposedly illegal investigative unit within the Revenue Service. Gordhan refused to do so, on legal advice. A letter from South African business leaders denounced these 'sinister manoeuvres', declaring that the investigation 'lacked credibility and legitimacy' and threatened South Africa's investment grade status.

What in effect was happening was a reversion to the methods employed under P. W. Botha, when a group of securocrats with no understanding of or interest in the economy, under the direct authority of the President, pursued against all comers the only objective of any interest to them, which was to maintain control by all means necessary and at any cost. Meanwhile, the Gupta-controlled Tegeta mining company sought an injunction to prevent the Treasury publishing its investigation into the licences awarded to Tegeta by Eskom.

The Deputy President, Cyril Ramaphosa, denounced the 'distasteful campaign' against Gordhan. Zuma, however, declared that he had no power to stop the investigation into Gordhan, then staged a further coup by seeking himself to take over the committee on the state-owned enterprises which Ramaphosa had been chairing. As the veteran anti-apartheid commentator Allistair Sparks pointed out in a valedictory column shortly before his death: 'This unschooled man has pronounced himself commander in chief of the economy. In doing so, he has grabbed control of all the big state feeding troughs on which the "tenderpreneurs" have been engorging themselves since he came to power seven years ago. There will now be no restraining them.'[35]

DISDAIN AND CONTEMPT

Zuma was not invited to attend the funeral at this time of the former ANC minister, the Reverend Makhenkesi Stofile. It was, however, attended by many of the old guard of the ANC and addressed by Sipho Pityana, formerly the ANC-appointed Director General of Foreign Affairs, detained and tortured by the apartheid security police, now a prominent business leader. He declared that the ANC's setbacks were self-inflicted. They had ceded the moral high ground. 'The President of our country takes every opportunity to show disdain and contempt for our constitution,' he added. They were falling over each other to steal from the poor. Were the latter-day ANC leaders of a revolution or thieves and looters? There was no accountability. 'Our movement is captured' and consequently the government was captured. Without new leadership, they would lose the next election.

On 26 August 2016, Pravin Gordhan was reported as telling Treasury staff that he was prepared to die to save the country from thieves. This was part of a bigger political battle. They should not be surprised if he and his deputy, Mcebisi Jonas, were removed. He added that he was being persecuted for doing his job by investigating contracts with companies owned by the Guptas.

Cyril Ramaphosa talked of a government at war with itself. F. W. de Klerk declared that the way in which black economic empowerment policies were being implemented would cause many white South Africans to emigrate. As the SACP members of the government also were threatened with dismissal because of the party's criticisms of corruption, their Deputy Secretary General and deputy Minister of Public Works, Jeremy Cronin, said that they would rather leave the government than remain silent in such circumstances. They denounced the attacks on Gordhan as politically motivated because of his stand against corruption and expressed scepticism as to whether the Guptas could find any buyers for or really intended to sell their thinly traded and overvalued assets. The veteran ANC and SACP anti-apartheid activist, Raymond Suttner, voiced concern that the only way an unreformed ANC could hold on to power would be by illegal means, which they were capable of employing.

Meanwhile, with Zuma intervening to chair the ministerial committee dealing with the state enterprises, Gordhan was unable to dislodge Zuma's closest female crony, Dudu Myeni, from her disastrous chairmanship of South African Airways, though he did achieve other changes to the board. The company had been kept afloat by 14 billion rand of government guarantees, plus now a further 5 billion rand. It also had been fined for anti-competitive practices in its efforts to put rival internal airlines out of business.

The Zuma securocrats continued the war against Gordhan. At a time when the Guptas were cash-strapped, the media were reporting that the head of SARS, Tom Moyane, had intervened personally to authorise the payment to them of a 70 million rand VAT refund. They were reported to have asked for this to be paid offshore, though this was *ultra vires* for SARS.

A PROSECUTING FIASCO

Shaun Abrahams's attempt to dislodge Gordhan for supposedly illegally approving the pension settlement for Ivan Pillay backfired badly, as a host of respected former ANC leaders, including former President Motlanthe, the surviving Rivonia triallists Ahmed Kathrada, Andrew Mlangeni and Denis Goldberg and many others rallied to Gordhan's support, threatening to attend the court hearing. Legal experts pronounced the case brought against Gordhan to be politically motivated. It then transpired that a senior SARS employee, Vlok Symington, claimed to have been held hostage and physically manhandled in the presence of the Hawks investigator Brigadier Xaba for refusing to hand over a memorandum in which he expressed ethical objections to the case against Gordhan.

Two days before the case was due to be heard, Abrahams abruptly withdrew the charges, rather than face a display of support for Gordhan and a fiasco in court. This caused a spectacular falling out between Abrahams, as head of the National Prosecuting Authority, and General Ntlemeza, head of the Hawks' investigators and Zuma's chief attack dog against Gordhan. Ntlemeza wanted indignantly to know why the case against Gordhan had been dropped. Abrahams responded furiously that the Hawks had withheld from him the evidence from Symington.[36]

After this fiasco, neither Abrahams nor Ntlemeza resigned. Abrahams received a letter from Zuma asking him to show cause why he should continue in office, but this turned out to be purely *pro forma*. Ntlemeza's response was to redouble his efforts to charge Pravin Gordhan.

THE LOOTING OF ESKOM

At a special late-night meeting after the South African banks declined to do further business with the Guptas because of concerns about over seventy questionable transactions, Eskom under Brian Molefe had agreed to bail them out by handing over the 586 million rand 'pre-payment' to the Gupta coal company Tegeta. It subsequently was revealed by the CFO, Anoj Singh, that with no Treasury authority, Eskom also had given them a 1.6 billion rand guarantee, intended to help the Guptas to overcome the withdrawal of their banking facilities, while acquiring Optimum with the connivance of Eskom management.

Eskom, in defiance of the Treasury, proceeded to start issuing the first contracts for 'consultancy services' for the nuclear programme, with Molefe claiming, contrary to all the evidence, that this could be financed without recourse to government funding, despite Eskom's critical dependence on government guarantees to fund its burgeoning 360 billion rand debt.

Molefe's successor as acting CEO of Eskom, Matshela Koko, endorsed this absurd claim. Despite his having denied this on live television, his signature also appeared on the document approving the pre-payment to Gupta-owned Tegeta, to help them to buy Optimum.[37] In January 2018, amid huge controversy, following an internal disciplinary hearing, he was reinstated in a senior position in Eskom, only for this to be reversed by the new leadership of Eskom.

CHAPTER XII

STATE OF CAPTURE

In her role as Public Protector, Thuli Madonsela and her staff had produced a series of impressive, thoroughly researched and well-written reports, not only about Nkandla, but also about the fiasco over locomotive procurement at the Passenger Rail Authority (*Derailed*) and the abusive regime of Hlaudi Motsoeneng at the South African broadcasting authority (*When Governance and Ethics Fail*), only for the government to find ways to do nothing about them.

Far from being ready to give up, her response was strongly influenced by her deep personal commitment to the constitution she had helped to write and to Mandela values. Recalling her own participation in the ultimately successful protests of the United Democratic Front, she ended up enquiring: 'Where are the people of South Africa?' Asked what ordinary citizens could do about a state that tore up the rule book, 'You must organise civil society to rise,' was her reply. And rise they did, as her courage was a catalyst for the extraordinary mobilisation of civil society in South Africa againt the misdeeds of the regime.

Working furiously against the clock in her last days as Public Protector, Thuli Madonsela, instead of retiring gracefully, produced her dramatic report on the allegations of state capture by the Guptas.

The Guptas' lawyer declared that the report would be published 'at her own risk and peril'. Zuma and Des Van Rooyen immediately sought injunctions to prevent its publication. The new Public Protector, Busisiwe Mkhwebane, declined to appeal against these interdicts, telling her staff that she wanted to work with government rather than against it and reportedly changing the news programmes in their offices from an independent channel to the Gupta-controlled news network. But the courts ordered the report to be published forthwith.

When the 335-page report, entitled *State of Capture*, was published on 15 October 2016, the contents were explosive, making an absolute mockery of the 'investigation' by Mantashe for the ANC into the same allegations.

AN OFFER NOT EASY TO REFUSE

Madonsela set out the allegation by the deputy Finance Minister, Mcebisi Jonas, that President Zuma's son, Duduzane Zuma, business partner of the Guptas, arranged a meeting with him in October 2015, then took him to the Guptas' residence in Johannesburg. Once there, according to Jonas, Ajay Gupta said that the family were earning 6 billion rand a year from state contracts. They hoped to increase this to 8 billion rand a year.

He allegedly told Jonas that he would be made Finance Minister, on condition that he removed several Treasury officials who
were a 'stumbling block' to the Guptas' commercial ambitions.
Jonas rejected the offer. Jonas added that, as he was about to
leave, Ajay Gupta offered him 600 million rand (around $45
million), which he rejected, then asked him if he had a bag
'which he could use to receive and carry 600,000 rand in cash
immediately', which Jonas also declined.

In December 2015, Zuma had astonished the country by dismissing Finance Minister Nene and replacing him by the virtually unknown Des van Rooyen. The report revealed that Van
Rooyen had been to the Gupta residence on seven occasions,
including the day before his appointment as Finance Minister.

Brian Molefe, CEO of Eskom, turned out to be a key figure
in the report, according to which he exchanged fifty-eight
phone calls with Ajay Gupta between August 2015 and March
2016 and was in the Saxonwold area on nineteen occasions between August and November 2015. He suffered much ridicule
for contending that he might have been in the area to visit a
shebeen, notwithstanding the fact that no such establishment
exists within the ritzy confines of Saxonwold. It was alleged
that he had deliberately weakened the financial position of
Optimum Coal, a major Eskom supplier, so as to enable it to
be bought by the Guptas.

The report began with a quotation: 'One of the crucial elements of our constitutional vision is to make a decisive break
from the unchecked abuse of state power' of the apartheid era.
It noted that the allegations made by Mcebesi Jonas and Vytjie

Mentor, though extremely serious, had never been investigated by anyone. It was 'worrying' that the Gupta family may have known in advance of Nene's dismissal as Finance Minister and that his successor, Van Rooyen, could be placed near Saxonwold on at least seven occasions, including the day before he was appointed a minister.

It reported 'allegations backed by evidence' of an allegedly cosy relationship between Brian Molefe and the Gupta family. It was extraordinary for the South African Cabinet to have intervened in a dispute between the banks and a private company owned by the President's friends and his son.

In the sale of Optimum, Glencore appeared to have been severely prejudiced by Eskom's refusal to sign a new agreement for coal supply. '*It appears that the conduct of Eskom was solely for the purpose of forcing Optimum into business rescue and distress,*' to the benefit of Tegeta. Minister Zwane's flight itinerary from Switzerland appeared to be irregular (he was reported to have travelled back on the Guptas' plane). It appeared that the awarding by Eskom to Tegeta of contracts to supply the Arnot power station was solely for the purposes of financing Tegeta and enabling it to buy Optimum.

The report noted that Tegeta having informed Glencore that they were 600 million rand short to buy Optimum, the Eskom board held the meeting at 9 p.m. on 11 April 2016 to authorise the pre-payment to Tegeta. Tegeta's conduct and misrepresentations about this could amount to fraud. The security of the Optimum rehabilitation fund, now held by the

Bank of Baroda, could not be guaranteed, as the funds were constantly moved around between accounts.

The Guptas indignantly denied the allegations, complaining that they had not been given a chance to reply. The report concluded that there was evidence of apparent corruption at the highest levels of the South African government, which needed to be investigated by a judicial commission of inquiry, which should be headed by a judge appointed by the Chief Justice, not Zuma.

The response of General Ntlemeza, head of the Hawks, was to hasten to assure the Guptas that no investigations were being conducted into them.

The head of the South African Communist Party and Minister for Higher Education, Blade Nzimande, denounced the 'parasitic' activities of the Guptas. The head of the ANC Youth League, Collen Maine, on the other hand, declared that the Public Protector's report was of no account and Brian Molefe was a 'shining diamond'.

AN EXPENSIVE CONSULTANCY

Brian Molefe burst into tears on television and resigned as CEO of Eskom. Mark Pamensky, one of the Eskom directors closely linked to the Guptas, also resigned. At Transnet, Molefe and his Finance Director, Anoj Singh, who accompanied him to Eskom, had awarded a 600 million rand contract to the Trillian consultancy, controlled by Salim Essa, the closest business associate of the Guptas. The international consultancy firm McKinsey subsequently suspended one of its South African executives for having given the impression that Trillian was acting as a sub-contractor for McKinsey, which had got itself awarded a 1 billion rand consultancy for six months' work.

ANOTHER STATE COMPANY SCANDAL

Appointed chairman of the Passenger Rail Agency of South Africa (PRASA), Popo Molefe had been a major figure in the struggle against apartheid inside South Africa, having been a leading figure in the Delmas treason trial. At the time, I visited the courtroom to show support for the defendants, who included also 'Terror' Lekota, and to seek to dissuade the judge from handing down a death sentence. Molefe had served as Premier of the North West Province under Mandela.

Popo Molefe found evidence that seven billion rand of contracts had been improperly awarded, including 3.5 billion rand spent via a black empowerment company, Swifambo Rail Leasing, on the Spanish locomotives that proved totally unsuitable for South Africa, as they were too high for the South African tunnel network. The Auditor General in 2016 had found 13.9 billion rand in irregular expenditure. Affidavits indicated that large payments were made to persons describing themselves as friends of the ANC and of President Zuma. Popo Molefe repeatedly attempted to get the Hawks under

General Ntlemeza to investigate, with no effective response from them.

Instead of pursuing what appeared to be well-founded allegations, the minister dismissed Molefe and the board. Molefe described PRASA as being operated like a 'farm' where ANC operatives went to 'harvest' for themselves. The courts subsequently adjudged the contract with Swifambo Leasing to be void, the company having only been formed just before the tender and having no railways expertise, leaving PRASA to try to recover the cost of the locomotives from the suppliers.

'SAVING SOUTH AFRICA'

In a thinly veiled attack on his successor, on 8 November Thabo Mbeki urged the government to 'act now and do the right thing, because time is not on our side'. The country was trapped in a deepening political, economic and social crisis. Negative features had emerged in the ANC, including the abuse of political power for personal enrichment, endemic corruption and the looting of public resources, 'tenderpreneurship' and state capture. Economic growth was too weak to raise living standards. One third of the population was effectively excluded from the economy. Parliament had failed to respond to the judgment about Nkandla.

As Sipho Pityana launched his 'Save South Africa' campaign, supported by former Robben Islanders, frustration with Zuma boiled over at a meeting of the National Executive

Committee (politburo) of the ANC on 26 to 29 November 2016. Derek Hanekom, a Cabinet member since the time of Mandela and a member of the Zuma government, tabled a motion of no confidence in the President. This was supported by the Health Minister, Aaron Motsoaledi, principal architect of the campaign against Aids; the Minister of Public Works; the ANC economic supremo, Enoch Godongwana; the ANC chairman in Gauteng, Paul Mashatile; and others.

Around one third of the NEC clearly wanted Zuma to go. With Zuma present in the meeting, those who wanted to oust him demanded a secret ballot, which was not agreed. He was fiercely defended by his ex-wife, Nkosazana Dlamini-Zuma who, otherwise, would have seen her own leadership ambitions go up in smoke, by the Security Minister, Mahlobo, and in threatening terms by Ace Magashule on behalf of the so-called Premier League. Zuma said that he was not going to stand down – if he did, his enemies would try to put him in jail.

No vote was taken and Zuma was enabled to carry on. Mantashe declared that there would be a change anyway in 2019 and no action should be taken against those who had demanded that the President should stand down.

The new Public Protector, meanwhile, threatened an investigation into her predecessor, Madonsela, for leaking the transcript of her meeting with Zuma about state capture, which she did to refute Zuma's claims that he had not been given a chance to answer the allegations against him. Mkhwebane's performance since taking office already had earned her the soubriquet of 'State Protector'.

'IT WAS ALWAYS ABOUT YOUR ETHICAL CONDUCT, SIR'

Before finalising her report, Thuli Madonsela had insisted on trying to interview the President herself. The transcript of the meeting showed Zuma's lawyer, Michael Hulley, who himself was caught up in the Aurora mining scandal, stonewalling for four hours while Madonsela tried to get Zuma to answer factual questions about his relationship with the Guptas. As not one of her questions was answered, with Zuma and Hulley pretending not to know what they were being asked about, the intrepid and tenacious Thuli Madonsela responded: 'It was always about your ethical conduct, sir.'

Madonsela observed that she was leaving her office with a cynical view of human nature, having witnessed people lying under oath without blinking.

*   *   *

As the year ended, Cyril Ramaphosa held talks with the trade unions and business representatives to try to help stave off a downgrade of the country's credit rating by the international credit rating agencies. It was agreed to recommend a minimum wage of 3,500 rand per month, to be phased in over two or three years, with exceptions for domestic work and agriculture. In future, ballots should be held before strikes, though several unions had no provision for this.

These efforts were rewarded, as the rating agencies refrained from downgrading South Africa to junk bond status. They did so less on the basis of fundamentals, which remained very weak (0.3 per cent growth in 2016 and continuing acute policy uncertainty) than from a desire not to undermine the efforts of Gordhan and Ramaphosa to avoid such an outcome. The government's debts in rand, however, had been downgraded to a level only fractionally above junk status, while Eskom's credit rating was downgraded by Standard & Poor's to BB with a negative outlook.

In March 2017, at a summit meeting with the most senior leaders of the ANC, including Zuma, their alliance partners in the South African Communist Party, concerned about corruption, demanded that the Guptas be stripped of their South African citizenship and Brian Molefe removed from the position he had just obtained, following his ignominious departure from Eskom, as an ANC MP.

By this stage the Minister of Social Security and Zuma's key ally as head of the ANC's Women's League, Bathabile Dlamini, was in serious trouble because of her failure to take any action in response to the Constitutional Court's finding in 2014 that the contract to pay the nearly 18 million social grants to the poorest South Africans awarded to a company called Cash Paymaster Services (CPS) was invalid as it had been awarded without any proper tender process, and should be reassigned.

Dlamini it was who, at a meeting of the ANC politburo, had declared that Zuma must be protected as 'we all have skeletons'. As, deliberately, she failed to make any alternative arrangements, the Constitutional Court delivered an even more damning judgment on March 2017 that, to enable the payments to be made at all, CPS would have to continue administering them for a further twelve months. Bathabile Dlamini was held responsible for this debacle. Replacement of the contract would now be under the direct supervision of the Court.

Following this judgment from the Constitutional Court, the office of the Chief Justice was the subject of a burglary, with those responsible making off with most of the computers.

ONE VILLAIN LESS

In the same month, in a victory for the Helen Suzman Foundation, which had brought the case against him, the Pretoria High Court ruled that the appointment of General Ntlemeza to lead the Hawks had been unlawful. In view of the earlier findings of dishonesty and bad faith against him, he was deemed to lack the integrity to hold any public office, let alone that of head of the Hawks.

CHAPTER XIII

OUSTING PRAVIN GORDHAN

Jacob Zuma had never been likely to take any of this lying down. At a meeting in KwaZulu-Natal, attended by Zuma, the head of the ANC youth league, Collen Maine, in a clear reference to the necklacing of 'collaborators' under apartheid, urged that Gordhan should be treated as an *impimpi* (informer). This about an ANC veteran who had risked his life in the resistance to apartheid. Zuma himself described the Treasury under Gordhan as an obstacle to 'transformation'.

In March 2017, Zuma made a mockery of the findings of the rating agencies by abruptly recalling Pravin Gordhan from meetings with the investment community in London and preventing his deputy Jonas from departing for a planned visit to the US. The Gupta news channel reported, correctly, that he had decided to remove Gordhan.

Zuma revealed that he had received what turned out to be a manifestly absurd intelligence report that they were meeting enemies of the government in London. The intelligence agencies apparently had concluded that foreign investors were the enemy. The South African Communist Party protested in vain. Zuma pressed for Brian Molefe to be appointed to replace Gordhan. Ramaphosa, Mantashe and the Treasurer General Mkhize opposed this, given Molefe's association with the Guptas. They tried also to secure the removal of notoriously incompetent or corrupt ministers, such as Dlamini, Muthambi (communications) and Zwane.

Dlamini subsequently was to destroy her own fragile credibility and damage that of the state broadcaster too by paying SABC 500,000 rand from the Social Security budget to broadcast an extended interview with her in the run-up to the ANC conference in December 2017 (having run the interview, only then did SABC decide not to accept the fee).

Action was held up for a day for the funeral of Mandela's great friend, the Rivonia triallist, Ahmed Kathrada. Zuma was asked by Kathrada's family not to attend the funeral. Zuma's former deputy, Kgalema Motlanthe, read out the letter Kathrada had written to Zuma a year before, calling on him to stand down, to a standing ovation.

None of this, and still less the remonstrances of his colleagues, had any effect on Zuma. Gordhan was replaced by the Zuma henchman and hitherto Gupta-friendly Malusi Gigaba. Hanekom, Jonas and Ramatlhodi were fired.

Gwede Mantashe, Secretary General of the ANC, felt that the list of changes had been drawn up 'elsewhere, and given to us to legitimise'. He was left lamenting that competent ministers had been dismissed and incompetents retained.

The dismissal of two highly capable ministers, Gordhan and Jonas, who had both exposed and fought against corruption, and the consequent departure of the highly regarded Director General Lungisa Fuzile, was seen as an assault on the institution of the National Treasury precisely because it was an obstacle to corruption. Another bane of the Guptas, chief procurement officer Kenneth Brown, already had left the Treasury.

The former head of Cosatu, Vavi, declared that 'the thieves have now taken over the Treasury'. The new deputy Finance Minister, Sipho Buthelezi, a Zuma loyalist, had been criticised in the Public Protector's report over his role in corruption at the Passenger Rail Authority. The ANC Chief Whip in Parliament, Jackson Mthembu, said that the only crime Gordhan and Jonas had committed was being incorruptible. The Mandela Foundation issued a statement entitled 'Time to account for crippling the state', demanding that Zuma be called to account and deploring the emasculation of the prosecuting authorities through 'political meddling to serve private interests'.

JOINING THE DOTS

As the presidency postponed the state memorial to Kathrada, Gordhan, by now dismissed, addressed a meeting convened by the Mandela and Kathrada Foundations at the Johannesburg City Hall, attended by Nelson Mandela's widow Graça Machel. Declaring optimistically that 'the ANC is ours', he said that 'our souls are not for sale', and that the reasons given for his dismissal were nonsense. Inviting people to 'join the dots' in understanding what had happened, he denounced the Gupta news channels for fabricating 'fake news' in attacking those who opposed them, and the British PR firm Bell Pottinger for aiding and abetting them. He added that the nonsensical intelligence report which had triggered his recall had referred to an intercepted telephone conversation with me, which he had made because I had arranged investor meetings for many members of the South African government – including Jacob Zuma.

A DEFLECTION CAMPAIGN

The role of Bell Pottinger in organising fake social media campaigns and helping to develop the narrative about 'white minority capital' in concert with the hitherto scarcely existent and Gupta-supporting Black First Land First group, set up ostensibly to counter the EFF, was denounced by one of South Africa's largest employers, Johann Rupert, chairman of Remgro, and in the Johannesburg *Sunday Times* on 2 April 2017, quoting former members of the firm alleging that this contributed to the departure from the company of its founder, Tim Bell. Johann Rupert had become a target for the regime by being the first major business leader to call for the resignation of Jacob Zuma ('I didn't trust the last [apartheid] lot, and I don't trust this lot either.')

The account for the Gupta company Oakbay Investments was managed for Bell Pottinger by one of their partners,

Nelson Mandela shortly after his release from prison on 11 February 1990.
MEDIA24/GALLO IMAGES/GETTY IMAGES

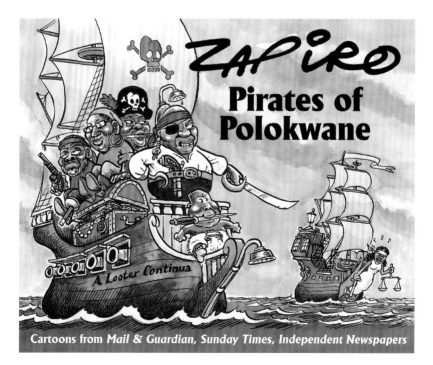

Jacob Zuma captures the ANC at the party conference at Polokwane in December 2008.
ZAPIRO

LEFT ANC President Jacob Zuma performing a Zulu dance during a Gift of the Givers event in Tembisa, before he became President of South Africa, 23 July 2008.
NEIL McCARTNEY/GETTY IMAGES

RIGHT The brothers Ajay and Atul Gupta together with Duduzane Zuma speaking to *City Press* from the *New Age* newspaper's offices in Johannesburg, 4 March 2011.
MUNTU VILAKAZI/CITY PRESS/GALLO IMAGES/GETTY IMAGES

The Gupta family compound in Saxonwold, Johannesburg, 7 April 2017.
FELIX DLANGAMANDLA/ GALLO IMAGES/ FOTO24 / GETTY IMAGES

Thuli Madonsela at a press conference while Public Protector, 14 July 2011.
LIZA VAN DEVENTER/ GALLO IMAGES/ FOTO24/ GETTY IMAGES

Nkandla: Questions to be answered – on Thuli Madonsela's investigation into public spending on the construction of President Zuma's private residence.
ZAPIRO: *THE TIMES*, 9 OCTOBER 2012

Finance Minister Pravin Gordhan is summoned by Hawks investigators.
ZAPIRO: *MAIL & GUARDIAN*, 26 AUGUST 2016

Thuli Madonsela's state capture report leaves President Zuma damaged.
ZAPIRO: *MAIL & GUARDIAN*, 4 NOVEMBER 2016

She's all yours, boss – one of Zapiro's most controversial cartoons, featuring President Zuma,
his allies Atul Gupta, Moegsien Williams, David Mahlobo, Bathabile Dlamini and the rape
of South Africa. ZAPIRO: *DAILY MAVERICK*, 11 APRIL 2017

The other gathering – on Atul Gupta's BBC interview stating he was proudly South African and denying claims linking his family to state capture as well as kickbacks.
ZAPIRO: *DAILY MAVERICK*, 4 AUGUST 2017

Losing it – on the escalating problems facing President Zuma and the Gupta brothers.
ZAPIRO: *DAILY MAVERICK*, 21 SEPTEMBER 2017

Budget statement – on Finance Minister Malusi Gigaba's maiden budget speech in Parliament.
ZAPIRO: *DAILY MAVERICK*; 25 OCTOBER 2017

Economic Freedom Fighters leader Julius Malema and DA leader Mmusi Maimane during the State of the Nation address debate, 18–19 June 2014. SOUTH AFRICAN GCIS

Mugabe gone – on President Mugabe's resignation.
ZAPIRO: *DAILY MAVERICK*, 22 NOVEMBER 2017

Deputy President Cyril Ramaphosa and Nkosazana Dlamini-Zuma at the 5th ANC
national policy conference, 1 July 2017. MUNTU VILAKAZI/FOTO24/GETTY IMAGES

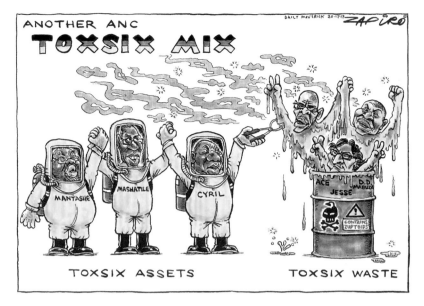

The ANC's 'Top Six' divided – political analyst claims that half the ANC's new 'Top Six'
– Gwede Mantashe, Paul Mashatile, Cyril Ramaphosa, Jessie Duarte, D. D. Mabuza
and Ace Magashule – are a disaster. ZAPIRO: *DAILY MAVERICK*, 20 DECEMBER 2017

Launch, dammit! – Ramaphosa encouraging Zuma to resign.
ZAPIRO: *DAILY MAVERICK*, 12 JANUARY 2018

Victoria Geoghegan, with the support of the chief executive, James Henderson. The firm denied stoking racial tensions by their 'deflection' campaign, based on the use of hundreds of fake social media accounts, and intended to draw attention away from their clients, contending that 'white minority capital' was the key problem in South Africa. In fact, white capital is indeed a reality, but far from being a monopoly. The only monopolies in South Africa are the state-owned companies, which had become the prime targets for 'capture'.

Having sought to present their efforts on behalf of the Guptas as being limited to Oakbay, following exposure by former employees, the *Citizen* newspaper and in a report by the South African Communist Party, Bell Pottinger finally claimed in April 2017 that it was severing ties with the Gupta family. No apology whatever was made at that time for their continuing disinformation efforts, even after the publication of Public Protector Thuli Madonsela's report about the methods the family were using to further their interests in South Africa, the resignation of the Guptas' auditors and their blacklisting by the South African banks. A report by the South African Communist Party gave details of a 'systematic campaign of disinformation and attacks on the opponents of corruption'. Pravin Gordhan compared their methods to those of Goebbels. The chief executive of Bell Pottinger, James Henderson, and the partner responsible for the Guptas' account, Victoria Geoghegan, remained unrepentant.

Ahmed Kathrada's partner, Barbara Hogan, ANC veteran and long-term prisoner under apartheid, dismissed by Zuma as

Minister of Public Enterprises because of her unwillingness to tolerate corruption in the state-owned companies, denounced the changes as 'dastardly deeds done in dark corners'. She declared that, the President having 'gone rogue', the time had come for him to be recalled.

Zweli Mkhize, Treasurer General of the ANC and former Premier of KwaZulu-Natal, declared that Zuma had ignored the views of other ANC leaders and damaged the ANC. Cyril Ramaphosa said that it was 'totally unacceptable' that Zuma had 'fired someone like Gordhan, who had served his country excellently, for his own gain and survival'.

In the following days, Ramaphosa called for the country to get rid of greedy, corrupt people. The ANC Integrity Commission, led by the veteran Robben Islander Andrew Mlangeni, renewed its call for Zuma to stand down, as did the trade union federation Cosatu. This meant that both the junior partners of the ANC in the 'tripartite alliance' were now calling for Zuma to go.

The Standard & Poor's rating agency, having reaffirmed South Africa's investment grade status in December, despite the weak fundamentals (close to zero growth in 2016) and political risks, responded to the dismissal of Pravin Gordhan by downgrading South Africa to junk status (BB+), contributing to an over 10 per cent fall in the value of the rand. Fitch followed suit, leaving Moody's alone in deeming South Africa still to be investment grade.

The new Finance Minister, Malusi Gigaba, former head of the ANC youth league, was denounced by the EFF as the 'chief enabler of state capture' and a 'Gupta stooge' because of his record as Minister of Public Enterprises. While Pravin Gordhan was still Finance Minister, battling against corruption entrenched at Eskom, Gigaba told the ANC leadership in Nelson Mandela Bay that the only state entity that had been captured was the Treasury – by 'white monopoly capital'.[38]

According to the subsequent Guptaleaks, on 22 March 2014 the Gupta associate Salim Essa circulated to Rajesh Gupta the CV of Collin Matjila, which then was sent on to Duduzane Zuma. At the end of the month Matjila was appointed as acting CEO of Eskom, and then approved 43 million rand in sponsorship by Eskom of *New Age* business breakfasts.

As Minister of Home Affairs, to the dismay of the Minister of Tourism, Derek Hanekom, Gigaba insisted on new visa requirements, including for anyone bringing a child into or out of South Africa without both parents present, which were so cumbersome as to be a serious disincentive to visitors. Well known for harbouring presidential ambitions of his own, as Minister of Home Affairs Gigaba had granted South African citizenship to the Guptas.

As a thoroughly researched report by the Public Affairs Research Institute (PARI), *Betrayal of the Promise*, pointed out in May 2017, as the minister responsible for the state-owned enterprises, it was Gigaba who in December 2010 appointed Iqbal Sharma to the Transnet board. In February 2011 Brian Molefe was appointed CEO of Transnet; in July 2012 Anoj Singh became CFO, signing off on various Gupta-related contracts, including Trillian.

On taking over the Finance Ministry, Gigaba declared his intention to pursue 'radical economic transformation'. Under him, the Treasury reacted to the downgrade of South Africa by Standard & Poor's with an extraordinary statement that 'reducing reliance on foreign savings to fund investment ... will secure South Africa's fiscal sovereignty and economic independence'. Once established as Finance Minister, however, Gigaba found himself having to battle to stave off further downgrades.

Eskom forthwith declared that they were seeking an exemption from the normal Treasury controls over the entire nuclear build procurement process.

'NO PUBLIC DISSONANCE'

Following meetings of the National Working Committee packed with unconditional Zuma supporters on 4/5 April, the Secretary General, Gwede Mantashe, leading the climbdown, announced the collapse of resistance in the ANC to Zuma's actions. Those involved were said to have acknowledged that there should not have been 'public dissonance': any arguments should have been behind closed doors. ANC members would not vote in Parliament or participate in demonstrations with the opposition parties against their leader.

Mantashe added that there was no question of voting with one's conscience in the ANC.

Despite tens of thousands of people demonstrating against the Zuma presidency in Johannesburg, Cape Town and Pretoria, Zuma's success in quashing this internal revolt appeared to have improved the prospects for his ex-wife, Nkosazana Dlamini-Zuma, to be elected President of the ANC ahead of Cyril Ramaphosa.

On 23 April 2017, Ramaphosa responded by taking the gloves off in a fervently applauded speech to the ANC faithful in the Eastern Cape. There were, he said, many who felt that the ANC was in a deep crisis and that the party no longer represented their hope for a better life. The allegations that there were private individuals who exerted undue influence over state appointments and procurement decisions should be a matter of grave concern. The ANC should support an investigation into these allegations. Otherwise 'our electoral support will continue to slide'. The ANC was losing the support of important constituencies. On 1 May 2017, Zuma was obliged to abandon an attempt to speak at Cosatu's May Day rally, due to persistent booing from a large section of the crowd.

Thabo Mbeki, Kgalema Motlanthe and F. W. de Klerk called for ANC MPs to have a free vote on the motion of no confidence in President Zuma. The board of Eskom exploited the dismissal of Pravin Gordhan to take the extraordinary decision to reinstate Brian Molefe as CEO of the utility, notwithstanding the conclusions of the Public Protector's *State of Capture* report.

This produced some interesting reactions, as the ANC Secretary General, Gwede Mantashe, called on the Minister of Public Enterprises to rescind this appointment.

The former Minister of Natural Resources, Ramatlhodi,

replaced by the Gupta associate Zwane, confirmed that Molefe and the Eskom chairman Ben Ngubane had pressured him to help the Guptas take over Glencore's Optimum coal mine in 2016. According to Ramatlhodi, they had urged him to suspend all Glencore's mining licences in South Africa pending payment of the 'insanely large' fine.

HOW TO ESCAPE A FINE

In April 2017 it was reported that the Gupta-owned Tegeta coal company had reached agreement with Eskom over the fine imposed on Glencore. Any doubts about the fundamentally corrupt nature of this transaction were removed when subsequently it was revealed that the 2.17 billion rand fine on Optimum, which had obliged Glencore to sell it, had been drastically reduced, now that Optimum was owned by the Guptas. Eskom tried hard to avoid revealing the revised amount, while claiming that the original amount had been incorrectly calculated, as the problem with the 'below-quality' coal alleged to have been supplied had lain mainly with Eskom's own coal crusher! The revised amount turned out to be first 557 million, then 225 million rand, a discount for the new owners of nearly 90 per cent.

In May 2017, Jacob Zuma told the ANC Integrity Committee that he refused to resign because he believed that there was a conspiracy by Western governments to get rid of him and thereby capture the ANC.

CHAPTER XIV

THE GUPTALEAKS

At the end of May 2017, the independent investigative group amaBunghane, the *Daily Maverick* and *News24*, joined by *Business Day*, *City Press* and the Johannesburg *Sunday Times*, started publication of huge batches of internal Gupta emails showing in explicit detail how billions of rand had been syphoned out of the state-owned enterprises and the extent of the state capture in which they were involved. Initially denounced as fake by the Guptas, they were full of circumstantial detail about journeys to Dubai, meetings and corporate transactions, which undoubtedly did take place, leading the Guptas to complain that it looked as if their server had been hacked.[39] Furthermore, the emails were corroborated by many of those mentioned in them. They triggered hugely embarrassing *mea culpas* from KPMG and Bell Pottinger and investigations by McKinsey and SAP into their local offices. Yet Atul Gupta in August 2017 still was telling the BBC that the emails were fakes.

The emails described the Guptas providing flights to and

accommodation in Dubai for Des van Rooyen, who they were understood to have helped to get appointed (briefly) as Finance Minister. They showed that on 1 August 2015 the CV of Mosebenzi Zwane was forwarded by Tony Gupta to Duduzane Zuma.[40] On 23 September 2015, Zwane was appointed Minister of Mineral Resources, in time to help deliver the Optimum mine to the Guptas. They also revealed the purchase of an 18 million rand apartment in Dubai for Duduzane Zuma, attempts in concert with Bell Pottinger to discredit the deputy Finance Minister, Mcebisi Jonas, who had accused the Guptas of trying to bribe him, and a close association with the new Finance Minister Malusi Gigaba in his previous role as Minister of Home Affairs.

The leaked emails showed that Gigaba's appointee to the board of Transnet, Iqbal Sharma, played a key role in helping a Gupta company to extract huge profits from the purchase of locomotives by Transnet from China. They included details of seven apparently Gupta-sponsored and paid-for visits to Dubai by the Chief Financial Officer under Molefe of first Transnet and then Eskom, Anoj Singh.[41]

The emails also included details of Bell Pottinger's support for the Guptas, orchestrated by their principal apologist, Victoria Geoghegan, writing in ingratiating terms to Duduzane Zuma, proposing a £100,000 per month fee and contributing to a violent speech by the ANC youth leader, Collen Maine. The accident-prone Duduzane received help from the Guptas over the settlement of maintenance for his child and an incident in which he drove his Porsche into a taxi in which a passenger was killed.

This was followed by a deluge of Twitter material seeking

to discredit the Finance Minister, Pravin Gordhan, and the Public Protector, Thuli Madonsela. Over 30,000 social media messages were generated against Gordhan, most of them from the same sites. An identical campaign was conducted by the leader of Black First Land First, Andile Mngxitama, an unconditional supporter of the decidedly capitalistic Guptas, who appealed to them for financial assistance. Mngxitama subsequently appeared at a *Daily Maverick* conference in a car which turned out to belong to the son of Brian Molefe.

The emails appeared fully to substantiate the allegations made by former Bell Pottinger employees in a memorandum dated 24 January 2017. As Marianne Thamm wrote in the *Daily Maverick* in July 2017, Bell Pottinger had engaged quite successfully in an attempt to deflect criticism of Zuma and the Guptas in a campaign to blame the country's ills on the whites, specifically 'white monopoly capital'. So much for the pretence that they had been working only for a single Gupta company, Oakbay, and did not have a broader agenda.

It took the Guptaleaks finally to confirm that the outrageously expensive 2013 Gupta wedding had been paid for with proceeds from the Estina dairy project in the Free State financed by the Free State government. A KPMG auditor, Rone Alex, queried why the 30 million rand bill for the wedding was being treated as a 'business expense', but was overruled by her superiors. They also forced the normally complaisant Minister of Public Enterprises, Lynne Brown, to fire her unusually influential personal assistant, Kim Davids, because of the revelation of her association with the Guptas.

Publication of the first batch of these emails coincided with a meeting of the National Executive Committee of the ANC at which a further effort was made to recall Zuma. This was supported by around forty-five of the members, with sixty opposing his recall or undecided. Zuma flatly refused to stand down, saying that he could only be recalled by the ANC branches.

The ANC did, however, demand an investigation into the leaked emails, stating that it had 'grave concerns' over the 'very worrying claims about the nature of the relationship between government and private interests' contained in them. It viewed the allegations in a very serious light as, 'if left unattended, they call into question the integrity and credibility' of the government.

A TARGET BITES BACK

Meanwhile, the state capturers found a new target in the highly respected and inconveniently independent South African Reserve Bank. The campaign was opened, extraordinarily, by the new and already discredited Public Protector, Mkhwebane, who argued in a report on the apartheid-era bailout of Bankorp that the Reserve Bank's mandate should be changed from its emphasis on price stability to promoting economic growth and socioeconomic wellbeing. This surprise intervention clearly did not come just from her.

At the time of her appointment, the DA had queried Mkhwebane's prior links to the State Security Agency, for which she was reported to have worked as an analyst. Her intervention brought a crushing response from the head of the SARB, Lesetja Kganyago, who said that it showed that she understood neither the constitution, nor the role of the Reserve Bank. Kganyago's subsequent comments suggested that he believed this attack on the Reserve Bank to have been motivated by the Guptas, because of the Bank's concerns about their activities.

On 11 August, Judge John Murphy declared Mkhwebane's proposal unconstitutional, adding that she seemed impervious to criticism and risked being charged with hypocrisy and incompetence if she did not hold herself to an equal or higher standard to those subject to her writ. Her crusade against the independence of the Reserve Bank, however, as the only as yet 'uncaptured' institution, subsequently was taken up by the ANC presidential candidate Nkosazana Dlamini-Zuma.

At the ANC Policy Conference in July 2017, Zuma supporters did not have things their own way on economic policy. The Gupta/Bell Pottinger slogan of fighting against 'white monopoly capital' was rejected by nine of the eleven commissions. The ANC's most respected policy leader, Joel Netshitenzhe, pointed out that it was necessary to work with white capital to help achieve economic growth. There was a lot of unhappiness about the exposure of the role of the Guptas and the huge profits they were making at the expense of the state-owned enterprises. The conference did conclude that the Reserve Bank, which hitherto had private shareholders, should be nationalised, though it should remain independent.

Following Kganyago's response and the failure of the ANC Policy Conference to support it, a filing by the Reserve

Bank's legal adviser revealed that, before making her proposal to change the Bank's mandate, Mkhwebane, the supposed Public Protector, had consulted members of the State Security Agency and the legal advisors of the President, despite her having denied doing so, leaving her reputation in further tatters. In those discussions, according to the affidavit, she had asked about the Reserve Bank: 'How are they vulnerable?' As the Reserve Bank pursued its case against her, her counsel was reduced to arguing that her job was at risk. All she had done was make 'an honest mistake'.

THE COMEUPPANCE OF BELL POTTINGER

On 7 July 2017 the chief executive of Bell Pottinger, James Henderson, made an abject, 'unequivocal' apology for the role the company had played on behalf of the Guptas. 'These activities should never have been undertaken,' he said. The account executive, Victoria Geoghegan, was fired and three other employees suspended. The Guptaleaks included a letter from Geoghegan advising the head of the ANC Youth League on an inflammatory speech about 'white minority capital'. Geoghegan's father, a senior executive of British Aerospace at the time of the arms deal, was reported to have introduced her to the ANC fixer Fana Hlongwane, who had facilitated meetings with the Guptas.

The 'Save South Africa' campaign was unimpressed by this belated repentance. 'Bell Pottinger – acting in partnership with its client – sowed racial mistrust, hate and race-baiting,' it declared. Pravin Gordhan, who had been the subject of attacks orchestrated by Bell Pottinger, described the 'apology' as disingenuous. Lord Tim Bell, founder of the firm, was not impressed either, stating that the account was one of the reasons he had left the company. The chief executive was accused of knowing all about the disinformation campaign that was being orchestrated in South Africa.

An investigation by the law company Herbert Smith reached some very damning conclusions. Following representations by the opposition Democratic Alliance, on 3 September 2017 Bell Pottinger was expelled from the UK industry body, the Public Relations and Communication Association (PRCA), for five years. The director general, Francis Ingham, accused the company of having brought the industry into disrepute. 'This is the most blatant example of unethical PR practice I have ever seen,' he declared. The CEO at last resigned. Following a general exodus of its clients, the company went into administration in September 2017, brought down by its association with the Guptas.

AND OF KPMG

KPMG in South Africa was equally heavily compromised in this saga, the Gupta leaks having revealed that the wedding at Sun City had been paid for by transferring funds in transactions that were supposed to be audited by KPMG.

On 1 July 2017 the head of KPMG South Africa still was defending their audit opinion and declaring that the firm had acted with integrity in its dealings with the Gupta vehicle Oakbay. Post the Guptaleaks, the tone changed dramatically to a chest-beating apology, with the announcement of action against three partners and the CEO of KPMG South Africa, declaring that 'Mistakes have been made and painful lessons learnt'. KPMG should have resigned from the Gupta accounts earlier than March 2016, he declared, and no fewer than four KPMG partners should not have attended the Gupta wedding.

On the most astonishing failure of all, the endorsement by KPMG of the phoney charges by Moyane against Pravin Gordhan about the supposed 'rogue' unit in SARS, it merely was stated that the partner responsible had left the firm.

KPMG also had been the auditors for the listing of Oakbay on the Johannesburg Stock Exchange. Following an exodus of clients and an internal investigation by KPMG, eight senior executives, including their CEO in South Africa, eventually were dismissed.

MULTINATIONALS BEHAVING BADLY

The Guptaleaks also shed a very unfavourable light on the payment by the German software company SAP of 100 million rand in 'sales commission' to CAD House, a company owned by the Guptas with Duduzane Zuma, to secure business from Transnet. As the commission was for 10 per cent of sales, this appeared to suggest that SAP won 1 billion rand worth of business from Transnet. The leaks showed that confidential SAP contracts were forwarded to the Guptas. SAP contended that the allegations were unfounded, but suspended four members of its South African management team pending an investigation.

In reality, a number of multinational companies had concluded that they were unlikely to be able to win government-related contracts in South Africa without an association with the Guptas.

The spread of the scandal also ensnared McKinsey which, with the Gupta/Salim Essa consultancy Trillian, extracted 1.6 billion rand in fees for 'turn-around' advice to Eskom. The contract was entered into despite warnings from Eskom's legal advisers that it favoured McKinsey and did not comply with the law. McKinsey suspended a senior employee, Vikas Sagar, for writing a letter stating that Trillian was a sub-contractor for McKinsey, when in fact it was not.

HOW TO OPEN THE TAPS

McKinsey did, however, have a business relationship with Trillian, no doubt to help with business access. Trillian turned out to be the recipient of 266 million rand of contracts from Eskom without, according to an enquiry by senior counsel Geoffrey Budlender, any convincing proof as to what work was done. The amount paid by Eskom to Trillian, which Eskom refused for a long time to disclose, soon was found to be far higher than that. Eskom senior management initially denied having made any payments to Trillian. The Guptaleaks indicated that McKinsey and Trillian between them hoped to extract a further 9.4 billion rand in fees by advising Eskom on the nuclear programme.

An early whistleblower, Mosilo Mothepu, told Thuli Madonsela that Trillian had known in advance that Zuma would fire the Finance Minister, Nhlanhla Nene, for which she was persecuted by the company. A graphic account of Trillian's modus operandi was provided, with supporting documents, by a subsequent whistleblower, Bianca Goodson. She described how Trillian ensured access for McKinsey to its highly lucrative consulting contract with Eskom, in return for which Trillian received huge payments while providing virtually no other services.

Goodson served as chief executive of Trillian management consulting from November 2015 until her resignation in March 2016. From December 2015, she declared, Trillian became the gatekeeper for consulting contracts at state entities. Work was secured through Salim Essa's contacts. If international companies wanted to participate, they needed to choose Trillian as their 'supplier development partner', giving it a large share of the contract.

According to Goodson, Trillian consulting did not at the time really conduct any work directly with Eskom, Transnet or Des van Rooyen's Department of Co-operative Affairs (supervising local government). It simply acted as the gatekeeper while seeking to secure 50 per cent of the ensuing revenues. The company had no relevant track record, starting with just Goodson and a chief operating officer. Yet soon it had 'earned' 595 million rand from Eskom by acting as McKinsey's supposed development partner. McKinsey itself received 1 billion rand for little more than six months' work.

When Goodson expressed surprise at the amounts earned by Trillian, despite its lack of capacity, she was told that the company was 'fortunate to have relationships with *the people who can open the taps*'. She resigned because of her concern not to be further involved with the owners of the business.

The Guptaleaks also revealed that a second German company, Software AG, entered into an agreement with another Gupta-controlled company to try to help secure a 180 million rand contract, also with Transnet. The company evidently believed that they would not otherwise win business from Transnet.

ESKOM BLED DRY

The departures from Eskom of the highly competent CEO Brian Dames, CFO Paul O'Flaherty and Treasurer Caroline Henry all had been driven by political interference, lack of any confidence in the appointments to the Eskom Board, in particular by Minister Gigaba, then in control of the state-owned enterprises, and concern at the contracts they were being asked to approve. As Pravin Gordhan put it, the boards and CEOs were changed to put in the 'right' people. The full extent of subsequent corruption in the state-owned company was further demonstrated when, on 11 July 2017, Eskom suddenly delayed releasing its full-year results. Things since then have got a lot worse for Eskom with, by year end, the once mighty electricity utility that had supplied power to most of southern Africa teetering on the brink of insolvency.

The *Mail and Guardian* revealed that its auditors had reported the company to the regulators due to serious irregularities in its accounts. The issues raised related to contracts awarded to a firm linked to Brian Molefe's deputy and for a time the acting CEO, Matshela Koko, and to the rehiring of the disgraced Molefe. The auditors were concerned that major contracts had been awarded to a company linked to Koko's stepdaughter, though he then was cleared in an internal inquiry. The CFO, Anoj Singh, was being asked to explain his involvement in numerous deals linked to the Gupta family, both at Eskom and in his previous role, also under Molefe, at Transnet.

On 29 July 2017 the Treasury's final report to Parliament into Eskom's supply contracts with the Guptas' Tegeta was released. This recommended that Brian Molefe and Anoj Singh should be investigated, including over the Chinese locomotives purchases when they were both at Transnet. A forensic audit was needed to establish whether they and Koko had received any 'gratifications' from the Guptas, why Molefe had given assurances that Tegeta had been supplying good-quality coal from Brakfontein, contrary to the evidence, whether Eskom had been overpaying for coal contracts awarded without tender to Tegeta and Singh's awards of huge contracts to Trillian.

The Minister of Finance, Malusi Gigaba, hitherto had been regarded as close to the Guptas. He now took steps to distance himself from them. Like millions of South Africans, he declared, he was 'very worried' about the influence they were said to exert.[42]

It was only at this point, at the end of July 2017, that Anoj Singh, very belatedly, was suspended as CFO of Eskom, despite the evidence that he had been entertained by the Guptas on several occasions in Dubai and the role he had played, also under Molefe, in awarding hugely lucrative contracts to Gupta-related companies at Transnet.

In 2016, Molefe and Singh between them earned 14 million rand from Eskom. Molefe, amazingly, also was deemed to be entitled to a 30 million rand pension, even though he did not appear to have been a permanent employee of the company. Both had mouth-wateringly expensive share incentive schemes.

By this time Salim Essa, so close to the Guptas that he was regarded as the 'fourth brother', had sold his holding in Trillian, leaving it under the control of the CEO Eric Wood, who lamented that the bad publicity was rendering it hard for the company to win business. According to former employees, it was Wood who had told them several weeks in advance that Finance Minister Nene, seen as an obstacle to the Guptas' ambitions, would be replaced. In his report on Trillian, commissioned by its outgoing chairman Tokyo Sexwale, the respected jurist Geoffrey Budlender found these allegations likely to be credible, extremely serious and needing to be investigated.

The former legal adviser of Eskom, Suzanne Daniels, told

the parliamentary inquiry that she had sent a comprehensive report on Eskom procurement irregularities to the Minister of Public Enterprises, Lynne Brown, as well as to management, but Brown had not acted on it. Instead, in October 2017, Daniels was suspended on grounds of 'misconduct'.

Daniels added that when she met Salim Essa, controlling shareholder of Trillian, in March 2015, he told her in advance that four senior Eskom executives would be replaced. In July 2017 she said that she was summoned to a meeting with Essa, Ajay Gupta, Duduzane Zuma and the deputy Minister of Public Enterprises, Ben Martins. According to her, Ajay Gupta wanted the court hearing about Brian Molefe's pension to take place after the ANC conference in December. Ajay Gupta denied ever having met her. She also was concerned that Molefe had been loaded into the system as a permanent employee of Eskom, when in fact he was on a contract.

She proved to be right about this, as the High Court struck down the 30 million rand payout for Molefe and ordered him to return the 11 million rand already received.

Daniels said that she was told by Brown's assistant, Kim Davids, that the minister had received complaints from Trillian about Eskom procurement and that she would get a letter from the minister telling her to give them more work.

Daniels added that she had received death threats, had suffered an attempted break-in at her home, had been followed in her car and had no doubt that her phone was tapped. She had been told on her phone that 'If you know what is good for you, you will shut up'.[43]

In June, the Johannesburg High Court had set aside a 4 billion rand boiler tender awarded by Eskom to a Chinese company despite a lower bid from the South African company Murray & Roberts and General Electric. Investors by now, very belatedly, were becoming seriously concerned at the deluge of evidence of massive corruption in the running of Eskom. In October 2017, Eskom was reported to Parliament for 31.3 billion rand in 'deviations' from normal procurement requirements.

At the parliamentary inquiry into Eskom on 22 November 2017, the former chairman Zola Tsotsi testified that Tony Gupta told him that he was not helping the family and that, therefore, his job was at risk, saying: 'We are the ones who put you in the position you are in. We are the ones who can take you out.' The Guptas said that they would report him to 'Baba' (Jacob Zuma). The minister, Lynne Brown, threatened him with dismissal for interfering in management. He added that the chairman of SAA, Dudu Myeni, had arranged for him to meet Zuma, a meeting in which she advised him to suspend several Eskom executives. He accused Brown of working with the Guptas and Salim Essa to decide which board members should serve on which committees. When he went to Brown's house to finalise the list, he found the Guptas and Essa there. The Guptaleaks emails showed that the Gupta executive Nazeem Howa prepared a statement about Tsotsi's resignation ten days before he was dismissed.

Despite this testimony, Lynne Brown indignantly denied that the meeting with the Guptas described by Tsotsi had taken place or that she had ever been influenced by them. The former Finance Minister, Pravin Gordhan, was unimpressed by her testimony, which he described as 'Denial, denial and denial'. Brian Molefe denied any knowledge of Eskom contracts with Trillian which, he said, were a matter for Anoj Singh.

The 'evidence leader' to the parliamentary inquiry into the state-owned enterprises, advocate Ntuthuzelo Vanara, reported that the Minister of State Security, Bongani Bongo, had offered him a blank cheque to resign from the inquiry.

The Guptaleaks also revealed the role of Malusi Gigaba's political adviser, Thamsanqa Msomi, in assisting the Guptas on various matters while Gigaba was Minister of Home Affairs.

CHAPTER XV

'MANDELA AND SISULU DID NOT STRUGGLE FOR THIS'

In July 2017 the Housing Minister Lindiwe Sisulu, earlier an ardent supporter of Zuma, including against Thuli Madonsela, launched her own campaign to become President of the ANC, invoking Mandela and her father Walter Sisulu who, she declared, 'did not struggle for this'. To save South Africa, they had to save the ANC. She described factionalism, corruption without limits, arrogance, loss of any sense of reality, impunity, greed, selfishness and total loss of value systems as the elements undermining the party. 'We must cleanse the ANC and recover its original values,' she said.

In a speech at the University of Johannesburg, Pravin Gordhan explained why the Guptas and their associates had not been convicted of any crimes. This, he contended, was because they had never been investigated. 'How many of you,' he asked, 'would refuse a 600 million rand bribe?' That was what, according to his deputy, Mcebisi Jonas, had been offered to him by Ajay Gupta to take over as Finance Minister and do the

Guptas' bidding. Jonas had turned them down and reported the attempted bribery – only for this not even to have been investigated by any of the prosecuting authorities. Instead, Gordhan himself had been investigated by the Hawks and the National Prosecuting Authority, whereas 'the criminal justice system does not chase the actual rogues'. Jonas added that 'We are increasingly becoming known as a capital of corruption and state capture. State-owned enterprises are centres for money racketeering.'

Since his appointment by Jacob Zuma, the head of the National Prosecuting Authority, Shaun Abrahams, had appealed against the High Court judgment reinstating the 783 corruption charges against Zuma. He then attempted to prosecute Pravin Gordhan for his involvement in setting up a supposedly rogue unit within the South African Revenue Service – a case which had collapsed ignominiously. The ruling by Thuli Madonsela as Public Protector that an independent judicial commission of inquiry should be appointed to investigate the evidence in her report on *State of Capture* still had not been acted upon. In September 2017 Zuma's lawyers admitted that it was 'irrational' for him to avoid dealing with the corruption charges against him, which already had been the conclusion of the Pretoria High Court.

In late July, the Johannesburg *Sunday Times* reported that the Guptas had been seeking advice on how to move tens of billions of rand to Dubai. South African legal firms declined to help over this. The Bank of Baroda was reported to be trying to close the Guptas' accounts, whch they set about doing in 2018.

A QUESTION OF CONFIDENCE

On 8 August 2017, amid scenes of high drama, MPs voted on the no-confidence motion introduced by the leader of the opposition Democratic Alliance and supported by Julius Malema and the EFF and the other smaller parties. The DA sought a ruling from the Constitutional Court that the voting should be secret. The head of the Constitutional Court ruled that this was a matter for the Speaker, Baleka Mbete. It came as a surprise when she ruled that the vote should indeed be secret. Thabo Mbeki and others urged ANC MPs to vote according to their consciences. The Secretary General, Gwede Mantashe, already had made clear that ANC members were not supposed to have consciences, but to act as disciplined party cadres.

An important intervention came from the ANC chief whip and Zuma critic, Jackson Mthembu. He argued that they all were concerned about corruption, the awarding of state contracts and the allegations about the Guptas. ANC members on the parliamentary committees had taken action to sort out the mess at SABC, helping to secure the removal of the chief operating officer, Hlaudi Motsoeneng (see Chapter XX) and were holding hearings on SAA. But to vote out the President would have 'nuclear' consequences, triggering the collapse of the government and creating a chaotic situation.

Maimane described the vote as being a choice between right and wrong. Malema said that they were trying to get rid of a criminal. Invited to withdraw, he replaced 'criminal' by 'crook'.

As the vote was taken, the outcome appeared uncertain.

It transpired that the President had survived by the narrow margin of 198 votes to 177. Twenty-six ANC MPs had voted against the President, with nine abstaining. It would have required only another dozen government MPs voting against to have removed the President.

So why did more ANC MPs not vote to remove a leader who clearly had become an electoral liability to them? The Gupta press had forecast accurately that no more than thirty-five ANC MPs would fail to vote for Zuma. Under the South African constitution, if the President were removed in a no-confidence vote, the government also would fall, costing seventy ministers and deputy ministers their posts. The Speaker would have thirty days to form a new government. The ANC MPs all were told that this would be impossible, given the divisions that would open within the party; they would have to face a fresh parliamentary election in the worst possible circumstances. Many of them would lose their seats. The party's own private polling already was showing ANC support down to 47 per cent.

This message was sufficient to bring waverers to heel and the tight result was hailed as a decisive victory by Zuma and his associates. And so indeed it was, as the rebellion had been limited to only 10 per cent of ANC MPs. Important losers included Cosatu and the SACP, who had been calling for Zuma to go, while the outcome also sent a clear message that Ramaphosa and those who wanted change would have a hard fight to prevail in the ANC leadership contest in December.

The very obvious problem with this denouement was that it did nothing to give any hope of improving South Africa's dismal economic performance, with near zero growth in 2016, with job creation falling well below the population increase, with Minister Zwane left to continue wreaking havoc on the mining industry and the Gupta network of contracts with the state-owned companies also untouched, despite all the controversy associated with them. Mmusi Maimane and Julius Malema, from their very different perspectives, were entitled to see the outcome as having created new opportunities for them. The ANC was liable to find it more of a struggle to stem the loss of support in nearly all the major urban areas, basing its hopes more than ever on retaining support in the rural areas.

The reaction of the former President and Deputy President of South Africa and ANC stalwart Kgalema Motlanthe was to tell the BBC that it would be better for South Africa for the ANC to lose the next election, as the only way of returning the party to its former values. The party had become associated with corruption. It needed to lose an election for 'the penny to drop'. The independent-minded KwaZulu-Natal MP, Makhosi Khoza, who had shown courage in her criticism of corruption, resigned from the party, declaring the 'new, alien and corrupt ANC' to be 'incapable of self-correcting'.

* * *

By August 2017 the Guptas were facing further serious banking problems. The Bank of Baroda had been trying to close down their accounts for some time, but were handicapped in doing so by the large loans they had made to Gupta companies.

According to Ben Theron of the Organisation Undoing Tax Abuse (OUTA), they had loaned several hundred million rand against the security of two properties worth barely more than a tenth of that. In a court hearing, the Bank of Baroda declared that it feared reputational damage if it continued doing business with the Guptas. The brothers had to look at creating new entities in the hope that the banks would deal with them.

'I AM DOING A VERY ETHICAL JOB'

On 20 August they announced that they had sold the *New Age* newspaper and ANN7 to the Gupta/Zuma acolyte Jimmy Manyi for 450 million rand, lent by them to him. Given Manyi's highly questionable reputation, it will be interesting to see which banks are prepared to deal with him. Manyi's most famous public intervention had been the suggestion that 'there is an over-concentration of coloureds in the Western Cape', where they showed a distressing tendency not to vote for the ANC, and 'they should be spread in the rest of the country'.

Three days later, the Guptas announced the sale of their coal company, Tegeta Resouces, to Amin al Zarooni via a Swiss shelf company, Charles King, with a capitalisation of 100,000 Swiss francs. The purpose evidently was to try to reopen bank accounts for Tegeta, enabling it continue to benefit from preferential contracts with Eskom.

The genuineness of this sale immediately was questioned by Pravin Gordhan and by amaBhungane, who pointed out that the Guptaleaks showed a previous effort by the family to set up a vehicle in Dubai that nominally would be 51 per cent controlled by al Zarooni, but would leave the entire economic benefit with the Guptas. The South African Communist Party denounced these 'dummy sales' and started talking about contesting future elections on their own, despite their lack hitherto of any substantial public support.

Atul Gupta continued to insist that there was no proof that he had done anything wrong. 'I am proudly South African,' he declared, describing himself as 'an example of financial liberation'. He added: 'I am doing a very ethical job'.[44]

Meanwhile the Guptaleaks continued to take their toll. The Minister of Public Enterprises, Lynne Brown, received a report recommending that action should be taken in relation to what was now described as the payment of 600 million rand to Trillian and 1 billion rand to McKinsey with no Treasury authority. On 22 September she instructed Eskom to take legal action against McKinsey, Trillian, Koko, Singh and the chief procurement executives. In November the Eskom spokesman alleged that the utility's problems stemmed from actions by the minister, Lynne Brown, such as delaying the suspension of the interim CEO Matshela Koko, though the company disavowed his statement.

McKinsey indicated that, if ordered to do so by a court, they would repay the 1 billion rand advisory fee earned for little more than six months' work for Eskom. They claimed not to have known that Trillian was controlled by Salim Essa. Thirty million rand turned out to have been paid by them via Regiments to Gupta-related companies for 'business development' purposes.

On 13 October 2017 the Supreme Court of Appeal had ruled that President Zuma should face eighteen charges involving the 783 allegations of corruption against him, thereby placing the head of the National Prosecuting Authority, Shaun Abrahams, who had opposed any reinstatement of the charges, now under an obligation to explain why he should not prosecute the President. The court noted that the President would continue to use all possible means to avoid prosecution and was scathing about the performance of the NPA in failing to prosecute.

In October 2017, Zuma carried out a further Cabinet reshuffle, dismissing Blade Nzimande, as both he and the SACP had been highly critical of the Zuma regime, and appointing his special confidant, David Mahlobo, former Minister of State Security, as Minister of Energy.

The Johannesburg *Sunday Times* reported in September that two prominent figures with criminal convictions, Gayton McKenzie and Kenneth Kunene, travelled with Mahlobo to Russia to present themselves as black empowerment partners for the Russian oil and gas company, Rosgeo. The Russians were reported to be agitating for Zuma to commit irrevocably to the nuclear procurement from Rosatom while he remained in control – the stumbling block being the judgment in May 2017 by the Western Cape High Court that no proper procurement process had been followed.

Rumours were disseminated by the Zuma camp that Cyril Ramaphosa risked being dismissed from the Cabinet before the December ANC conference and 'exposed' as, supposedly, an agent of the CIA.

Sipho Pityana of the 'Save South Africa' campaign expressed scepticism that the ANC any longer was capable of reforming itself. There were contests and legal challenges in the provinces as to who the legitimate party delegates actually were. If the forces of state capture succeeded in cementing their takeover of the ANC at the conference in December, which was a realistic possibility, genuine supporters of the party would have to resist calls for unity at all costs and choose whether to break ranks.[45]

The *Financial Times* reported on 18 October 2017 that the US Justice Department and the FBI were looking into individuals, bank accounts and companies in the US with ties to the Gupta family. In Britain, the Financial Conduct Authority announced that it was in touch with HSBC and Standard Chartered banks over their dealings with the Gupta family. HSBC in Dubai and Hong Kong were alleged to have arranged bank transfers for the Guptas in 2013 related to the China South Rail transaction with Transnet. The former anti-apartheid campaigner Peter Hain used a money-laundering debate in the British Parliament to demand action against any financial institutions that had done business with the Guptas. The Guptas, who have always denied any wrongdoing, continued to point out that they have never been convicted of any crime.

A THREAT TO THE ENTIRE ECONOMY

On 25 October, Malusi Gigaba presented to Parliament his Medium Term Financial Strategy, revealing an even larger than expected deficit in the public finances for the next three years. The bailout for SAA increased to 10 billion rand. Ironically, Gigaba railed against the mismanagement of the state-owned enterprises and the threat this posed to financial stability, notwithstanding the role he played in appointing Molefe and packing the boards of Transnet and Eskom with Gupta associates. Eskom was described by him as a 'significant risk to the entire economy'.

Gigaba would not be the first political figure to have to try to clear up the mess he helped create in the first place.

The rand took a serious hit and the Fitch rating agency concluded that it could see no prospect of fiscal consolidation. South Africa was caught in a slow-growth trap. Indebtedness had doubled to 52 per cent of GDP under Zuma and was trending towards 60 per cent – a very hazardous level for a developing country – while tax revenues and per capita incomes were falling. Fitch had been proved right in its assessment that the removal of Pravin Gordhan was likely to result in the burgeoning debts of the state-owned enterprises ending up directly on the balance sheet of the government.

Gigaba did, however, acknowledge that the nuclear programme was simply unaffordable 'at the present time'. South Africa had a serious surplus of power capacity, due to much lower than anticipated economic growth. He also was concerned about the performance of SARS where, following an exodus of qualified personnel under Tom Moyane, and Moyane's preoccupation with pursuing Pravin Gordhan, the agency had been failing in its primary task, contributing to a 50 billion rand tax revenue shortfall. To Moyane's dismay, he announced an inquiry into SARS. Moyane's acolytes responded by saying that he could not be removed by Gigaba, but only by the President.

In mid-November the rand took a further hit with the resignation from the Treasury of the long-term budget director, Michael Sachs, following pressure from Zuma to offer free tertiary education before the 2019 elections and further revelations that Eskom risked running out of money in the new year, with lenders increasingly nervous about extending further credit.

The German software company SAP announced that it had reported itself to the US Justice Department for paying 107 million rand in commission to Gupta-related companies on 660 million rand in sales to Transnet and Eskom. Three employees were suspended and SAP apologised 'wholeheartedly' for its actions.

A situation had now been created in which no Western company any longer could afford to do business with the Guptas. But this did not stop the Minister of Public Enterprises, Lynne Brown, appointing as CEO of what was supposed to be the new and cleaner Denel board Zwelakhe Ntshepe, who had been heavily involved in the Guptas' tie-up with Denel. Denel too by this stage was in dire financial difficulties, struggling to roll over its loans.

On 27 July, *News24* had published a report showing that the Gupta-related companies with Dubai addresses mentioned in the Guptaleaks as benefiting from the family's business operations in South Africa did not have meaningful offices or any permanent staff, but were simply shell companies there. The Gupta mansion in Emirates Hills, on the other hand, really did exist, having been bought in 2015 for 331 million rand.

The ANC spokesperson, Z. G. Kodwa, published an emotional letter to Oliver Tambo on the anniversary of his birth: 'The challenge confronting the movement today is not a vicious apartheid state, but *the vultures within*.'

A RUSSIAN CONNECTION

Zuma's response to Gigaba's statement that the nuclear programme currently was unnecessary and unaffordable was to declare that for South Africa it was vital. It was being opposed by Western interests. The Soviet Union always had been the ANC's best friend.

Although Zuma in his 'struggle' days had been on very friendly terms with the British intelligence services, his association with the Guptas had long since driven him into the arms of Putin and his associates, with no likelihood of any criticism of corruption coming from them. It was to them that he had turned to arrange treatment in Moscow for his alleged poisioning, while working with the Russians on the planned nuclear deal.

A study by Eskom had demonstrated that nuclear energy was not needed and was by far the most expensive option. But this did not stop the new Energy Minister, David Mahlobo, declaring:'Nuclear will happen.' The insistence on pursuing an unnecessary and unaffordable nuclear programme come what may was deemed to be related to undertakings given to Putin, while if it stalled the Guptas' investment in uranium would turn out to be valueless.

ESKOM ON THE BRINK

In November 2017 Standard & Poor's lowered South Africa's local currency borrowing to sub-investment grade, having already lowered its foreign currency rating to junk status. Moody's put South Africa on review for a downgrade. This temporary stay of execution meant that the country for the time being could remain in some key global bond indices, which require an investment grade rating for US and many other investors to be able to buy their bonds. Every downgrade to date, however, already had the effect of increasing borrowing costs for most major South African entities including, especially, the state-owned enterprises. The downgrades forced the government to say that it was envisaging 50 billion rand in spending cuts for 2018, and 30 billion rand in tax increases in an already weak economy.

In November, the World Bank and five other major international development institutions wrote to the minister, Lynne Brown, that they were 'extremely concerned' about the governance issues at Eskom and 'severe allegations of wrongdoing against members of Eskom management as well as compromised internal controls and procurement processes'. Faced with this clear warning and urged to act 'without delay', Brown did nothing. Instead, Eskom were permitted to reappoint, after a pro forma internal inquiry, the severely compromised Matshela Koko and the head of capital, Prish Govender. As soon as they were appointed in January 2018, the new management at Eskom suspended Koko once again, alleging that he had lied to Parliament about his involvement with Trillian and visits to Dubai.

As Eskom's major lenders had made clear their unwilling-ness to lend to Eskom so long as Koko was still there, it was impossible to understand the failure of the minister, Lynne Brown, to take any action to deal with this. But that was true of her oversight of the state-owned enterprises in general, throughout her disastrous tenure as the minister responsible for them.

Her director general, Richard Seleke, was a former associ-ate of Mosebenzi Zwane in the Free State. According to the Guptaleaks, before being appointed to oversee the state-owned enterprises, he sent his CV to Duduzane Zuma – though he denies this. By the end of 2017, Eskom was on the verge of a debt default, with Gigaba declaring that the Treasury did not have the funds to bail it out.

* * *

In November 2017, the investigative journalist Jacques Pauw who, with Max du Preez, and at risk to their own lives, had led the way in exposing the death squad activities of the security forces under P. W. Botha, sought to do the same to the secu-rocrats around Jacob Zuma in his book *The President's Keepers*, which the State Security Agency (SSA) and others tried, un-successfully, to stop being distributed.[46] Pauw alleged that the SSA had wasted over 1 billion rand on a programme rife with corruption, called the Principal Agents Plan. Three hundred vehicles were said to have been purchased by this unit, which put the Agency's own auditors under surveillance when they tried to inspect it! Despite his leadership of this programme, Arthur Fraser was recalled to be appointed head of the SSA, perhaps because of the help he was believed to have given Zuma at the time he was being investigated under Mbeki.

A Russian oligarch connected to Putin and the Russian intelligence services, Vladimir Strzhalkovsky, at the time CEO of Norilsk Nickel, was reported to have flown a large amount of cash as well as medical supplies into Durban for Zuma at his estate in Nkandla in 2011, briefly impounded by Durban customs, who were said to have released the consignment on the instructions of the Security Minister. A former KGB agent, Strzhalkovsky served previously with Putin in St Petersburg.[47]

The hitherto respected South African Revenue Service (SARS) had been captured, Pauw contended, through the appointment of Tom Moyane, with high-level investigations into cigarette smugglers and other businessmen connected to the Zuma family, especially Duduzane and Edward Zuma, being interrupted as Ivan Pillay, head of the investigative unit, was ousted, along with his senior colleagues. In the other investigative agencies, anyone who attempted to reveal corruption was targeted through dismissals, intimidation and trumped-up charges, thereby creating a shadow state to circumvent the constitution.

Tom Moyane, as head of SARS, launched legal action against Pauws for revealing sensitive tax information, thereby seeming to confirm the quality of his sources. The overall picture of state capture and the workings of the 'shadow state' described in his book is not easily contestable.

As if to validate Pauw's account, a well-known figure in the police's Crime Intelligence division, Morris ('Captain KGB') Tshabalala, turned out to have been sentenced to ten years for armed robbery in the 1990s, but never to have served his sentence as he had not bothered to present himself to do so. While on the run, he joined Crime Intelligence. In 2013 he was arrested, then acquitted, over a cash-in-transit robbery, but had to serve two and a half years of his earlier sentence. He then immediately rejoined Crime Intelligence! This interesting career only ended with him finally being dismissed for stealing from his employers in 2018. In this case and others, the distinction between Crime Intelligence and crime was no longer visible to any dispassionate observer.[48]

Pauw's account of the workings of sections of the security services under Zuma, including fraud, corruption, racketeering, incompetence and close relationships with connected criminals, were a mirror image of those he had described in the apartheid era – with the important difference that they no longer were engaged in murdering their opponents. Political killings in post-apartheid South Africa have largely been confined to KwaZulu-Natal. Whereas these used to be a result of Inkatha/ANC rivalry, in recent years they have more often been attributed to faction fighting within the ANC.

CHAPTER XVI

THE OPPOSITION RIGHT AND LEFT

B orn in Johannesburg to parents who left Germany in the 1930s (her maternal grandfather and paternal grandmother were Jewish), Helen Zille began her career as a reporter on the staunchly anti-apartheid *Rand Daily Mail*. She made her reputation by exposing police lies that Steve Biko had died on hunger strike, when in fact he had been battered to death. For this, she and her editor, Allister Sparks, were convicted by an apartheid judge of 'tendentious reporting'. She was heavily involved in other anti-apartheid activities, before holding the public affairs post at the University of Cape Town. In 2004, she became an MP for the opposition Democratic Alliance.

The Democratic Party (then Alliance) was the successor to the anti-apartheid Progressive Federal Party, inspired by Helen Suzman and whose leader at the time was Colin Eglin. The 'Progs' never succeeded in winning more than a fraction of white votes against the National Party, but left a valuable legacy in contributing to the adoption of a genuinely liberal constitution for South Africa, which under Zuma was coming under increasingly serious threat.

They fared very poorly in the 1994 elections, winning only 1.7 per cent of the vote. The National Party under F. W. de Klerk represented the main alternative to the ANC at the time. Under the combative but abrasive Tony Leon, the DA vote increased to 9 per cent in the 1999 elections.

But in the 2006 municipal elections, the DA won 42 per cent of the vote in Cape Town and, with the support of the smaller parties, Helen Zille became mayor of the city. There were constant battles with the local ANC who tried to keep her out of the Cape townships, but failed to do so, as it proved impossible to intimidate her. In her autobiography, *Not Without a Fight*,[49] she describes the numerous occasions when, at serious personal risk, she had to try to save DA members suffering physical intimidation at the hands of ANC supporters in the townships, with the police siding with the ANC. She consolidated support among the coloured population and speaks fluent Xhosa. She established a remarkably effective and corruption-free administration and in 2008 she won the international World Mayor of the Year award.

In 2007, she was elected leader of the Democratic Alliance. In 2009, the DA won over 50 per cent of the vote in the Western Cape and Zille was installed as Premier, with Patricia de Lille succeeding her as mayor of Cape Town in due course. De Lille had led the calls in Parliament for an independent inquiry into the arms deal and described the ANC under Zuma as 'a liberation party that has no respect for the constitution and the rule of law'. In the 2009 election, the party won 3 million votes, helping to keep the ANC just below the two-thirds majority needed to amend the constitution.

As leader of the opposition, Zille proved extremely effective, and the Western Cape was administered far more efficiently than the other provinces. Before the 2014 election, Zille tried but failed to persuade her friend Mamphela Ramphele, former partner of Steve Biko, to merge her small party with the DA. Nevertheless, in the general election, the DA advanced to win 4 million votes, 22 per cent of the vote nationally, including 30 per cent of the votes in Gauteng (which includes Johannesburg). They won nearly 60 per cent of the votes in the Western Cape, with the ANC there faction-ridden and facing charges of corruption, and the national leadership close to giving up on the province. Zuma's response in 2016 was to suggest that the site of Parliament should be moved from Cape Town to the north.

Helen Zille by now had concluded that the party must have a black leader. There had been friction between her and one potential candidate for the post, Lindiwe Mazibuko, but finding that few of her senior party colleagues were willing to make way for black colleagues, Zille decided to do so herself, resigning as leader of the party and supporting the election of the DA's parliamentary leader, Mmusi Maimane, to succeed her, while remaining Premier of the Western Cape. Mazibuko contends that the party's 'brains trust' remains dominated by white males.

The until recently pretty effective ANC mantra against the

DA has been that the party exists to support the interests of the whites. The Democratic Alliance today has more non-white than white support, the bulk of it coming from the coloured community, but continues to be represented as white-dominated. The challenge for the party in the 2016 municipal elections was to demonstrate that it could break out of its stronghold in the Western Cape and capitalise on the progress it had been making in the Eastern Cape, Johannesburg and Pretoria as a result of dissatisfaction with the ANC.

* * *

While the Democratic Alliance was posing an increasing challenge to the ANC among the better off and better educated, based on claims of greater competence in 'delivery' and less corruption, the Economic Freedom Fighters were making inroads from the left. The new party quickly formed an effective organisation. Malema's deputy, Floyd Shivambu, is a highly capable pragmatic Marxist, with stronger ideological moorings than his leader.

Malema, however, is not to be underestimated. Lacking virtually any formal education, he has studied successfully for a degree from the distance-learning University of South Africa (UNISA). He is a charismatic speaker and leader, with huge self-confidence and a clear view of his political constituency. The EFF won over 6 per cent of the vote and twenty-five seats in Parliament in the May 2014 elections. They became a familiar feature on the nation's TV screens, clad in red berets and overalls and made Zuma's life in Parliament a nightmare whenever he appeared there, chanting 'Pay back the money!' At the opening of Parliament in February 2016, the EFF members were hauled out of the chamber for demonstrating against Zuma.

Malema contends that he and the EFF represent the vast army of the unemployed, those who have nothing and no expectations of a better life. Though he faced corruption charges himself, he has proved exceptionally able at exploiting popular dissatisfaction with what are seen as the self-enriching practices of the ANC and of Zuma personally, appealing to a constituency the DA cannot reach.

The EFF are, ideologically, polar opposites of the DA, leading the ANC to assume that the two could never combine against them. The opposition to the ANC has been given entirely new credibility by its success in winning control of the major urban conglomerations of Gauteng, Tshwane and Port Elizabeth and the fragile alliance between the DA and the EFF so far has held in all three municipalities.

When Malema, Shivambu and Dali Mpofu, a well-known lawyer and former boyfriend of Winnie Mandela, visited London in November 2015, I participated in a meeting with them, at which they were warned against using threats of violence. In a discussion of nationalisation, they appeared to have no strong commitment to the policy if other ways could be devised to help farm and other workers, for example, through co-ownership. Asked about corruption charges against him too, Malema's response was 'Only three!' as against the 783 charges awaiting President Zuma.

* * *

At a time when the DA appeared to be gaining some momentum and Zuma was struggling, the party enmired itself in an extraordinary squabble of its own. The politically incorrect Helen Zille, at the end of a visit to Singapore, proceeded to emit a factually accurate but politically unwise and provocative tweet that colonialism had brought some benefits, such as infrastructure and an independent judiciary.

In the racially charged atmosphere of South Africa, this triggered a firestorm of abuse on social media, with calls for her immediate resignation. Instead of reprimanding her and urging her to get on with her day job of governing the Western Cape, the leadership instituted protracted 'disciplinary proceedings' against her.

The uncompromising Zille had made enemies in her climb to the top of the DA, now keen for revenge, while supporters of the new leader, Mmusi Maimane, wanted to neutralise her future influence in the party and try to increase its appeal to black South Africans. Zille was obliged to accept that she would play no future role in the party leadership, while remaining Premier of the Western Cape until 2019. But the spat distracted from the DA's attacks on the government and disregarded Zille's continuing popularity, above all in the Cape. The hope is that these negatives will be offset by the demonstration that Maimane is firmly in charge.

The opposition then suffered a further setback over moves by DA members to oust the mayor of Cape Town, Patricia de Lille, who was said to have been acting in an autocratic and dysfunctional manner and possibly to have been involved in tender fraud, though this was unproven. With Zille's term limited and war declared on De Lille, both of them high-profile politicians, popular with their constituencies, the DA could find itself losing ground in its home province.

The risk is the greater as a serious dent in the DA's claims to greater competence was made by the problems over water supplies in Cape Town. Having failed to anticipate a severe drought (the worst in nearly a century), the municipality struggled to find medium-term solutions, leaving the city critically short of water for the foreseeable future. The central government, which is supposed to have responsibility for bulk water supply, failed to offer any support or to relax budgetary restrictions until very late in the day. The population of the municipal region had increased from 2.5 to nearly 4 million since 1994. Sufficient new ground water was proving difficult to access. A first small desalinisation plant was not ordered until August 2017; more have followed since, but too few and ordered very late. Water supplies have been severely rationed in the city, which has had to plan for the possibility that on 'day zero' it might become the first major city where the taps run dry. 'Day zero' may not happen but, in Maimane's words: 'I wish we had done better.'

*   *   *

When Johannesburg was run by the ANC, Adam Habib, Vice Chancellor of Wits University, asked how it was that a business friend of Zuma, Vivian Reddy, was able to win a major power contract with the city, despite being one of the highest bidders. He never received a reply.

The new DA mayor of Johannesburg, Herman Mashaba, a successful businessman and unabashed capitalist, has made an impact with an anti-corruption campaign, suspending 100 city officials and making numerous arrests. His estimate of the value of dubious contracts awarded by the city is 16 billion rand; the figure certainly does run into billions. General Sibiya, wrongfully ousted from the Hawks, was hired by Mashaba for his anti-corruption campaign. Mashaba developed a plan to rescue tenements in Hillbrow from criminals who, literally, had hijacked them from the municipality. His campaign against the huge number of people from other African countries in Johannesburg has been controversial and inflammatory, but popular when it has come to cracking down on criminal gangs from Nigeria. A recent attempt by the ANC to remove him was defeated with the help of the EFF, supporting the anti-corruption campaign.

In Tshwane (Pretoria) too, the DA regime, supported by the EFF and led by Solly Msimanga, sought to crack down on corruption, complaining about the large number of city employees who, allegedly, were employed only because they were ANC, and selling the mayoral mansion to help finance basic services.

The DA regime in Port Elizabeth has struggled with coalition problems with smaller parties with very different agendas, though here too the mayor has engaged forcefully in a campaign to try to clear up the network of corruption graphically described in Crispian Olver's *How to Steal a City*.[50]

The DA has played a positive role in South African politics since apartheid, based on support for the constitution and the rule of law. It has avoided the arrogance of power of the ANC, its leaders typically travelling economy class. With good access to very competent legal advice, it has proved very effective at holding the government to account through legal challenges, with victories in several high-profile cases, including the reinstatement of the corruption charges against President Zuma.

The party, however, will badly need to get the problems in Cape Town behind it if it is to perform as well as it hopes in 2019. It can look forward to continuing support in the municipalities. It is less clear that it is yet making any further breakthrough in the rural areas or at the national level. Ramaphosa as President will draw away some business and middle of the road support, provided he can demonstrate his ability to really do something about corruption. Flanked as he is by colleagues regarded as robber barons within the ANC, the DA and the EFF will question how far he will be able to take the anti-corruption campaign.

Indisputably the main opposition party, the DA does not yet have the breadth or depth of support simply to take over from the ANC. That would require a wider 'Anyone but the ANC' coalition, of the kind governing the municipalities. But it would be much harder at the national than at the local level to reconcile the polar opposite views of the DA and the EFF. With Zuma gone and the ANC now committed to land expropriation, the EFF have far more in common with them than with the DA.

CHAPTER XVII

HOW TO UNDERMINE
AN INDUSTRY

To illustrate the practical effects of a combination of questionable policies, corruption and the collapse in political standards, it is worth considering the fate of the South African mining industry and the manner in which its travails even under Mbeki have become a full-blown crisis under Zuma.

While Thabo Mbeki, the Reserve Bank, Trevor Manuel and Pravin Gordhan never had any difficulty understanding that the capital-intensive South African economy could not prosper without inward investment and that such an inflow was vital to job creation, other government departments, including under Mbeki, were bent on pursuing policies that had the opposite effect.

Much of South Africa's wealth was built around the mining industry. The country to this day has some of the world's best mineral resources and the industry still contributes 25 per cent of the country's export earnings (over 40 per cent if manufactured goods from minerals are included). Currently,

450,000 people are directly employed in mining – about half the number employed thirty years ago. Over 1.3 million people have jobs in or derived from mining, with family dependents increasing that number many times.

South Africa, however, long since has lost the position of pre-eminence that it once enjoyed. In the 1980s, South Africa represented nearly 40 per cent of the global mining industry. Today it represents less than 5 per cent, a percentage that is continuing to shrink.

In part this was due to factors beyond the government's control. Declining ore grades in the country's ageing deep-level gold mines have meant that South Africa now accounts for only around 5 per cent of world gold production, behind China, Australia, Russia, the US and Peru, having dominated the industry for the prior century and more.

Successive ANC governments have given absolute priority to improving safety in the mines and, thanks to a concerted and sustained effort from the industry, there has been a dramatic improvement in safety performance.

When it comes to mining production and job growth or at least job preservation, all the trends have been in the opposite direction. The China demand-driven mining boom in the period from 2001 gave a strong boost to mining growth and employment in Australia, Brazil and Chile and other jurisdictions, whereas in South Africa there was no growth in output at all. The country failed almost entirely to benefit from the ten-year bull market in commodities.

Each year in this period, on behalf of investors, the South

African government was given a paper entitled: 'Why there is no job creation in the South African mining industry.' New investment was only very belatedly committed for vital new infrastructure. The worst impediment, however, was the extraordinarily cumbersome and protracted bureaucratic process, which meant that those seeking new mining licences in many cases had to wait for several years. Separate licences were required from the Departments of Mineral Resources, Environmental Affairs and Water Resources, with these in practice having to be obtained *consecutively* rather than simultaneously. While investment would have benefited South Africa, officials in all three departments displayed an apparent determination to keep it at bay.

Nor was there any hope of obtaining licences anyway without the choice of the 'right' empowerment partner. In the case of one well-known mining investor seeking to develop a new mine, the process took seven years. In the cases of a good many others, they gave up midway through. A perception of corruption and of excessive political influence in the choice of empowerment partners contributed to the exit of major international mining companies.

Overseas investment in the industry has been throttled by the uncertainties over mining legislation, black economic empowerment and delays in securing licences. Successful battles for higher wages pushed up costs, as did annual double-digit increases in electricity prices, which have trebled in real terms over the past decade. The crisis over power supply from Eskom constrained production for several years, with mines rationed to 90 per cent of normal power, bringing forward the closure of marginal shafts.

In 2012, extreme labour militancy resulted in a violent five-month strike in the already barely profitable platinum mining industry, as a radical new union, the Association of Mineworkers and Construction Union (AMCU), threatened the position of the incumbent National Union of Mineworkers (NUM).

International mining companies have been voting with their feet. The world's largest mining company, BHP, exited South Africa in 2015. Rio Tinto has only a minimal presence there. GoldFields is now down to one mine and AngloGold to just two mines in South Africa. The South African industry's return on equity fell to almost zero in 2015. In the words of Neal Froneman, CEO of Sibanye-Stillwater, which is close to employing 100,000 people in mining in South Africa, 'there is not an investment-friendly climate ... there is a toxic cocktail of issues that need to be addressed.'

The government were forewarned that amendments to the Mineral Resources Development Act were being put forward in a form – insistence on a massive free carry for the state in oil and gas projects – that was certain to bring oil and gas exploration in South Africa to a complete halt. Yet the proposed legislation was not amended, while major exploration was being undertaken in neighbouring Mozambique.

The legislation also gave the government the power to declare any mineral 'strategic' and to require 'beneficiation' by processing in South Africa of a proportion of the minerals produced, requirements that demonstrate the statist mentality of the ministries involved. This was a particular hobby horse of the SACP Minister of Trade and Industry, Rob Davies. As the industry pointed out, with no success, where beneficiation was economically viable, it would be undertaken by the private sector without the need for legislation to force them to do so.

These problems have been compounded by ever greater uncertainty about black empowerment. Most of the major deals under which 26 per cent ownership was required to be sold to black partners were financed by the South African mining companies lending the empowerment partners the money to buy the shares. When black partners have sold their interest, the government's view is that the company then must be 'empowered' all over again, a requirement now being tested in the courts. If the government's view were upheld, this could leave South African companies permanently subject to 're-empowerment', rendering shares in these companies of questionable value in the future.

When I suggested to the then minister, Susan Shabangu, that some serious scandals could have been avoided by broader-based empowerment transactions benefiting communities and employees, this met with a diatribe from the Director General, declaring that this was not at all the intention of what was supposed to be 'broad-based economic empowerment', which should be confined to the promotion of (politically connected) black entrepreneurs. Any sensible policy should have been designed to do both (absent the political connections).

The past two decades have seen the emergence of important mining companies led by highly competent black South Africans, in particular African Rainbow Minerals (ARM) led by Patrice Motsepe, the mining interests of the Shanduka group of Cyril Ramaphosa, Exxaro under Sipho Nkosi, Seriti Resources led by Mike Teke, and Kalagadi Manganese. But implementation of the new legislation also has been marked by a number of scandals, such as the unexplained grant of mining rights to the Gupta-connected Imperial Crown Trading (ICT), subsequently struck down by the Constitutional Court.

In 2010, when Tokyo Sexwale's Mvelaphanda Group suddenly sold its vendor-financed interest in Gold Fields, the company had to look for another empowerment partner to be allowed to develop South Deep – the only new deep-level gold mining project in South Africa. A consortium called Invictus Gold was formed, including a lot of politically connected names, but approval was not secured until a stake in Invictus reportedly worth 28.6 million rand was allocated to Baleka Mbete, who had become chairperson of the ANC and currently is Speaker of the Parliament.[51] The US Securities and Exchange Commission launched an investigation into this transaction, though no one in the South African mining industry thought that Gold Fields had much option but to do what was necessary to secure the licence to develop the mine.

HOW THINGS ARE IN A PREDATOR STATE

When Harmony Gold believed it had sold shares to women's and veterans' groups in the Free State, it found that these had ended up in the hands of a businessman called Mzi Khumalo, who hired a yacht to entertain his friends at the Athens Olympic Games. In 2008, Harmony sold two mines to a BEE entity called Pamodzi Gold. When it ran out of money, Aurora Empowerment, led by Khulubuse Zuma, nephew of the President, famous for his vast girth and expensive lifestyle, and Zondwa Mandela, a grandson of Nelson Mandela, was appointed with promises to re-finance the mines, despite a lack of any prior experience of mining. Instead the mines were stripped of all saleable assets and the workers went unpaid for months before the venture collapsed. Frans Baleni, President of the National Union of Mineworkers, declared that 'This is how things are in a predator state.'

In 2010 the Department of Mineral Resources suddenly ordered Lonmin to stop selling the valuable nickel, copper and chrome by-products from its Marikana platinum mine. Lonmin had not believed that they needed a separate licence to sell by-product minerals and by the time they applied, they were informed that a prior application, including for prospecting rights, had been made by Sivi Gounden, former senior civil servant and subsequently a director of Lonmin. As Gounden's claim was upheld by the Minerals Department, Lonmin had to pay Gounden's company, Keysha, $4 million to recover the prospecting rights.

Meanwhile, from mid-2009 Julius Malema began campaigning for nationalisation of the mines, and in September 2010 the ANC agreed that this could be studied in the run-up to the 2012 party conference in Mangaung. The ANC party leadership had no intention of going down this route, with the minister, Susan Shabangu, declaring that nationalisation would not happen 'in her lifetime', and duly pronounced against it at Mangaung, but not before the debate had spooked the more nervous overseas investors.

In 2016, South Africa was ranked by the Fraser index eighty-fourth out of 104 countries for uncertainty in mining policy, leaving only the Congo and Zimbabwe ranking behind it in Africa. With the Zuma appointment in September 2015 of Mosebenzi Zwane as Minister of Mineral Resources, the situation has become very much worse, posing a serious threat to employment and investment in the industry. All mining investors are aware of his role in forcing the sale of Optimum to the Guptas, of his longstanding association with them and his ardent defence of the family when the South African banks withdrew their credit lines. His subsequent actions appeared to be designed to try to deliver the coup de grâce to the industry in its present form.

Breaking off any semblance of consultation with the industry, in 2017 Zwane announced the unilateral imposition of the new Mining Charter, wiping $3 billion off the value of mining stocks listed on the Johannesburg Stock Exchange. The black empowerment threshold was raised from 26 to 30 per cent, which would readily have been accepted, but a raft of other conditions were added too, including that 70 per cent of goods and 80 per cent of services must be procured from black-owned entities.

In addition, the new Charter contained an extraordinary provision mandating a distribution of 1 per cent of revenues from new order mining rights to black empowerment share-holders before any other distributions are made, which appears to be at odds with the constitution. Black shareholders are required to be debt-free within ten years, otherwise existing shareholders would have to write off this expense. Companies where black empowerment partners have sold their shares would be expected to 're-empower' themselves at the further expense of existing shareholders.

The Charter also seeks to set up a Mining Transformation Development Agency, whereby about 3 billion rand in extra taxes from the industry would be diverted into a fund entirely controlled by the minister.

MAKING THE COUNTRY UNINVESTIBLE

Froneman, Mark Cutifani of Anglo American and other mining leaders declared that the minister was making the country uninvestible. Zwane had ploughed ahead despite the opposition of the industry and of several of his colleagues, in-cluding the Deputy President, Cyril Ramaphosa, who was left urging the need for 'dialogue', all attempts at which had been rejected by Zwane.

As the Chamber of Mines applied for a court interdict, implementation of the Charter has been suspended pending a court hearing. The industry has shrunk by 70,000 jobs in the past five years with another 24,000 currently subject to retrenchment notices. The Charter made no allowance for previous empowerment, financed by the companies themselves, if black empowerment shareholders subsequently sold their shares, as Tokyo Sexwale did in the case of Gold Fields and, therefore, Sibanye.

As for the requirement that a royalty of 1 per cent of revenues must be paid to empowerment shareholders before any dividends were paid to others, the Chamber of Mines pointed out that, on this basis, in the previous year no other dividends would have been paid out at all. These requirements clearly would leave existing shareholders, domestic and foreign, with little further incentive to invest or even to continue to hold their shares.

The CEO of the Chamber of Mines, representing 90 per cent of the South African industry, Roger Baxter, had played a major role in reaching agreements with previous mining ministers. But he told a mining conference in Australia that the industry had lost all confidence in Minister Zwane, given significant corruption allegations that had not been cleared up, and the fact that his plans had created a crisis for the industry.

Given these major uncertainties and headwinds, it is a tribute to the skill and determination of people at all levels in the South African mining industry that it still makes the contribution it does. It has been kept afloat to a significant degree by the devaluation of the rand. There will need to be a further expansion of the coal mining industry to cope with demand from Eskom as its major new power plants finally are commissioned, several years later than planned. But any hope of a return of overseas investment was dispelled by the appointment of Zwane as Minister of Mineral Resources and his subsequent actions.

The major mining conference (*Indaba*) held for the international mining industry every February will continue to attract the attendance of those who enjoy visiting Cape Town at that time of year. But none of those attending have been looking at investment opportunities in mining in South Africa. To reverse that trend will require amendment of the Mining Charter and replacement of the minister.

At last, however, there are now some hopeful signs. Sibanye-Stillwater has stepped in to buy Lonmin, which otherwise was likely to have ended up in administration. This should save 20,000 jobs, though 12,000 will still be lost.

One of Cyril Ramaphosa's first acts as President was to replace Mosebenzi Zwane as Minister of Mineral Resources with Gwede Mantashe, enabling negotiations to be engaged with the industry on amendments to the Mining Charter.

CHAPTER XVIII

'SOUTH AFRICA BELONGS TO US'

Having described the looting of the state-owned enterprises in South Africa to the extent – so far – of tens of billions of rand and the extraordinary self-enrichment, at the expense of the South African state, of three Indian brothers, it is time to consider how on earth this could have been possible. How is it that a once great liberation movement, which played so critical a role in the liberation of South Africa from apartheid, the party of Mandela, Tambo and Walter Sisulu, could have descended to the level and state of disrepute in which it finds itself today, struggling to remove a blatantly corrupt leader, notwithstanding the damage he had been inflicting on it? Is there something in the nature of these liberation movements that leads them, once in power, to the authoritarianism and kleptocracy in evidence in Angola and Zimbabwe today? As Alec Russell observed in *After Mandela*, such movements do not have a habit of ageing gracefully.[52] What is the future likely to hold?

The comparative study of the performance of *Liberation Movements in Power* by Roger Southall is not an encouraging document.[53] In most cases, the parties that considered they had won independence entered, and then held, office with a special sense of entitlement and disregard for those not within the magic circle, even when those who had done the actual liberating were replaced by ambitious apparatchiks with no convincing struggle credentials. The objective then became simply to hold on to power.

In the whole of southern Africa, the party that led the country to independence or 'liberation' remains in power, the only exception being Zambia, where after nearly three decades in office President Kenneth Kaunda was obliged to accept a multi-party democracy, then lost the elections to the former union leader Frederick Chiluba. Botswana has enjoyed a fairly benign paternalist regime since independence, which does still appear to have extensive support. Mugabe was able to 'win' the 2008 election in Zimbabwe only by printing an extra half-million votes. The Swapo regime in Namibia has been accompanied by some corruption, but not on anything like the scale in South Africa under Zuma. Angola is a fully fledged one-party kleptocracy and the Frelimo government in Mozambique also has been marked by some serious scandals. This is not a neighbourhood that as yet has proved conducive to democracy.

Which does not mean that South Africa is condemned to follow the example of its neighbours, the fundamental difference being that elections in South Africa since 1994 indisputably have been free and fair. The press has remained unmuzzled, the judiciary independent.

Any post-apartheid government in South Africa had to contend with enormous challenges in terms of redressing historical imbalances, overcoming the desperate skills deficit resulting from Bantu education and attempting to address the problems of the millions of have-nothings, while also promoting the development of the black middle class.

Among the problems from hell confronting the new government was that of land reform, where radical change was liable to disrupt food production and the massive sums spent have resulted in only around 10 per cent of the land so far transferred being farmed productively by black farmers.

In a predominantly arid country, there is limited scope for successful small-scale farming, rather than subsistence agriculture. The innumerable land claims resulting from the displacements under apartheid have nearly all been cash settled. The former editor of the *Sunday Times*, Mondli Makhanya, declared 'at the risk of being lynched, tarred and feathered', that most South Africans did not want to engage in farming but to seek opportunity in the cities.

Twenty-four years after majority rule, the number of white, mainly Afrikaner farmers has fallen below 35,000, many of them barely making a living, but they still own 70 per cent of commercial agricultural land. In the past decade there has been an increasing number of cases of farmers being murdered on their land, in most cases in robberies with extreme violence but, in the belief of the farmers, in some cases possibly also with a racial motivation.

Confronted by these vast problems, it was Thabo Mbeki and his colleagues who, determined to avoid the post-independence economic catastrophes in several other African countries, eschewed fresh socialist experiments and fiercely redistributive policies in favour of a serious attempt at redistribution through economic growth. An effect of the fact that radical socialist policies have not as yet been tried in South Africa is the temptation to try them in future, though they have never yet succeeded elsewhere.

Mbeki's intelligence and competence were offset by his tragic denialism about Aids, only for this to be followed by the far greater tragedy of the Zuma regime, with no redeeming features. Under him, the party has been following a trajectory described also by some other liberation movements, with the denouement in South Africa bound to have a far bigger impact on the continent than in other cases.

Most of the evidence in other countries and cases suggests that it is extremely difficult for a major political party to reinvent itself without losing power. But for a liberation movement, and specifically for its leadership, this is something it is never supposed to do. Jacob Zuma has declared that in South Africa the ANC will rule 'until Jesus comes'. Whether he meant that literally, he certainly did not envisage the ANC ever giving up power and nor do many of his associates. The official history of the ANC, published during the struggle against apartheid, was entitled 'South Africa belongs to us'. This, however, is a notion that persists within the ANC today.

* * *

So how did this morphing of large sections of the party from would-be liberators, prepared to make great personal sacrifices for the cause, into a predatory class come about? By what process did the admirable history of opposition to apartheid turn into the abuses evident today? To what extent are these inherent in the sense of entitlement of liberation movements? What are the chances of reversing such a process?

Nelson Mandela, having studied law at Fort Hare and Wits universities, had become a leader of the defiance campaign in the Transvaal and founder of the youth wing of the ANC. He and most of his senior colleagues were prosecuted unsuccessfully for treason from 1956 to 1961. It was in December 1961 that Mandela, concluding that non-violent methods would never work against the apartheid state, joined with the SACP to found the military wing of the ANC, Umkhonto we Sizwe (MK). Mandela claimed later to have consulted Chief Albert Luthuli, then President of the ANC, confined to his homestead in rural Natal, but there is no evidence for this and Luthuli was known to be unhappy about the abandonment of non-violence.

Concerned to avoid civilian casualties, Mandela's activities consisted of an (unsuccessful) attempt to blow up some electricity pylons. In 1964, Mandela, who was already in jail, and the senior ANC leaders arrested on the Liliesleaf farm at Rivonia were convicted of conspiracy to overthrow the state.

In his speech at the Rivonia trial, Mandela said that he was against white domination, and against black domination. He had cherished the ideal of a democratic and free society, which he hoped to see realised. 'But, my Lord,' he added, 'if needs be, it is an ideal for which I am prepared to die.'

The prisoners knew that they faced the very real danger of a death sentence. When they were sentenced to life imprisonment, one of the triallists, Denis Goldberg, exclaimed 'Life is beautiful!'

Nearly all those imprisoned with him were members of the South African Communist Party as, briefly and nominally, Mandela had been himself. Having done what I could to help speed up their release, it was a great occasion to meet Walter Sisulu, Ahmed Kathrada and their colleagues in Soweto on the day after the end of their imprisonment. These elderly, immensely dignified gentlemen, clad in cardigans, all seemed unlikely revolutionaries. In meetings with them then and later, I found that they all were socialists, but with no deep commitment to communism, least of all in its Soviet guise. They had joined the party as the most extreme and organised manifestation of opposition to apartheid. As with Mandela, they were remarkably devoid of bitterness and, instead, were hopeful that they would live to see the outcome for which they had sacrificed half their lives. The sacrifice they had made was equal to that of Mandela, and their ideals were the same.

Leadership of the ANC, banned in South Africa, passed to the exiles, led by Mandela's friend and former partner in their law firm, Oliver Tambo. At a time when we were supposed not to be talking to the ANC, I arranged a couple of meetings with the scholarly and kindly Tambo, demonised at the time in South Africa, during his exile in Muswell Hill in north London, with his formidable wife, Adelaide, dispensing helpings of currant cake.

Tambo too was an improbable revolutionary, driven to it by the apartheid state, and almost as remarkable an individual as Mandela. It was largely thanks to his leadership that violent factional disputes within the exile movement were contained, as were the vast frustrations resulting from the lack of success and often incompetent leadership of the military wing. Tambo was an African nationalist and never a communist, but the SACP, led by Joe Slovo, established a virtual stranglehold over the secretariat, publications and much of the rest of the leadership of the ANC.

Protected by the police in London, he became an anglophile. Following Mandela's release, my doubts about the revolutionary nature of Oliver and Adelaide Tambo were confirmed when I received an engraved invitation: 'The President of the ANC requests the pleasure of your company at a dinner in honour of the Deputy President of the ANC (Mandela)', followed by 'Carriages at Eleven O'Clock'. On his return to South Africa, I was summoned to meet him, having been told by a colleague that he wanted to see 'our ambassador'. He proceeded to tell the first ANC conference able to be held in South Africa for decades that it was a waste of time calling on other governments to treat de Klerk as if he were P. W. Botha. They needed to get ready for a new challenge: that of participating in government. It was a tragedy for South Africa that he was by then too frail to play any further role, his ideals being exactly the same as those of his lifelong friend Mandela.

But there was a much darker side to the movement too, reflected in the 'necklacing' of real and supposed collaborators in the townships. Many of the young men leaving South Africa to fight apartheid found themselves consigned to remote, badly run and ill-supplied camps a very long way from the front line. The miseries they suffered were recounted to me in graphic detail by the MK veteran Zola Zkwewiya. The security wing of MK, paranoid about South African spies, were both brutal and violent. Among those arrested and interrogated by them was Pallo Jordan, regarded as a leading intellectual within the movement, subsequently a Cabinet minister from 1994 to 2009. He has become a leading dissident again today.

In Angola, the MK trainees found that, having signed up to fight apartheid, they were required instead to fight the UNITA rebel movement. Having sustained heavy casualties, in January 1984 they tried to protest to Tambo himself, who was visiting Angola at the time. They also protested about the security branch and demanded an investigation into the notorious Quatro punishment camp.

Tambo did not meet them. Instead, the MK leaders asked the Angolan army to suppress the mutiny. Joe Modise and Chris Hani both were involved in arresting leaders who had been promised a fair hearing, but instead were shot. Resistance continued for several weeks at the Pango camp in Angola, until most of the mutineers were executed. News of the mutiny was successfully suppressed. Many years later, Tambo declared that in 1984 'enemy agents' had started a mutiny in Angola, though this was belied by the ANC's own internal investigation, led by James Stuart, which set out the real reasons for the mutiny.[54]

For those who did enter South Africa, many MK recruits displayed no lack of courage. An operation was conducted in 1980 against a SASOL (oil from gas) facility in South Africa and another in 1981 against a South African air force base. But in general life expectancy was short, as MK units could not match the firepower of the South African army and police and, within South Africa, they very often were penetrated by informers; the South African military responded by launching lethal attacks on ANC operatives in Maputo, Harare and Swaziland.

The paranoia about informers affected MK operations in Natal, overseen by Jacob Zuma. As infiltrated MK operatives more often than not were quickly captured, suspicion fell on his colleague, Thami Zulu. Zuma appears to have been involved in his arrest and interrogation, following which Zulu died.

The great achievement of the ANC in exile was not on the battlefield, but in mobilising international support against apartheid and explicitly for the ANC in opposing it. This was the achievement above all of Tambo and, by far his most effective deputy, Thabo Mbeki. Guaranteed the support of the Soviet Union and its satellites for the military wing, ANC representatives were thrilled to be granted an audience with Mao Tse-tung, though Chinese support turned out to be largely rhetorical.

It was with the principal Western countries that Tambo and Mbeki had their greatest successes. Aided by the black caucus in Congress, they overcame Reagan and Bush's resistance to isolating South Africa. The Nordic countries became principal funders of the ANC. The British Council of Churches and the World Council of Churches became unconditional supporters, despite SACP domination of the leadership, and appeared remarkably unconcerned by announcements by Chris Hani and others that the military wing would henceforth be targeting 'soft' (i.e. civilian) targets, which, in fact, they were already doing. The ANC led the international campaign for sanctions against South Africa. They also succeeded in attracting to the party the lion's share of the external funding for the resistance in South Africa, giving them a huge advantage vis-à-vis the other much less well-organised resistance groups, such as the Pan Africanist Congress.

The ANC by this stage were experiencing the familiar problems of exile movements, including an understandable degree of paranoia, given the capabilities and methods of their opponents, overreliance on often questionable intelligence operatives and sources, and sharply conflicting leadership ambitions. The fiercest of these was between Thabo Mbeki and Chris Hani. Unlike most of the other MK commanders, Hani had distinguished himself in action, albeit in Zimbabwe. The ANC doctrine at this stage remained that of a 'seizure of power', whereby the enemy would throw in the towel and the liberation movement would take over without the need for much of a negotiation.

Oliver Tambo was never a believer in this concept and nor, in jail, was Nelson Mandela. Mandela, who had founded MK, knew that it would be a very long time indeed before it could hope to overcome the resistance of the South African army and police. He wrote that 'in our circumstances, the aim of a people's war was not to "win", but gradually through a process of attrition to bring the government to the realisation that we could not be defeated and they could not win' (Mandela's foreword to O'Malley *Shades of Difference* p 11).[55]

Chris Hani himself acknowledged that the military achievements had been modest, but he argued – without doubt correctly – that it had been a formidable recruiting factor for the ANC. Tambo himself regarded the military campaign as an exercise mainly in 'armed propaganda'. The conviction in the townships that MK was engaged in a military confrontation with the apartheid regime was a vitally important recruiting factor with township youth and persists in ANC mythology today, according to which MK 'liberated' South Africa. The reality was more clearly expressed in an internal ANC report, inadvertently read out publicly in 1990 by the secretary general, Alfred Nzo. He declared that it had to be admitted that the armed struggle was making no progress in South Africa. Whatever those dreaming of a seizure of power might think, there was going to have to be a negotiation.

Whatever the divisions within the movement even then, the history of the struggle against apartheid was one in which, as Kgalema Motlanthe observed: 'We did not join the ANC to get rich: we joined it to go to jail.'

CHAPTER XIX

'I DON'T KNOW WHERE THIS NOTION COMES FROM THAT WE HAVE CONSCIENCES'

The negotiation initiated by Mandela and Thabo Mbeki, and carried forward by Cyril Ramaphosa, having succeeded, the ANC exile leaders, now re-established in South Africa, lost no time in elbowing aside the army of the interior, the ANC-supporting United Democratic Front (UDF) who, arguably, had done more actually to liberate South Africa than the exiles had. For many of those fighting apartheid through mass demonstrations and constant repression within South Africa, the faraway external leaders had been organising an 'armchair revolution'. Oliver Tambo, by the time he returned to South Africa, was in very poor health. He would have tried harder than his external colleagues did to bridge this gap.

Mandela apart, even leaders as prestigious as Walter Sisulu and Ahmed Kathrada swiftly were sidelined by Mbeki among others, and Cyril Ramaphosa was told by the exiles that he was not 'one of us', putting paid to his own leadership ambitions at the time. Following their own convictions about the levers of power that actually mattered, the exiles colonised the defence, police and intelligence ministries, on which Jacob Zuma continues to base his power today.

While the practice of corruption (in the cases, for instance, of Allan Boesak and the questionable activities of Ismail Ayob) was the exception in the UDF, it was habitual in the upper echelons of Umkhonto we Sizwe, and was epitomised by its commander, Joe Modise.

There was at the time a great deal of concern that the ANC might actually implement the Marxist policies to which they were formally committed, including nationalisation of the banks and the mines. On the basis of my own meetings at the time with Mandela, Sisulu, Kathrada, Tambo and other ANC leaders, I told Margaret Thatcher, among others, that I did not believe there was any serious likelihood of their doing so. On returning to South Africa, Mbeki and Zuma already had abandoned their membership of the SACP. Neither had ever been anything remotely resembling a committed Marxist. Mbeki had embarked on his campaign to establish an economic policy framework (GEAR) based on fiscal discipline and the need to achieve a balance between growth and redistribution.

There was another equally important issue on which I was able to offer no reassurance at all. For the ANC, having abandoned their SACP mentors on economic policy, had embraced wholeheartedly the Communist doctrine of the supremacy of the party over the institutions of the country, as evidenced in the quotation from Zuma at the outset of this book. A large fraction of the party contended, with the SACP, that the, to them, unpleasant compromises involved in coming to power by relatively peaceful means must lead on to the second phase of the 'national democratic revolution' in which such constraints on transformation and economic liberation would be set aside. Even the most thoughtful and serious of Mbeki's advisers, Joel Netshitenzhe, declared in 1998 that the party's goal must be 'extending control over all levers of power: the army, the police, the bureaucracy, the intelligence structures, the judiciary, the parastatals and regulatory bodies, the public broadcaster, the central bank and so on'. Netshitenzhe at this time described the opposition Democratic Alliance as 'undermining the state'.

This declaration of intent represents the heart of the problem for South Africa today and was followed to the letter by the Zuma regime. For this is the policy that has been pursued ever since by those who believe that the party should stay in power 'until Jesus comes'. As the ruling party's popularity declined, the danger was obvious that this ambition could bring it into ever greater conflict with the safeguards in the constitution, a clash that the more moderate wing of the party was concerned to avoid.

Following the euphoric celebration of the 1994 elections the ANC found itself in power at every level of government and in every region except KwaZulu-Natal, where the elections were won by Inkatha. Many now in power entered it with a genuine determination to redress the wrongs of the past and to serve the people who had elected them. There are plenty of

ANC members and some leaders who are just as committed to serving the people today.

But there are others who are not. Those arriving in power, for instance in the municipalities, had no prior experience of government. The ability to allocate contracts to political supporters or personal beneficiaries proved too much for most municipalities to resist, with similar effects at the regional level as well. The ANC cadres in the regions found that those particularly disposed to contribute to party coffers and the enrichment of individuals were the less reputable members of the local business communities, expecting commercial favours to be delivered in return, and bringing the party into close contact with criminal syndicates, as described by Crispian Olver in *How to Steal a City* and in Sizwe Yende's *Eerie Assignment*. The Guptas did not invent 'tenderpreneurship'. Rather they displayed an exceptional ability to profit from it. For corruption had by now become structural and a way of life within the ruling party.

BLACK ECONOMIC EMPOWERMENT

The equally exceptional opportunity they were able to exploit resulted from the policy of black economic empowerment (BEE) – or rather the way it has been implemented, which, as numerous critics have pointed out, has turned out to have very little to do with uplifting the poorest in society.

The redressing of historical economic imbalances through

black economic empowerment has been a cornerstone policy of ANC governments since 'liberation'. There can be no reasonable argument with the objective of correcting the manifest injustices of the past, creating a fairer society and giving 'hitherto disadvantaged South Africans' the hope and promise of a better future.

A starting point was Thabo Mbeki's declaration that 'South Africa is a country of two nations. One of these nations is white and relatively prosperous ... The separate and larger nation of South Africa is black and poor.' The eventual aim of the Employment Equity Act of 1999 was to seek to ensure that jobs at every level should reflect the make-up of the population. Mandela initially urged white civil servants to stay at their posts. But this was incompatible with the ANC's determination to reward their supporters and to establish control over all the levers of power through the 'deployment of party cadres to positions at every level of the bureaucracracy'.

The target of 70 per cent representation of black South Africans in senior levels of the civil service, both nationally and in the provinces, has long since been achieved, but the tidal wave of appointments based on political patronage was criticised by Mamphele Ramphele, when Vice Chancellor of the University of Cape Town, as compromising both the independence and competence of the civil service. In presenting the National Development Plan, Trevor Manuel acknowledged that the 'development state' could achieve little without a 'capable state', requiring more competent administration.

In the private sector, from 2008 black empowerment codes

prescribed black representation at 60 per cent in senior and 75 per cent in middle management. A problem with this quasi quota approach, which has promoted the advancement of black professionals, has been that it does nothing for the seriously disadvantaged, the destitute and workless, accentuating the gap between the increasing number of black haves and the also increasing number of black have-nots.

The Employment Equity Act especially, benefiting a far wider category of people, has made a major contribution to the rapid growth of the black middle class. Black economic empowerment also has contributed, though far more selectively, to this. The opposition Democratic Alliance, as it focuses on winning more black South African support, after a fierce internal debate, also has accepted a version of empowerment to help overcome centuries of discrimination. It was difficult to see how the horrendous inequalities of opportunity resulting from apartheid could otherwise have been addressed. The programme could and should have been used to benefit a far wider spectrum of the 'historically disadvantaged'. But successive empowerment programmes, although ostensibly intended to promote 'broad-based' black economic empowerment, have never yet been operated in that way (except by individual companies).

The programme instead has been criticised on both sides of the political spectrum for having benefited mainly politically connected black businessmen. Archbishop Tutu has argued that black economic empowerment as it has been applied to date has served mainly the black elite, while leaving millions in dehumanising poverty.

Another notable critic has been Moeletsi Mbeki, brother of Thabo, who has argued that BEE entrenched economic inequalities by creating a culture of entitlement and cronyism, discouraging genuine black entrepreneurship by creating a class of unproductive but wealthy 'crony capitalists' linked to the ANC.[56] Senior figures in the trade union movement and the SACP denounced the 'parasitic nature of the emerging BEE elite', arguing that the programme was encouraging corruption and diverting the ANC from focusing on improving the situation of the poor.

In 2007, Kgalema Motlanthe, then secretary general of the ANC, stated that BEE was fuelling corruption at all levels of government. He told the journalist Carol Paton that corruption in South Africa was far worse than most people realised. Almost every project offered the 'opportunity for certain people to make money'. The ruling party, allocating tenders and contracts, both nationally and in nearly all the provinces, was preoccupied with 'business opportunities and who should profit from them'.

This often was accompanied by blatant displays of wealth. In September 2009, Cosatu denounced the 'crass materialism' that had become 'a social norm amongst the elite'.

Every significant transaction from which the Gupta family has benefited has exploited the black economic empowerment model to secure an advantage and achieve their objectives, even though they cannot conceivably be considered to be 'historically disadvantaged South Africans', a role performed for them, along with others, by Duduzane Zuma.

The way in which black empowerment policies were

implemented appeared to reflect a belief, prevalent elsewhere in Africa, that the poor have no political influence. Instead of promoting broad-based empowerment, in a new version of 'South Africa belongs to us', the programme has been used to create and reward an entire class of frequently now very prosperous black business leaders closely connected to the ANC. It was this orientation of a policy that could have been used to benefit a far broader segment of the population that created an irresistible opportunity for exploitation of the system for the Guptas, among others. Combined with the prevalent phenomenon of 'tenderpreneurship', the opportunity was created for malfeasance on an epic scale.

The ANC's own 'empowerment' investment vehicle, Chancellor House, was set up to fund the needs of the party and has made a major contribution to doing so. Chancellor House acquired a 25 per cent interest in Hitachi Power Africa which, to no one's surprise, then won contracts valued at 40 billion rand for the supply of steam generators for the two massive new Eskom power stations at Medupi and Kusile. The second contract did not even go out to tender. Chancellor House's stake in Hitachi Power Africa eventually was sold for 50 million rand. These and other commercial operations gave the ANC sources of funding that no other political party could begin to hope to match.

* * *

The anti-apartheid campaigner Helen Suzman, who got to know the ANC leaders through her efforts on their behalf through their long years in jail, used to express to me her worries about what she regarded as the Manichaean nature of the ANC. On the one hand there were those, who she admired wholeheartedly, who were immensely courageous fighters for freedom, on the other those who were fighters mainly for power, and the ability to use it in much the same ways as their predecessors had done. The genuine fighters for freedom she found to be more prevalent among the older than in the younger echelons of the ANC.

The latter-day counterpart to the former Robben Islander and interim President Motlanthe's declaration about joining the ANC not to get rich, but to go to jail, and Mandela's statement that 'This is a principle for which, if necessary, I am prepared to die', came from the Secreatary General of the ANC, Gwede Mantashe. Urging support for Jacob Zuma in the no-confidence vote, he declared: '*I don't know where this notion comes from that we are a collection of individuals who have consciences.*'

The Zuma regime sought, pretty successfully, to negate the safeguards in South Africa's constitution by neutralising the prosecuting agencies and seeking to circumvent and subvert the constitution, rather than mounting a full-scale attack on it. As the party came under ever greater political pressure, there were a good many within it as well as outside it who worried that the reaction – as in Zimbabwe and Angola, both of them more advanced kleptocracies than South Africa – would be to seek to hold on to power at any cost, including authoritarianism, a crackdown on the press and rigged elections. The

Financial Times, in an editorial, wrote of a possible 'descent into despotism'.[57]

That was indeed not just a possible but a likely future scenario, which certainly would have been favoured by the securocrats around President Zuma and the unimpressive leaders of the women's and youth leagues. There was on their part a keen desire to limit freedom of the press, the more so as they had never yet succeeded in doing so. There are plenty of leaders within the ANC, however, who would very strongly oppose tearing up the constitution or implementing self-defeating economic policies, with at their head a principal architect of the constitution, Cyril Ramaphosa. His wafer-thin victory in the ANC presidential election was of capital importance in arresting the prospect of a descent into authoritarianism.

The electorate in 2019 no doubt would have sought to do so as well. With the ANC led by Dlamini-Zuma, the likelihood was of a hung election, with the EFF holding the balance. With the DA and EFF polar opposites in their political philosophies, and the ANC bound then to try at almost any price for a rapprochement with Malema, the outcome would have been highly uncertain. If Ramaphosa were to prove unable to assert his authority, it could still be.

The raison d'être of the ANC has become to hold on to power. It continues to benefit from a deeply ingrained tendency to hold on to the mothership, and fear of the consequences of abandoning it. While many still say they support it because of its role in the liberation struggle, the truth in other cases is more prosaic. Meeting members of a family of ANC royalty after criticising the government over Eskom, I found them all to be ardent critics of Zuma, but not prepared to say so. For if they did, they volunteered, they would stand to lose all the government contracts that had enriched them.

In a BBC interview in September 2017, Kgalema Motlanthe followed Archbishop Tutu's example in calling for the ANC to lose the next election unless it returns to the mission of serving the people, reflecting his apparent belief that the party will only really reform itself once it loses power. Ramaphosa will now have the chance to prove this wrong. But it is not a given that he will succeed in doing so.

CHAPTER XX

THE FOURTH ESTATE

'Burke said there were three Estates in Parliament; but in the Reporters' Gallery, there sat a Fourth Estate more important than them all.' – Thomas Carlyle, *On Heroes and Hero Worship*

So what were the countervailing forces that gave hope for the future in South Africa? High among these must be rated the extraordinary continuing performance of the South African press, despite partially successful efforts to undermine media independence.

For a brief period, around the time of liberation, there were hopes that the South African Broadcasting Corporation (SABC) might cease to function as the mouthpiece of the government, as it had under apartheid, and become a genuinely independent broadcaster. The BBC was eager to offer advice on how to do this. These hopes were quickly disappointed, even under Mandela, as the ANC government lost no time in asserting its control. The leadership of the broadcaster since has gone through various crises, but reached a new low with the appointment from 2008 of Hlaudi Motsoeneng to senior positions in SABC despite his prior abysmal record (he was described in a Deloitte report as 'semi-literate') and lack of any relevant qualifications. By 2011 he was acting chief operations officer and also acting, in effect, as editor in chief.

SABC's own legal team told a tribunal that Motsoeneng had 'abused his power and must be dismissed'. The charges included the fact that he had lied about having a high school certificate when first appointed. His lawyer said that he had been portrayed as a 'slimy character'.

Motsoeneng's response was that a good brain was more important than a piece of paper. He decreed that whenever the ANC was discussed on SABC, an ANC representative must be present. In 2013 he further decreed that there must be '70 per cent positive news'. Eight senior journalists dismissed by him accused him of being responsible for 'the death of public service journalism' and of instituting a reign of terror at SABC. The Minister of Communications, Faith Muthambi, also interfered directly in the newsroom, telling journalists what to do.[58]

The Public Protector, Thuli Madonsela, in her report entitled *When Governance and Ethics Fail*, found that Motsoeneng had lied about his qualifications and that his salary had increased from 1.5 to 3.7 million rand plus a reported 30 million rand bonus for selling the entire SABC archive for use by the commercial channel MultiChoice. In response to demands for his removal following the Madonsela report, Minister Faith Muthambi told the SABC Board 'But Baba loves him, he loves him so much' – Baba being Jacob Zuma. Far from being disciplined, Motsoeneng was appointed permanent COO.

During the 2014 election campaign, the SABC refused to broadcast campaign advertisements of the opposition parties. It also censored the proceedings in Parliament during Zuma's 2015 State of the Nation address. It earlier was revealed to have compiled a blacklist of commentators who must not be permitted to broadcast.

In April 2014 SABC reporters were warned by the chairperson, Ellen Tshabalala (who turned out also to have lied about her qualifications), that their phones were being tapped by the National Intelligence Agency and that they must remain loyal to the ANC. Despite court judgments against him, in a disciplinary hearing on 13 December 2015, Motsoeneng was mysteriously cleared of charges that he had claimed to have a high school certificate on the grounds that, supposedly, it was well known that he did not have any formal qualifications when he was first appointed, so all his misrepresentations about this did not matter, thereby enabling him to continue running the SABC on behalf of the Zuma faction of the ANC.

In June 2016, to justify his decision to suspend senior journalists who had defied his orders that protests against the government should not be shown, he said that they must follow his leadership or 'get off the bus'. He had previously been dismissive of journalists with degrees. In the following month he intervened to extend a programme produced by one of Zuma's daughters for three years, at a cost of 167 million rand. SABC were showing the Guptas' ANN7 business breakfast events on their main TV channel.

In 2016, following a Western Cape High Court ruling that

his appointment had been illegal, he finally was obliged to step down as chief operating officer – only to be reappointed as head of corporate affairs. This in turn was challenged, including by the ANC members of the relevant parliamentary committee.

The committee were told in December 2016 that no processes were followed before appointing Motsoeneng as permanent COO. The board were simply told to do so by the minister. The head of the audit committee, who resisted the appointment, was ousted. The chairman of the SABC board responsible for keeping Motsoeneng in office, Mbulaheni Maguvhe, claimed that he was unable to remember most of what had happened on his watch.

By this time ANC members of the parliamentary committee on broadcasting had had enough and the court judgments proved impossible to set aside. The reign of terror by this totally unqualified person, who should never have been appointed in the first place, came to an end. The SABC, however, remains tightly under the control of the government.

*　*　*

The Independent Media group of newspapers in South Africa, so long as it was owned by the Irish businessman Tony O'Reilly, tended to be circumspect about directly attacking the government, but employed a raft of respected editors, journalists and columnists who did not hesitate to expose corruption and abuses of power. When the group and its owner fell into financial difficulties in 2013, Independent Media was bought by the businessman Iqbal Survé, reported to have been a struggle activist and Mandela's doctor, though not in the period when I knew Mandela. The mystery as to how he could afford to buy the group was solved when Parliament required the Public Investment Corporation (PIC) to declare its major investments, obliging the PIC to reveal that it had loaned Survé 1 billion rand to enable him to buy Independent Media.[59] The PIC justified this on the grounds of the group's predominant position in the South African press, controlling several major titles (including the *Argus, Star, Cape Times* and the *Sunday Independent*, together amounting to a quarter of the English language newspapers sold in the country) and the need for 'transformation'. This was a long way from its mandate, which is to look after the savings of all state-sector employees.

The takeover of the Independent Media group was followed by an exodus of experienced, independent-minded journalists. Following Nelson Mandela's death in December 2013, the *Cape Times* carried an extended tribute, but also a damning report by the Public Protector, which found that the Fisheries Minister, Tina Joemat-Pettersson (subsequently Energy Minister) had been guilty of 'improper conduct' in the irregular awarding of an 800 million rand fishing contract to a Survé company. This was followed by the dismissal of the editor, Alide Dasnois. The Survé newspapers subsequently were obliged to apologise to Dasnois for suggesting that a settlement with her had 'vindicated' the media group.

In January 2015, Helen Zille questioned the

independence of the group after it apologised to President Zuma for an article written by the respected columnist Max du Preez describing him as a 'one-man wrecking ball' causing devastation that would take years to overcome.

As the editor of the fiercely anti-apartheid *Vrye Weekblad*, Du Preez and his colleague Jacques Pauw had done more than anyone at the time to expose the activities of P. W. Botha's death squads and the dirty tricks of the security forces.

His response was to write to the then editor in chief, Karima Brown, that he no longer wished to be associated with the group, following the dismissal of Alide Dasnois as editor of the *Cape Times* and allegations that the journalist Tony Weaver (another anti-apartheid veteran) had 'disrespected the authority' of his superiors. He was astonished that Karima Brown and her deputy had chosen to wear ANC T-shirts at a party celebration. He concluded: 'The transformation the media needs is not a replacement of critical voices with loyal ANC cadres. The transformation we need is for the media to fight harder for clean and accountable government.' Karima Brown, after leaving the group, became a severe critic of the Zuma regime and showed support for the distinguished columnist Peter Bruce when he suffered attempted intimidation by Black First Land First.

The *Star*, *Argus* and *Cape Times*, nevertheless, have continued to publish content critical of government misdemeanours. The editor of the *Sunday Independent*, Steve Motale, however, having publicised allegations about Cyril Ramaphosa's private life at the height of the ANC election campaign which, given the use of intercepted emails, clearly were planted by the intelligence services, also was reported to be trying to investigate the sources used by Jacques Pauw in *The President's Keepers*.[60] Survé had been at odds with the Guptas over a share they hoped to obtain in Independent Media, and the *Star*, *Argus* and *Cape Times* reported objectively on the ANC presidential campaign.

In December 2010, the Gupta family launched a new daily newspaper, the *New Age*, intended, they said at the time, to present a positive picture of the South African government and the ruling party. The paper claims a circulation of over 100,000 – a figure that has never been audited. Of this, some 50,000 copies are sold via sweetheart deals with the South African parastatals. The Guptas also launched their Zuma-friendly news channel, ANN7.

The former government spokesman declared that Zuma had asked him to 'help the Guptas' by boosting the circulation of the paper. The state-owned corporations – Transnet, Telkom and Eskom – all funded *New Age* breakfasts at the Gupta mansion in Saxonwold. In November 2014, Eskom's auditor questioned the company spending 43 million rand sponsoring these breakfasts. The *Mail and Guardian* was correct in suspecting similar practices at South African Airways and PetroSA.[61] As the Gupta media engaged heavily on Zuma's side in his conflicts within the party, attacking Pravin Gordhan and any other actual or potential critics of the President, they went so far overboard that the ANC required the Gupta channels to apologise for 'reckless journalism'.[62]

In their campaign on behalf of the President and his supporters in the ANC, the Gupta media channels have given a great deal of air-time to a faction entitled Black First Land First, led by Andile Mngxitama, calling for all land to be distributed without compensation. Mngxitama fell out with his former colleagues in the Economic Freedom Front and ever since, along with the Guptas, has been an ardent defender of the President, with tweets about 'Hands off Zuma' (and the Guptas) and 'Pravin must go' and the struggle against 'white minority capital'. Favourite targets have been Johann Rupert, Trevor Manuel, Thuli Madonsela, Pravin Gordhan and any other critics of the President. While their site makes a lot of noise, supporters seem to be few and far between. The site is alleged to have been in large part the creation of the PR firm, Bell Pottinger, as part of the effort to divert attention from the misdeeds of the President and the Gupta family through attacks on their critics and the dissemination of fake news.

* * *

So much for the bad news about attempted state capture of the media in South Africa. For alongside the 'captured' entities, there exists an extremely impressive, passionate and vibrant free press, bent on exposing corruption and holding the government accountable, and an equally impressive array of journalists and commentators determined to report and opine without fear or favour.

The largest-circulation newspaper, the Johannesburg *Sunday*

Times, owned by the Times Media Group (now Tiso Blackstar), remains indisputably independent. It has a circulation of over 440,000 and a readership estimated at over 3 million. It went through a period when three of its reporters allowed themselves to be used by the intelligence services to plant stories about those chasing the real wrong-doers, but its current leadership definitively put that episode behind it. It frequently leads with headlines extremely embarrassing to the government about its performance. It has on many occasions infuriated the ANC and Zuma personally and continued to publish cartoons by Zuma's nemesis, Zapiro.

Given its circulation and the large number of titles it controls, there were persistent rumours of a desire on the part of the government to try to buy indirect control of the group and in particular of the *Sunday Times*, which under the current editor, Bongani Siqoko, remains fiercely independent today.

The group also controls the newspaper with the largest circulation among black South Africans, *The Sowetan*. It has a circulation of around 120,000, but a readership estimated at nearly 2 million. Under its remarkable former editor, Aggrey Klaaste, *The Sowetan* played an honourable part in the struggle against apartheid, but also showed itself to be highly resistant to bullying by the ANC.

Times Media also owns the two main business publications, *Business Day* and the *Financial Mail*, which have been highly critical of the Zuma government's failures in economic policy. They have several very influential and highly respected columnists. *Business Day* claims, with some justification, to be the country's most respected daily newspaper, though its circulation is only 23,600, with a readership around three times that. The *Financial Mail* has a circulation of around 30,000, but claims a readership of around 180,000. Both publications were strong supporters of Pravin Gordhan in his attempts to avoid a ratings downgrade and keep the South African economy on an even keel. Both magazines are close in their opinions to the business community, viewing as extremely dangerous for the South African economy the populist policies of the Economic Freedom Front and, increasingly, of President Zuma and his acolytes.

In the last two decades of the apartheid era, the *Weekly Mail*, now the weekly *Mail and Guardian*, had been the leading press critic of the apartheid regime. In 1988, when the paper was suspended by P. W. Botha, on behalf of the British government, I provided it with funding to tide it over until the courts enabled it to start publishing again. In 1993 it formed a joint venture with the Guardian group in the UK.

To the dismay of ANC leaders, following majority rule, the *Mail and Guardian* proved just as independent of government as it had in the past. In particular, it played a leading role in exposing corruption and maladministration in the arms deal, followed by fierce criticism of Thabo Mbeki's denialism about Aids. Ever since, it has played a role in holding the government to account, especially in relation to the innumerable scandals under Zuma. It recently was sold to an independent media group in the US, with the editorial staff remaining firmly in control.

The Nasionale Pers group, owned by Naspers, controls much of the Afrikaans press, in particular the two leading titles,

Beeld and *Die Burger*. *Die Burger* has a circulation of around 55,000 in the Western Cape, including many readers from the Afrikaans-speaking Coloured community. *Beeld*, published in Johannesburg and the north, has a circulation of 40,000 and a readership estimated at around 380,000. Both titles have been highly critical of the new regime, especially under Zuma.

Nasionale Pers has been reaching an increasingly wide audience in the English-speaking media with its outstanding news service *News24*. The group has been embarrassed, however, by the revelation of payments by its entertainment channel, MultiChoice, rising from 50 million to 141 million rand a year, plus a one-off payment of 25 million rand, to the Gupta ANN7 TV channel. In 2018 MultiChoice decided to end the relationship with ANN7, which will make a serious dent in ANN7's finances, without explaining why such generous payments were made in the first place. MultiChoice at the time was lobbying the government, in the end successfully, to secure digital migration in a form that would safeguard its monopoly of South African pay TV.

The newspaper which, after *The Sowetan*, also has a strong following among black South Africans is *City Press*, with a circulation of around 80,000 and an estimated readership of 1.5 million. It too is owned by Nasionale Pers. Under a remarkable former editor, Ferial Haffajee, and since, it has been highly critical of the Zuma regime.

In 2009, Branko Brkic founded a new online newspaper in South Africa, the *Daily Maverick*. Since then it has become a cutting-edge critic of President Zuma, based on extremely good sources and highly competent commentators and contributors. Starting with a cult following, the *Daily Maverick* has become indispensable reading for anyone wanting to know what really is happening in South Africa.

Often working closely with the *Daily Maverick* has been the extraordinary association of independent investigative journalists, amaBhungane (this being the Zulu name for the extraordinarily determined and tenacious dung beetle!).

Their effectiveness in exposing corruption already was formidable. Since the Guptaleak emails fell into their hands, it has become even more so. Analysis of the material has become a joint venture with the Scorpio investigative unit of the *Maverick*, in a joint venture with *Business Day*, *City Press*, the *Sunday Times* and the *News24* group, working on a treasure trove of revealing information, the publication of which has forced government action against executives at Eskom as well as exposing the roles of Bell Pottinger and KPMG and the manner in which normally reputable multinationals sought to use the Gupta connection to win business in South Africa.

I would like finally to express my conviction that of all the many distinguished commentators on events in South Africa, none has been more effective, trenchant or accurate than Zapiro. I do not believe that there is any more effective, or funnier, political cartoonist anywhere. It is an honour to be able to accompany this account with his more telling contributions.

*   *   *

South Africa also has a thriving publishing industry, which has published memoirs like that of the former prosecutor, Vusi Pikoli, whose book *My Second Initiation* describes the systematic interference, followed by dismissal, he suffered in his attempts to do his job, and those of other prosecutors and investigators ousted for the same reason.

In 2014, Alex Boraine, who played as distinguished a role as Van Zyl Slabbert in the fight against apartheid, published *What's Gone Wrong?*, attributing the ANC's excesses to the conviction that the party should rank above all the other institutions of the state, including the press and judiciary. In 2015, Justice Malala published the seminal *We Have Now Begun Our Descent*, describing the high hopes of the early years of majority rule. Visiting Lagos in 2004, he was appalled and disbelieving to find his Nigerian hosts telling him that 'before long you will be like us', only then to witness the prophecy coming true under Zuma. 'I never thought it would happen to us, this relentless decline, the flirtation with a leap over the cliff.' His book reflects the disillusion of many members of the black South African intelligentsia, even and in some cases especially among those who remain, partly for historical reasons, supporters of the ANC.[63]

In *How Long Will South Africa Survive?* R. W. Johnson forecast a rapid continuing downhill slide, until the country needs to be rescued by the International Monetary Fund. Ferial Haffajee published the thoughtful and entertaining *What If There Were No Whites in South Africa?* Pieter-Louis Myburgh analysed brilliantly the influence of the Gupta family in *The*

Republic of Gupta. Crispian Olver painted a vivid picture of ANC-led corruption in Port Elizabeth in *How to Steal a City*. Adriaan Basson and Pieter du Toit described in comprehensive detail the tidal wave of corruption under Zuma and the resistance to it in *Enemy of the People*. Jacques Pauw, who had risked his life to expose the police death squads operating under apartheid, rendered his country another major service with his exposé of the murky world of the State Security Agency and its semi-criminal associates in *The President's Keepers*.[64]

One of the most remarkable commentators on post-apartheid South Africa has been Moeletsi Mbeki, brother of the former President, who was blacklisted by SABC because of his criticisms of the government run by his brother! His scathing critique of the way black empowerment to date has benefited mainly the politically connected has been accompanied by the demand of most black South African commentators for more genuine transformation targeted on benefiting the vast army of unemployed.[65]

While Zuma and his associates have continued to try to portray criticism of the President, government and ruling party as coming mainly from the white-owned press, this has long since ceased to be the case. The revelations about the looting of the state-owned enterprise and the Guptaleaks have been fastened on by a host of fiercely independent black commentators determined to expose corruption and hold the government to account. The performance of the media in South Africa has been admirable, often in difficult circumstances, and a major element of hope for the future.

The media can heave a sigh of relief at the election of Cyril Ramaphosa as ANC President. He is used to dealing with a demanding press and consistently has pronounced against those who have wanted to curb press freedom. The ultimately costly relationship of his opponent, Dlamini-Zuma, with the media was one of mutual hostility, compounded by her refusal to give interviews to anyone except the Gupta news channels.

CHAPTER XXI

THE JUDICIARY AND
CIVIL SOCIETY

The independence of the judiciary is solemnly enshrined
in Chapter 3 of the South African constitution. The same
has been true of constitutions in a good many other African
states, only for the principle to be honoured more in the breach
than the observance. In South Africa, however, the judiciary
to date has well and truly lived up to the intent of those who
drafted the constitution. They have done so despite the deeply
ingrained and quite frequently publicly expressed belief of the
ruling party that the judges should be answerable to it.

This is not a new phenomenon. There is within the ANC
no more respected intellectual than Joel Netshitenzhe. Yet it
was Netshitenzhe who, reflecting liberation movement dogma,
declared in 1998 that the ruling party must control all the levers
of political control, including the press and the judiciary. The
frequent attacks on the judiciary by the Secretary General of
the ANC, Gwede Mantashe, and his deputy, Jessie Duarte,

show that, notwithstanding the constitution, the desire to control the judges, far from abating, has intensified over time.

The Chief Justice under F. W. de Klerk, Cambridge-educated Michael Corbett, was a wise and humane person. In the case of the disappearance and murder of Stompie Moeketsi, I had to warn him that, even though he was fast losing his illusions about Winnie, Nelson Mandela would be unable to cope with his wife, whose conduct he blamed on his 27-year absence, being sent to jail. The Chief Justice spared Winnie Mandela a jail sentence, even though the evidence pointed towards it. On his retirement in 1996, Nelson Mandela paid tribute to his 'passion for justice'.

In the post-apartheid era, Corbett was succeeded by Ismail Mahomed, a leading jurist of Indian origin, then by Arthur Chaskalson, who had played a prominent role in the struggle against apartheid. The roles of Chief Justice and head of the Constitutional Court were merged in 2001.

Chaskalson was succeeded by Pius Langa, then Sandile Ngcobo, on whose death it was widely assumed that the Deputy Chief Justice, Dikgang Moseneke, would succeed him. Moseneke, however, though a long-term prisoner on Robben Island, had been there as a member of the Pan Africanist Congress, not of the ANC, and was reported to have made private criticisms of the government. To the dismay of his supporters, the choice fell instead on Mogoeng Mogoeng, who was felt to have a clearly inferior record as a jurist and had served for only two years on the Constitutional Court. He also was criticised for the relative leniency of his sentencing in cases of violence against women.

As Chief Justice Mogoeng has confounded his critics well and truly by upholding very firmly the independence of the judiciary vis-à-vis the government and ANC officials led by Gwede Mantashe, who denounced members of the judiciary who ruled against the ANC as 'counterrevolutionary forces'. Mogoeng ruled against the government in several high-profile cases. In 2016, Mogoeng himself wrote the judgment that Zuma had violated the constitution by failing to act on Thuli Madonsela's Nkandla report.

The televised spectacular of the Chief Justice, backed by the full bench of the Constitutional Court in their ceremonial robes, publicly and unanimously sanctioning the President for violating the constitution was a dramatic moment in South African history, creating a hope and conviction that the judiciary will continue to call government to account. The Constitutional Court judge Albie Sachs, who barely survived a bomb attack by the apartheid security police, hailed it as the judiciary's finest hour.

The South African bench has been distinguished by jurists of exceptional calibre, such as Moseneke and Edwin Cameron, and such remarkable characters as Albie Sachs. But the judges at other levels have mostly also shown neither fear nor favour in cases involving the government, consistently ruling against what they have regarded as abuses and government overreach. While ANC leaders have clamoured for faster 'transformation' of the judiciary, the judgments of most black South African judges generally have been no different from or more favourable to government than those of their white colleagues.

In 2012, the Democratic Alliance was able to use the courts to get rid of Menzi Simelane as the National Director of Public Prosecutions (NDPP), as he had been found guilty of dishonesty in a parliamentary inquiry into the campaign against his predecessor, Vusi Pikoli. They got the courts eventually to set aside – seven years later, in 2016 – the decision of the acting NDPP, Mokotedi Mpshe, in 2009 not to pursue the corrupton charges against Zuma, thereby opening the way for him to become President. They also secured a court ruling that helped to bring an end to the disreputable career of Hlaudi Motsoeneng at the SABC.

Freedom under Law successfully challenged the dropping of murder and fraud charges against Richard Mdluli, the powerful and feared head of intelligence under Zuma. As the Zuma government redoubled its attempts to force through the acquisition of unaffordable and superfluous new nuclear reactors from Rosatom, its efforts were interrupted by two environmental groups who secured the important judgment by the Western Cape High Court in April 2017, stalling the nuclear programme because of the lack of any due process in procurement.

Blots on this generally positive picture have been the apparently very political judgment of Judge Chris Nicholson, which saved the day for Jacob Zuma, and the case of Judge John Hlophe. Hlophe was appointed head of the Cape Town High Court in 2000. When a ruling in favour of the Aids-denialist Health Minister, Tshabalala-Msimang, was challenged, Hlophe refused any right to appeal, only to be overruled by the Supreme Court in a damning judgment. Various scandals followed, including his involvement with an asset management company and demand that his official car should be upgraded to a Porsche.

In 2008 he ruled in favour of the removal of 20,000 shack dwellers in Langa, a judgment overruled by the Constitutional Court, as the eviction order made no provision for their re-housing. A fervent Zuma supporter, he urged colleagues in the Constitutional Court that the charges against him should be dismissed. The Judicial Services Commission, which has four presidential appointees, failed to find against him and has proved a potentially vulnerable aspect of the independence of the judiciary, declining to endorse some outstanding candidates for appointment to the Supreme Court. As a result of court judgments, the case against Hlophe, eight years later, still proceeds, though with little chance of his being formally removed from the bench.

The attitude of the courts, however, and the genuine independence of government that has been displayed by the great majority of the judiciary, does mean that any government bent on staying in power at any price would have to find a way to neutralise the judiciary in general as effectively as it has done with the investigative and prosecuting agencies, a task that would entail a head-on assault on the constitution.

The other outstanding feature of the resistance to arbitrary and corrupt government in South Africa has been the role of civil society. In 2017 the ANC veteran and former Director General of Foreign Affairs Sipho Pityana launched the 'Save

South Africa' movement, which has attracted tens of thousands of people to anti-Zuma demonstrations. Pityana, who founded the Council for the Advancement of the South African Constitution (CASAC), belonged firmly in the camp of those who believed that the ANC must reform itself from within – if it could. More recently he argued that if the 'state capturers' prevailed at the ANC conference in December 2017, reputable members of the party would have to consider breaking away.

The Helen Suzman Foundation, led by the formidably effective and tenacious Francis Antonie, has mounted numerous legal challenges to the government's actions, several of them successful, and was instrumental in getting General Ntelemeza dismissed as head of the Hawks. They pursued the government over the visit of President Bashir of Sudan, wanted by the International Criminal Court in The Hague for suspected war crimes. During the municipal elections in 2016, the Foundation secured an interdict overturning a ban by management on the reporting of anti-government demonstrations by the SABC.

They frequently have acted in concert with Freedom under Law, led by the highly respected Judge Johann Kriegler, former member of the Constitutional Court and head of the Electoral Commission for the 1994 elections, joining forces to get rid of Ntelemeza and in opposing Shaun Abrahams's failed attempt to charge Pravin Gordhan with fraud. Sipho Pityana's CASAC has made a significant impact, including in a court case against Busisiwe Mkhwebane for failing to live up to her role as Public Protector.

In December 2017, Freedom under Law, Corruption Watch

and CASAC won a ruling from Judge Dunstan Mlambo of the Pretoria High Court that Shaun Abrahams must vacate his position for failing to carry out his duties as the National Director of Public Prosecutions. Furthermore, the court ruled that, as President Zuma was himself facing corruption charges, a replacement needed to be appointed within sixty days by the Deputy President, Cyril Ramaphosa. Zuma immediately appealed, but the judgment shredded the already close-to-zero credibility of Shaun Abrahams.

The Section 27 organisation, referring to the relevant provisions of the constitution, has made a positive impact in the fields of social justice and health care. Corruption Watch and Right2Know also have done much to help expose abuses. The Institute of Race Relations for decades has played an important role, as these days does Business Leadership South Africa, now led by Bonang Mohale.

The activities of these non-governmental organisations, and their success periodically in calling the government to account in the courts, has caused great concern to the security agencies, with the Security Minister Mahlobo accusing them of acting for foreign governments, while maintaining his own close associations in Moscow.

The F. W. de Klerk Foundation has devoted itself to defence of the constitution. The Centre for Development and Enterprise, led by Ann Bernstein, has produced numerous papers on economic policy, including on such subjects as land reform, which, if acted upon, would significantly improve South Africa's growth prospects. The Nelson Mandela Foundation has come out firmly against the Zuma regime, as have the Ahmed Kathrada, Oliver Tambo and Thabo Mbeki Foundations, Neeshan Balton having been particularly active and effective, with Barbara Hogan, on behalf of the Kathrada Foundation.

The Organisation Undoing Tax Abuse (OUTA) has launched legal actions to seek to prevent the 1.7 billion rand mine rehabilitation funds held by Gupta companies being diverted to be used for any other purpose. They also have laid charges against ministers and senior officials they believe to have been guilty of corruption.

There are numerous other instances of civil society organisations and spokespersons exposing and resisting corruption at every level of government. One of the most remarkable of these has been the academic grouping, the Public Affairs Research Institute, which published in 2017 the seminal and meticulously researched paper, *Betrayal of the Promise*, on which all subsequent commentators, including the present author, have come to rely.

CHAPTER XXII

THE BATTLE FOR THE SUCCESSION

Jacob Zuma initially had not ruled out standing for a third term as ANC President, just as Thabo Mbeki had tried unsuccessfully to do. The municipal election results and the slew of scandals around his presidency put paid to any ideas of doing so. All his efforts, therefore, instead were devoted to safeguarding the continued dominance of the Zuma faction within the ANC and, he hoped, guarding himself against the consequences of future prosecution by ensuring that he was succeeded as President of the party by his ex-wife Nkosazana Dlamini-Zuma vis-à-vis his deputy, Cyril Ramaphosa, who he did not trust to protect him.

As the struggle to succeed him as President of the ANC was seriously engaged in 2017, the battle lines were drawn between two utterly dissimilar candidates representing entirely different strands of the movement.

Born in Soweto in 1952, the son of a retired policeman, Cyril Ramaphosa never completed his studies at the University of the North as, for his role as a student activist, he was detained in solitary confinement for nearly a year in 1974 and again for six months at the notorious John Vorster Square detention centre in Pretoria in 1976.[66] He graduated subsequently with a law degree from UNISA and devoted himself to what were still barely legal trade union activities, emerging as head of the National Union of Mineworkers, which he helped to found in 1982. On the first anniversary of the anti-apartheid *Mail and Guardian*, which they both attended, he launched a fierce public tirade against Harry Oppenheimer, head of Anglo American and De Beers, for the treatment of workers on their mines. Characteristically, however, he insisted on silence from his supporters to allow Oppenheimer to reply.

In 1987, he organised a massive strike on the mines, marked by violence by mine security staff and the killing of several miners who failed to go on strike. Following a lock-out by employers, the strike ended without having made any major gains beyond the 15 per cent plus pay increase already offered by the employers. But the union had demonstrated its ability to call out over 250,000 mine workers for three weeks. In successive negotiations it secured improved pay and conditions for its members and Ramaphosa had become a major figure on the political scene.

As leader of the most important union and a key figure in the ANC-aligned United Democratic Front, Ramaphosa played a leading role in the struggle against apartheid throughout the 1980s. Although the bearded youthful Ramaphosa on the hustings could look and sound like a firebrand, knowing him at this time, I always found him to be extremely effective at calculating how much he could achieve. He had, he told me, no intention of 'doing a Scargill', and risking destroying his own union by extreme militancy, as Arthur Scargill had done to the miners' union in Britain. When Margaret Thatcher visited South Africa, not appreciated by the ANC, we cut a deal. There would be no demonstration against her in Johannesburg, provided she declined the freedom of the city offered by the all-white municipality (which was her intention anyway).

As the exile leadership in Lusaka became alarmed at the out-of-control antics of Winnie Mandela and her 'football team' (in fact young thugs) in Soweto, Ramaphosa was one of those critical of her behaviour.

With the ANC unbanned, the UDF leaders were not supposed to challenge the returning exiles. It came as an unpleasant shock to them when Ramaphosa did just that, standing for election as Secretary General of the ANC against the well past his sell-by date veteran exile, Alfred Nzo – and defeating also Jacob Zuma for the post!

There followed a 'mini coup'; with Mandela overseas but with his support and Mbeki and Zuma away at a conference in Cambridge, Ramaphosa, not Mbeki, was appointed to lead the ANC team negotiating the new constitution. Zuma found that as the ANC's head of intelligence, he had been replaced by 'Terror' Lekota.

As the ANC's chief negotiator on the new constitution, Ramaphosa formed a friendship with his National Party counterpart, Roelf Meyer, including a couple of fly-fishing trips together. An extremely effective negotiator, he subsequently was felt to have outmanoeuvred the National Party, securing the ANC's key objectives. To this day, in contrast to those of his ANC comrades who find the constraints imposed by it irksome, Ramaphosa is proud of and committed to the constitution he helped to negotiate.

He was favoured by Mandela to succeed him, given Mandela's reservations about Thabo Mbeki's personality, and also because Mandela wanted a leadership less dominated by Xhosas from the Eastern Cape. But when it came in 1997 to the election of Deputy President of the party, the exile leadership pushed him aside, installing Mbeki and embittering Ramaphosa. Mandela tried to persuade him to become Minister of Foreign Affairs, which he declined, choosing instead to retreat into a very successful business career.

Unless you happen to be one of his political adversaries, it is extremely difficult to dislike Cyril Ramaphosa; and many of them quite like him too. A person of great charm and also of great ability, gregarious, with an attractive personality, he became the partner of choice for many South African enterprises and business leaders, the more so as he soon showed himself to be an extremely capable chairman or director on the boards of several major companies, including Standard Bank and SABMiller. He became chairman of the MTN telecoms group and of the international paper and packaging group Mondi. He benefited from a series of black economic empowerment transactions in building up his own successful holding company, Shanduka, with investments in mining, energy, real estate and finance. In the process, he became very wealthy, with an estimated net worth over $400 million.

He also played a supporting role in the Northern Ireland peace process, as he and the future President of Finland, Martti Ahtisaari, were asked to verify that the Irish Republican Army were taking steps to disarm. This entailed highly secretive night-time visits, escorted by the IRA, to inspect their arms caches on the Northern Ireland border. More nimble than Ahtisaari, it was Ramaphosa who had to climb down into the cellars to inspect the guns, then return in equal secrecy months later to confirm that they had not been used.

Concerned about the low quality of basic state education, Ramaphosa and his wife established their own educational trust to fund scholarships. Ramaphosa launched his Adopt a School Foundation to encourage companies and groups to adopt local state schools to help improve their standards.

Ramaphosa is married to Tshepo Motsepe, sister of the most successful black South African business figure, Patrice Motsepe. There has never been any hint of corruption around Ramaphosa. On becoming Deputy President, his business holdings were placed in a blind trust. He has been careful not to flaunt his wealth, save in one famous instance. In 2012 he offered to pay a reported 18 million rand for a steer from the Central African Republic – though, in the event, he was outbid for it! He subsequently apologised, but since has published a book about his favourite cattle.

Apart from his wealth and generally business-friendly attitude, the Zuma camp and leftist sections of the ANC also held against him his role as a director and key shareholder of Lonmin in the Marikana massacre, Ramaphosa having asked for police protection against violence from elements of the radical mining union AMCU who had killed several members of Ramaphosa's former union, the National Union of Mineworkers. The South African Communist Party, however, and the trade union federation Cosatu both backed Ramaphosa in the battle to succeed Zuma. In an attempt to dent his generally clean image, the security services planted in the so-called *Sunday Independent* allegations about his personal life, with little impact, given the sources from which they came.

* * *

Ramaphosa found himself, at any rate nominally, pitted against a number of other declared candidates – the Speaker of the National Assembly, Baleka Mbete, the Minister in the Presidency, Jeff Radebe, Zweli Mkhize (Treasurer General of the ANC), Lindiwe Sisulu and Mathews Phosa.

Apart from Mkhize, none of these were taken very seriously. Mkhize, however, had served as an impressive and successful Premier of KwaZulu-Natal. As Treasurer General of the ANC, he was prepared to engage seriously with the business community in efforts to find solutions to the country's problems. For a time he won tactical support from David Mabuza as a candidate who could restore unity in the ANC, but this was always subject to Mabuza's overriding ambition to end up as Deputy President.

The main fight, however, was always going to be between

Ramaphosa and the chosen candidate of the Zuma camp, Nkosazana Dlamini-Zuma. A medical doctor, who graduated from Bristol University, Dlamini-Zuma was Minister of Health under President Mandela in a period when her response to the Aids pandemic was to finance an outrageously costly (14 million rand) Aids awareness play, called *Sarafina II*, commissioned from a personal friend, with no tender process, despite much lower competing bids. She misled Parliament, but got away with it, thanks to an intervention from Mandela.

Next, she presented to the Cabinet, with no validation from the Medical Research Council, a locally produced quack remedy for Aids based on an anti-freeze solution and called Virodene. She appeared to be encouraged to do this by the then Deputy President and Aids denialist Thabo Mbeki. Her response to criticism from the Medical Research Council was to seek to abolish it.

In 1998 she suspended pilot testing of the provision of anti-retrovirals to prevent mother-to-child transmission of Aids, declaring this to be unaffordable. The health care administrators in the Western Cape insisted on continuing the distribution of anti-retrovirals despite her best efforts to prevent them from doing so. Obliged to back down, she eventually conceded that she could not actually prevent this, provided it was described as a 'pilot' project. Other provinces were not so courageous, leading to vast numbers of avoidable infections.

More positively, she campaigned for international pharmaceutical companies to reduce prices for their products in South Africa and passed legislation limiting smoking in public places.

She then served as Minister of Foreign Affairs for a decade from 1999, for most of it in a very subordinate fashion under Thabo Mbeki, who acted largely as his own Foreign Minister. She did, however, show herself to be a fierce Africanist, reacting strongly to any Western criticisms about abuses of power and human rights, regarding these issues as being for Africans to sort out themselves. In relation to Zimbabwe, she showed herself to be just as complaisant towards the ruling party as Mbeki, reacting furiously to any criticism for this. She had a tense relationship with senior officials in her Department, including her Director General, Sipho Pityana, later founder of the 'Save South Africa' movement. He departed during her tenure, describing her as a 'difficult woman'. At the ANC conference in Polokwane, she was nominated by Mbeki to become Deputy President of the ANC, only to lose out to to Kgalema Motlanthe, nominated by her ex-husband, Jacob Zuma.

More of a genuine leftist than her ex-husband, she was extremely resentful of criticism from 'white' South Africa. In foreign policy, she had been a fierce critic of any external interventions in Africa, for instance in Libya – in which respect she was probably right.

In her one and only meeting with the US Secretary of State, Colin Powell, she was advised to concentrate on trade access and other areas where the United States could help South Africa. Instead, she launched into a tirade about the, in her view, disgraceful treatment of the Palestinians by the US, not pausing for breath for the next forty-five minutes. The normally affable Colin Powell then terminated the meeting, telling his staff that there was never going to be another one with her. (Colin Powell had tried, unsuccessfully, to get Israel/Palestine negotiations resumed.)

Capable and very hard-working, Dlamini-Zuma fared much better as Minister of Home Affairs under her ex-husband, Jacob Zuma, where she was regarded as having put up a very competent performance in a hitherto mismanaged department. She has never appeared to be interested in personal self-enrichment. She was, however, close to and assiduously courted by the Guptas.

Then, in 2012, she was elected by the English-speaking bloc as chairperson of the African Union. In that capacity, she was criticised for spending time pursuing her political ambitions in South Africa. She tried hard, but struggled to make a success of efforts to mediate in regional conflicts, though that had more to do with the weakness and divisions of the African Union than with her own performamnce.

Given the support of Zuma and KwaZulu-Natal and the pro-Zuma Premiers, as well as of the ANC Youth and Women's Leagues, she was regarded by many insiders as having a better chance than Ramaphosa of becoming the next President of the ANC. The press tended to be more optimistic about Ramaphosa, given the lack of charisma of his opponent and his greater popularity in the population at large. *City Press* published a poll showing that only 16 per cent of the population thought she would make a good President of the ANC, against 43 per cent for Ramaphosa.

However, as she pointed out, the election would not be decided by the population at large, but by the ANC branches. She complained about the 'media onslaught' against her, but gave interviews only to the Gupta media channels and did nothing to dissociate herself from them. This enabled her, throughout her entire campaign, to avoid having to answer any awkward questions, such as whether she supports the constitution, which the President has to pledge to uphold, or what she intended to do about state capture, a subject on which she avoided giving any undertakings whatever.

Having run an assiduous but very lacklustre campaign, her hopes had to be based on the support of the 'Premier League' and on the fact that Zuma consistently had shown that he has no equals in terms of exercising authority within the party, with the assistance of patronage, threats and intimidation and the active involvement of the intelligence services.

Regarded as being dour and devoid of charm, Dlamini-Zuma has a more colourful history than one might expect. As a student in Britain, she was the girlfriend of the Marxist head of the Anti-Apartheid Movement, Mike Terry, who had expected them to get married. Instead Nkosazana returned to Africa, reappearing as the first wife of Jacob Zuma.

In the ANC leadership discussions of the numerous scandals around Zuma, she was an unconditional supporter of his performance as President, despite having suffered a torrid time with him when they were married. She declared herself shocked at what she regarded as *lèse-majesté* on the part of those who dared to criticise him, giving the impression that, while not corrupt herself, she would, if elected, not have much appetite to combat corruption within the party.

CHAPTER XXIII

A REMARKABLE VICTORY

So far as the Zuma camp and the 'security cluster' of ministries around him were concerned, Cyril Ramaphosa was not supposed to be allowed to win the election for the presidency of the ANC. For many in this camp, that could create a serious risk of their going to jail. They were determined to avoid 'regime change', which for them meant a loss of power by the dominant faction in the ANC. There was no intention of playing by the Queensberry rules in the effort to avert this.

As Ramaphosa observed about the attempts to smear him, 'I have not committed any crimes. I have not stolen any money.' But he had to be prevented 'at all costs' from winning the election. So state institutions had been used to hack into his emails. Unfortunately from their point of view, the provisions of the constitution, which the security services had been so successful in circumventing, proved in the end too resilient to be simply set aside.

So how was the election decided? How was it that Ramaphosa was able to overcome the forces arrayed against him?

The first mistake they made was that of underestimating their opponent. For three and a half years, Ramaphosa had been obliged to be deferential to Zuma. When he finally erupted over the dismissal of Pravin Gordhan, he was obliged to recant, with Mantashe and others declaring that such differences should not have been 'aired in public'. When it came to the no-confidence vote in Parliament, Ramaphosa had no option but to vote for Zuma.

This led to some unpleasant chanting at his expense at Zuma-supporting rallies in KwaZulu-Natal. Listening to members of the Zuma camp in the run-up to the election, it was remarkable to hear how dismissive they were of their goody two-shoes colleagues in the ANC who, in their view, had no idea how to exercise power. They were supremely confident that Ramaphosa could be elbowed aside and that, having lost, he did not have it in him to split the ANC.

They probably were right about that as, in the run-up to the vote, Ramaphosa told close friends that if he lost, he would retire and would not split the party. Some of his supporters might still have staged a breakaway, judging the ANC by then to be beyond redemption, but without a major leader, the impact would have been limited.

The second mistake of the securocrats was to underestimate the damage they had done to the electoral chances of the ANC. They were behaving exactly as their counterparts had been doing, with impunity, in several other African countries, with the disadvantage that South Africa still was a functioning democracy. Many of the ANC delegates who voted for

Ramaphosa did so because they feared that with Dlamini-Zuma, they would lose the next election.

Who can really doubt, however, that if the intelligence services so closely supervised by Jacob Zuma had realised that Ramaphosa might prevail by a mere ninety delegates voting the wrong way, they would have found the means to beg, borrow or (preferably) steal sufficient votes to prevent this disaster happening? Two days before the vote, they were still telling not only Zuma but also any others willing to listen to them that the election was 'in the bag'. If the Zuma camp had been less confident, they would have found a way to postpone the conference.

It was not only in this respect that they proved to be incompetent. In the course of the campaign, Ramaphosa was accused of beating his first wife, which she indignantly denied. Leaked emails were used to accuse him of having numerous affairs, which students sponsored by him also denied. Plans to 'expose' him as an agent of the CIA, who would break off relations with Russia, leaked and were covered with ridicule. A wilder plan to charge him with treason was felt to be impractical. The idea of dropping him from the government and replacing him with Dlamini-Zuma before the conference also was canvassed, but not pursued. The relevant services remained confident, however, that with their allies they could help to secure the right result through the ANC's voting processes, only to encounter an unexpected difficulty.

In KwaZulu-Natal, the courts declared the ANC's provincial elective conference, massively favouring Zuma, to be null and void. In 2016, Zuma had ousted the Premier of KwaZulu-Natal, Senzo Mchunu, who did not take this lying down. Attempts to engineer a near-unanimous 800-plus votes for Dlamini-Zuma from KwaZulu-Natal failed, as Gwede Mantashe insisted on vetting the delegates' elections, opening the way for Ramaphosa to win a significant minority vote in Zuma's principal stronghold.

When it came to self-preservation, however, which was his overriding objective, Zuma knew that he could count on some important allies, notably the loyalty of the Premier of the Free State, Ace Magashule, who, cut from the same cloth, is described by the opposition as having turned the province into a 'banana republic'. In 2015 he was reported to have spent 8 million rand on 'aesthetic' improvements to his residence, followed in December by a Mercedes with a panoramic sunroof and entertainment centre costing 2.3 million rand. He allowed the Free State government to plough 220 million rand into the Guptas' Estina dairy farm project, with one of his sons being employed by the family.

The other main members of the Zuma-supporting 'Premier League' were the Premier of Mpumalanga, David ('DD') Mabuza, who had been at the centre of a lot of controversy in that province, and the Premier of the North West Province, Supra Mahumapelo, an ardent supporter of the Guptas. In 2010, 14 million rand was reported by the press to have been stolen from Mabuza's farm near Barberton and his supporters in Mpumalanga did not hesitate to use violence against his critics there.

In a recent book, *Eerie Assignment*, a *City Press* journalist,

Sizwe sama Yende, paints an alarming picture of corruption, violence and gangsterism in the province, described by him as the 'Wild East'. Yende's own life was threatened, armed men appeared at political rallies, and whistleblowers about corruption came to a sticky end. The most prominent of them, having exposed corruption over the construction of a huge stadium for the soccer World Cup, was gunned down in his driveway, with the wrong people being arrested for the crime. All charges were dropped against those he had accused. When Mabuza's predecessor and nemesis, Mathews Phosa, was scheduled to address a SACP meeting in the province, it was broken up with extreme violence by Mabuza supporters. Mabuza then was hospitalised for two months, complaining he had been poisoned.[67]

Mabuza, however, is a former maths teacher, highly intelligent and with a genuine passion for education. This got him into trouble earlier in his career when he inflated the matriculation results in his province to make them look better than they were. In recent years, however, Mpumulanga apparently genuinely has produced impressive exam success rates. His opponents found that it was extremely unwise to underestimate his political skills. He was to confound everybody, by withstanding intense pressure from the Zuma camp, including threats of investigations targeted on him, and putting up a nerveless performance in the ANC succession contest.

The province has only 4 million people, as against over 12 million in Ramaphosa-supporting Gauteng. But Mabuza, a master of manipulation and what he himself describes as 'shenanigans', ensured that the province has ANC membership second only to KwaZulu-Natal, giving him disproportionate influence over the outcome of the ANC leadership election.

Mabuza declared himself from the outset to be the king-maker. Initially, he alarmed the Zuma camp by declaring that if Dlamini-Zuma were elected to succeed her ex-husband, they would lose the 2019 election, and announcing his support for Zweli Mkhize, as a candidate who could restore party unity. Mabuza's main objective, however, was to secure the position of Deputy President, which Ramaphosa was not prepared to pledge to him. Dlamini-Zuma assured Mabuza that he would become Deputy President if she won, confident that this would be sufficient to secure his support and that of Mpumalanga.

As the provinces sought to choose their delegates for the party conference, faction fights broke out in nearly all of them. In the Eastern Cape, fists flew and chairs were thrown before a majority of delegates opted for Ramaphosa. Zuma had long since had problems in Gauteng, where he is felt to be an embarrassment by much of the black elite. At the time of the ceremony in Soweto in honour of Nelson Mandela after his death in December 2013, Zuma was booed on entering the stadium, causing a senior ANC official to scream into her mobile phone to the chief operating officer of the SABC to ensure that this was cut out of the television coverage. F. W. de Klerk was applauded on entering the stadium. The chairman of the ANC in Gauteng, Paul Mashatile, was a strong critic of Zuma's failure to pay back part of the cost of upgrading his homestead at Nkandla, but found himself being wooed by Mabuza as part of his campaign to preserve ANC party unity.

* * *

In the ANC electoral contest, Dlamini-Zuma campaigned on the basis of speeding up 'radical economic transformation' land transfers without compensation, plus free tertiary education, regardless of its affordability.

While having strong political opinions, she has never shown much understanding of economics. Denouncing 'white monopoly capital' and their 'imperialist backers', she envisaged ending the independence of the so-far uncaptured South African Reserve Bank. There was in her campaign no undertaking to do anything about the looting of the state-owned enterprises or the neutering of the investigative and prosecuting authorities. On state capture, her response was that white South Africans had no right to charge others with looting, having, under apartheid, looted everything for them-selves.[68] Her dependence on the support of Magashule, the ANC Youth League leader Collen Maine and the Women's League leader Bathabile Dlamini created a valid concern that, as President, her protection against corruption charges would extend not just to Zuma, but to all the key figures who helped to elect her.

Those who wished to see the party change, return to some-thing more like what it had been and get rid of the Gupta influence found themselves aligned with Ramaphosa. But many in the party wanted someone who could be counted on not only to grant immunity against prosecution for Jacob Zuma, but also to protect the very large number of ANC cadres who, as the head of the Women's League had reminded them, had skeletons to hide themselves.

And not only the head of the Women's League. For in ANC discussions about him, Zuma had reminded senior party members that he had files on all of them, some of which he brandished. Given his extremely close involvement with the intelligence services, they also were aware that he knew all about the doubters and those leaning towards Ramaphosa, for whom there would be consequences. No one who knew Jacob Zuma was ever wise to underestimate his skill in the art of party management by fear.

For those who knew him too, the question about Ramaphosa was whether he really had the burning desire, killer instinct and ruthlessness required to rise to the very top of the greasy pole. He had displayed real toughness and fighting spirit at the head of the NUM and in the negotiations on the new constitution. But during the battles between Mbeki and Zuma, he told his friends of his determination to keep his head down. The same formula was used again by him when he joined the Zuma government. It is to Ramaphosa's credit that he does not enjoy confrontation, but that could be a handicap in dealing with those arrayed against him.

As the Zuma/Gupta scandals spiralled out of control, Ramaphosa became far more forthright in his criticisms and the demand for change. In July 2017 he told the SACP conference that '*We now know without any shred of uncertainty that billions of rands of public resources have been diverted into the pockets of a few*' and that public money had been used to fund a lavish wedding in Sun City. For several months before the elective conference, he toured the country, conducting a far more effective campaign in the provinces than that of his opponent to secure the succession to Zuma. But Zuma remained dominant – and domineering – in the meetings of the ANC.

* * *

So what helped to sway the cliff-hanging vote in the direction of Ramaphosa, confounding those who believed the odds were stacked against him?

Gwede Mantashe served as Secretary General of the National Union of Mineworkers before being elected Secretary General of the ANC in 2007. He was re-elected on the Zuma slate, against that of Mbeki, at the Polkwane conference. Controversially, he served also as chairman of the South African Communist Party until standing down for tactical reasons in 2012, though he remains a member of the SACP politburo. In September 2008, following a closed-door meeting of the party leadership, he announced that Thabo Mbeki was being 'recalled' from his post as President of South Africa.

Mantashe is highly intelligent and has tried to be a stabilising force within the ANC, but his unquestioning devotion to the party at times could lead him to some strange conclusions, such as, until latterly, that the ANC and the country could somehow afford a second full term for Jacob Zuma. He also could be erratic. In February 2016 he suddenly declared that the US embassy was organising meetings to promote 'regime change'. In fact these were to select candidates for short-term scholarships in the US. The US ambassador responded: 'Let's not blame others for our own challenges.'

The SACP had been increasingly openly critical of Zuma, as had the Congress of South African Trade Unions (COSATU). Mantashe was publicly critical of Zuma over Nkandla and on several other occasions. Whenever the chips were down, however, he never hesitated to defend the indefensible, leading the charge to oppose Zuma being 'Thaboed' – that is to say re-called – as his predecessor had been. His response to the Chief Justice's observations that South Africa needed ethical leader-ship and it was 'time for a change' was to threaten the judiciary with political attacks. In terms of the inability of the ANC to stand up to Zuma, despite the damage he was inflicting on the party, Mantashe had a good deal to answer for, one of the low points being his non-investigation into the allegations about the Guptas.

As the preparations advanced for the ANC conference to elect a new President in December 2017, there was general scepticism that anything approaching a properly accredited conference could be convened, offering Zuma, if he felt his candidate was in any danger of losing, the chance to postpone it. With faction fights and legal challenges in nearly every prov-ince, the chances of an uncontested conference looked bleak indeed. Mantashe exerted himself to try to counter prevalent skulduggery, intimidation and vote-buying and in seeking to vet who precisely were the legitimately elected delegates from the provinces, nearly all of them efforts that went against the

Zuma camp. He invalidated some very dubious delegate nom-
inations from KwaZulu-Natal, the Free State and the North
West Province, which would have more than sufficed to ensure
a Zuma victory. Without his campaign to try to ensure a rea-
sonably orderly and fair process, Ramaphosa would have had
no chance whatever. Mantashe by this stage had had enough
of Zuma. He appeared on the Ramaphosa slate as the future
chairman of the party and there wasn't really any doubt that he
wanted Ramaphosa to win.

As his running mates, Ramaphosa nominated the respected
ANC Cabinet minister Naledi Pandor to be Deputy President,
the leading ANC dissident against Zuma in KwaZulu-Natal,
Senzo Mchunu, to be Secretary General, the head of the
party in Gauteng, Paul Mashatile, to be Treasurer and Gwede
Mantashe to become chairman of the party. It was not clear
what additional electoral muscle in the ANC branches these
candidates would bring, apart from Mchunu, who helped to
deliver nearly a quarter of the branches in KwaZulu-Natal,
as compared with Dlamini-Zuma's promise to make Mabuza
Deputy President.

In the run-up to the elective conference, Zuma sought
to demonstrate again who was really in charge by dismissing Blade Nzimande, head of the SACP, from the Cabinet.
Nzimande left in tears, shed, he claimed, not for him, but for
South Africa.

On 27 November, Zuma summoned the candidates to a 'last
supper' at which he was successful in getting them – particularly
Ramaphosa – to pledge loyalty to whoever won the election, the

nightmare of the Dlamini-Zuma camp being that her victory might trigger a split in the party. It was Zuma also who had suggested that there should be two Deputy President posts, one for Ramaphosa, if he could be persuaded to stay in a devalued role, the other for Mabuza. Ramaphosa, however, rejected the idea of the loser in the election becoming the winner's deputy.

In the days just before the elective conference, Jacob Zuma suffered two setbacks in the North Gauteng (Pretoria) High Court which showed just how high the stakes were for him. First was the finding by Judge Mlambo that Shaun Abrahams had proved unfit to serve as head of the National Prosecuting Authority and that, Zuma himself being conflicted, a new National Director of Public Prosecutions should be appointed by his deputy, Cyril Ramaphosa, within sixty days.

With Thuli Madonsela present, the same court then ruled unanimously against Zuma for his failure to appoint an independent judicial commission of inquiry, as required by the Public Protector in her report on state capture. The court found that a bid by Zuma to appoint the commission himself was 'ill-advised and reckless'. By refusing to appoint an inquiry, Zuma had acted in flagrant disregard of the constitutional duties of the Public Protector, whose findings were 'extremely serious'. The President had no justification to simply ignore the impact of corruption on the South African public. The court ordered him to pay the costs of the litigation personally.

Zuma announced forthwith his intention to appeal to the Supreme Court against both judgments, and then no doubt to the Constitutional Court, so as to drag things out until, in due course, his ex-wife might be in a position, if necessary, to pardon him.

The judgments showed the incompatibility of so corrupt a regime with the independence of the judiciary. The head of the ANC Youth League, Collen Maine, threatened an insurrection against the judges. They would not have been able to co-exist much longer. The security 'cluster', bent on avoiding what they regard as regime change, if given the chance, would be bound at some future point to try to muzzle first the press, then the judges. It was not the lack of desire that had prevented them from trying to do so before.

Mandela's widow, Graça Machel, called for a return to Mandela's values and new leadership in the ANC. As the voting started, the Finance Minister, Gigaba, said that it was all-important to achieve a resumption of economic growth and called for new discussions about the Mining Charter. His efforts to keep expenditure under control were undercut by Zuma's pledge at the conference to provide free tertiary education for all poorer students, with no indication as to how this was to be financed. Zuma used the accounting scandal engulfing the South African-controlled Steinhoff conglomerate to claim that there was as much wrongdoing in the private as in the public sector. The head of the Women's League proposed that there should be forgiveness for state capture, just as there had been for apartheid.

As the results from the branches came in, they showed Ramaphosa winning easily in Gauteng, Limpopo and the Eastern, Western and Northern Cape and doing better than expected in KwaZulu-Natal. But Dlamini-Zuma, as expected, won large majorities in KwaZulu-Natal, the Free State and North West Province and, nominally, drew with Ramaphosa in Mpumulanga where, however, Mabuza as king- or queen-maker withheld over 200 'unity' votes for him to deploy. To Dlamini-Zuma's alarm, he still had not pledged that these votes would go to her.

These results, showing Ramaphosa in the lead, caused a sense of optimism among his supporters and in the financial markets, but were greeted with caution by those familiar with the capacity for manipulation of the Zuma ANC. The Zuptas, it was thought, simply had too much at stake to be able to afford to lose and, almost to the end, they remained confident that they would win.

As the votes were counted, the cameras focused on Jacob Zuma, sitting on the podium. When Thabo Mbeki was voted down (and out) at Polokwane, he had appeared thunderstruck and ashen-faced. In a moment of delicious irony, the same fate now overtook his successor. He too had been advised that the result was 'in the bag'. But Mantashe's efforts and the defection of David Mabuza had sufficed to change the calculation. Although he had just been told the result, as the vote confirming Ramaphosa's victory was read out, the thunderous expression on Zuma's face turned into one of near desperation, his head swinging to and fro with the expression, as one observer put it, of a strangled tortoise. No one who knew Jacob Zuma, however, believed that he was the least bit likely to withdraw gracefully from the scene.

CHAPTER XXIV

WHAT NEXT?

The other major victor of the conference, apart from Ramaphosa, was David ('DD') Mabuza, who turned out to have led Dlamini-Zuma up the garden path about his voting intentions. All through the campaign, in return for the promise of the deputy presidency, she had sought to get a public promise from Mabuza that his vote would be hers. They always were counted in her column by the members of her camp. But as the campaign advanced, Mabuza became convinced that he had the votes to become Deputy President anyway. According to Julius Malema, 'DD doesn't like Nkosazana.' More importantly, he was increasingly convinced that she would lose the next election. He had no wish to end up in the opposition. In the event, the votes in Mpumalanga were split between the two candidates, including Mabuza's 'unity' votes, kicking away one of the main pillars of Dlamini-Zuma's hoped-for support.

Ace Magashule, Premier of the Free State, won the election to become Secretary General of the ANC by an even narrower margin than Ramaphosa. Thanks to sixty-eight 'missing' votes, he defeated Ramaphosa's candidate, Mchunu. A hitherto un-conditional supporter of Zuma, he has extremely close links to the Guptas, as does the Deputy Secretary General, Jessie Duarte. It will be interesting to see how he performs, especially with the media, in his new role, his methods in the Free State having been based on intimidation, rather than any more so-phisticated approach.

Within the new top six, Ramaphosa could count on the support of Mantashe and Paul Mashatile, elected as Treasurer General, and the increasingly influential David Mabuza forth-with attempted, without success, to persuade Zuma to stand down. The new National Executive Committee did not initial-ly look to have a clear enough majority to force Zuma out. The balance soon started shifting, however, with the Zuma camp shrinking rapidly as former supporters sought to make their peace with Ramaphosa.

The ANC conference ended with a supposedly unanimous, but fiercely debated decision, pressed for by the KwaZulu-Natal supporters of Zuma and his ex-wife, that the ANC will seek to amend the constitution to provide for land expropria-tion without compensation, the proviso being that this must not harm agricultural production or food security. Ramaphosa has had to pledge himself to this. To secure the necessary two-thirds majority in Parliament, the EFF are being asked to join in supporting it, which they say they will do.

Ramaphosa and the ANC economic supremo, Enoch Go-dangwana, tried to limit the damage by declaring that this power will only be used in cases where the outcome will be 'sustainable'. There will now be a long, drawn-out process of implementation and they will seek to contain the fallout. To overseas fund managers, particularly in the US, this otherwise could look like the road to Zimbabwe. It will be the first major breach in the constitution, which protects property rights.

The resulting policy uncertainty will have unintended effects. White commercial farmers, now down to 35,000, will become more cautious about investing in their farms. Only 10 per cent of the land transferred so far has ended up in the hands of black farmers. The rest has gone to local communities for subsistence agriculture, to be leased back to farmers, or is lying fallow. The power to expropriate, once enshrined in law, will have to be exercised, in response to the political pressures to do so – a poisoned chalice for Ramaphosa and his colleagues.

Ramaphosa, with help from Pravin Gordhan, has a coherent economic programme, including an attack on mass unemployment through much greater support for small business development and a nationwide programme of skills training. He envisages a potentially 1 trillion rand programme to repair badly decaying infrastructure (the potholes in David Mabuza's Mpumulanga are large enough to swallow a truck). A more serious effort will be made to get the teachers' union to accept greater efforts to improve basic education, which is badly needed, as comparative studies of basic education in developing countries sadly have shown South Africa to be among the very worst. This will be no easy task, as the ANC-supporting union to date has resolutely opposed the testing of teachers or even checking if they turn up, which an alarming number of

them don't. There will be tax incentives to encourage manu-
facturers to employ more young people. Relations are to be
repaired with the mining industry and policy uncertainty to
be ended. The state-owned enterprises must be reformed and
boards appointed with the requisite skills. Investor confidence
must be restored.

None of this is going to be easily affordable within the extremely tight budgetary constraints, the pledge of free tertiary
education and Eskom representing a black hole in the public
finances.

Ramaphosa also is committed to transforming the still
white-dominated 'economy', which, for the ANC, means the
private sector, the huge swathe of the economy dominated
by central, regional and local government and the massive
state-owned companies having already been well and truly
'transformed'. Boards can be made more representative, but
need to have skills and experience. The public sector is scarcely
likely to be a good model to apply to private business in South
Africa. Zuma's more extreme demands for Africanisation of
the private sector were based on regarding the whites as not
really South African. Mandela had a different view, regarding
the economic contribution of the white community as vital for
the success of the new South Africa.

Ironically, on the land issue the ANC conference also made
a more positive move, pronouncing in favour of giving property
rights to the millions of people still living in a feudal system
in the former homelands, whereby land and housing is simply
allocated by the traditional chiefs and no one has any title to

it. The effect has been to exclude millions from any access to credit and the modern economy.

Ramaphosa's victory will hugely improve the ANC's chances of retaining a majority in the 2019 elections. He will be depicted by both the DA and the EFF as being not really in charge of a fundamentally corrupt organisation, incapable of being reformed by him (or anyone else). But he will have much broader appeal and be a far harder target than Dlamini-Zuma, even though he has had to adopt part of her programme.

Having majored on the fight against corruption, the problem Ramaphosa will face, after twenty-four years of the ANC in power and a decade of Zuma, will be that of dealing with colleagues who know no other way of operating. No effective campaign can be launched without reform of the investigating, prosecuting and tax authorities, neutered by Zuma so long as he was in control.

The new year opened with some positive news. The long slumber of the National Prosecuting Authority at least partially ended, as the asset forfeiture unit secured a court order requiring McKinsey to pay back the 1 billion rand it had received for not much more than six months' work at Eskom. While McKinsey continued to contend that they had done nothing wrong, a number of South African companies declined to do further business with them. The unit also was demanding the return of 600 million rand from Trillian, declaring both contracts to have been corruptly awarded, in the absence of any competitive tender process.

The unit also obtained a court order to seek to recover the

220 million rand paid to the Estina dairy project in the Free State, naming Atul Gupta as a beneficiary and contending that this was a straightforward case of money-laundering. The investigation extended also to the roles in this affair of the Mineral Resources Minister Zwane and the Free State Premier Ace Magashule, now Secretary General of the ANC. A report by the so-called Public Protector, Busisiwe Mkhwebane, was greeted with derision, as she failed to make any mention of the role of Zwane or the Guptas, though she did conclude that Des van Rooyen had lied to Parliament about his relationship with them.

With Eskom in extremis, Ramaphosa was able to secure the appointment of the respected chairman of Telkom, Jabu Mabuza, as the new chairman of the board and other well-qualified appointees, enabling Eskom to secure a short-term loan from the Public Investment Corporation to bridge its critical funding requirements. Criticised for allowing pension funds to be used for this purpose, the head of the PIC declared that without the loan, Eskom would have been forced to default. Struggling under its huge burden of debt, Eskom's financial position remains extremely precarious.

For the first time in this long saga, companies benefiting from the exploitation of the state-owned companies were being obliged to pay a price for having done so. At this stage, however, none of those responsible for the looting of the South African state have yet been convicted of any crime. There will be no lasting deterrent effect until some hitherto protected high-profile villains *and the politicians who protected them* are seen to suffer unpleasant consequences for their behaviour.

* * *

To try to prolong his tenure, Zuma at last accepted the inevitability of appointing the judicial commission of inquiry into state capture demanded by Thuli Madonsela in October 2016, while trying to broaden the terms of reference away from his activities and those of the Guptas. He gave notice of his intention to appeal against the court ruling that Ramaphosa should appoint a new Director of Public Prosecutions in lieu of Shaun Abrahams, which annoyed Ramaphosa and backfired, as the ANC politburo concluded that he must stand down in due course, leaving it to Ramaphosa and his colleagues in the 'top six' to find a way to make this happen. The response of the two Zuma loyalists and Gupta-connected members of the six, Magashule and Jessie Duarte, was to declare that they could see no reason for Zuma to stand down before 2019.

The narrow margin of his victory and the need to avoid a fracturing of the party and problems in KwaZulu-Natal caused Ramaphosa to try to negotiate a 'dignified' exit for Zuma, while ruling out an amnesty or indemnity, for which there was no basis in South African law, only to find Zuma determined to cling on for several months and trying to lay down unacceptable conditions. Zuma was warned that unless he gave way, the government could lose the no-confidence vote in Parliament tabled by the opposition. There also would be an attempt to impeach him.

It never looked likely, however, that Zuma could be removed without being voted out. The state of the nation address, which Zuma had been determined to deliver at the opening of Parliament, at the last minute was postponed as, otherwise, the EFF would have had a field day disrupting it. With Zuma continuing to look for ways to delay his exit and for protection thereafter, he was given an ultimatum to resign or be recalled.

On 13 February 2018, the National Executive Committee of the party announced their decision to recall Zuma, as they had Thabo Mbeki, with Magashule having to fall in line behind those who had swung over to Ramaphosa. Foreseeing that he might still refuse to resign, Zuma was told that, if necessary, the ANC would table their own no-confidence vote in Parliament to remove him. After a rambling, brazen, shameless and self-pitying TV interview, in which he too kept asking, 'What have I done wrong?' on the evening of 14 February Zuma resigned, paving the way for Cyril Ramaphosa to take over as the new President of South Africa.

* * *

In the new government, David Mabuza became Deputy President and Nkosazana Dlamini-Zuma accepted a position in the presidency. Ramaphosa took the hugely positive steps of bringing back Nhlanhla Nene as Finance Minister and Pravin Gordhan as Minister of Public Enterprises, and several compromised ministers left. Gwede Mantashe became Minister of Mineral Resources, but the continued presence in the government of Gigaba and Bathabile ('We all have skeletons') Dlamini showed that this was no clean sweep. He will now be able to change the heads of the NPA, Hawks and SARS, restoring the credibility of those institutions.

A major effort will be made to attract investment back into the country and to achieve higher rates of economic growth. With Pravin Gordhan, Ramaphosa should now be able to end the looting of the state-owned enterprises and drastically to limit theft at the centre. What he almost certainly will not be able to do is to end endemic corruption in the ANC-run provinces, of the kind at present so prevalent in virtually all of them. The Democratic Alliance, for all the limitations in its national support, has a far better record from this point of view. Mmusi Maimane argued that the problem has been 'not Jacob Zuma, but the ANC'. From this perspective, it remains to be seen if the ANC will turn out to be reformable.

The real significance of Ramaphosa's incredibly narrow victory was in pulling South Africa back from the brink. A continuance of the Zupta regime could not have been sustained without measures to muzzle first the press and then the judiciary. The country would have faced a real possibility that 2019 might be the last free and fair election and the pressures on the Independent Election Commission in the run-up to it would have been alarming.

For the avoidance of this denouement, the country owes a huge debt to its remarkable free press, to its incorruptible judiciary and to the most effective agencies of civil society I have ever witnessed operating anywhere. Thanks to their efforts, as *The Economist* pointed out, what is unusual about South Africa is not that corruption thrived, but that it did so *in plain sight*.

The sky has darkened dramatically for the Guptas, the Guptaleaks having proved a disaster for them. They are being pursued by Eskom and the Industrial Development Corporation for nearly 1 billion rand – a modest fraction of their earnings from the state-owned enterprises over the past five years. Their businesses in South Africa have imploded or been abandoned, leaving them holding on to the vast sums they have transferred abroad, and they are facing probes by the US and other overseas financial institutions. On the day of the resignation of their chief protector, the Hawks arrested senior Gupta associates over the fraud in the Free State. As the net, very belatedly, started to close around them, the Gupta brothers and Duduzane Zuma were reported to have left the country.

The looting of the South African state, however, has not primarily been a result of the Guptas. Corruption had become endemic before they appeared on the scene. Maimane described them as 'sordid people exploiting a vulnerable country'.[69] They were merely exploiting an opportunity, though in the process holding in thrall a President and many others besides. The responsibility lies squarely with those in the state-owned companies who diverted contracts in their direction, and the ministers who appointed them and de facto approved their activities.

The ultimate responsibility self-evidently rests with their mentor in chief, Number One, the 'one-man wrecking ball', who will be remembered not for the honourable role he played in the liberation struggle and in trying to end the violence in Natal, but for having compromised the ideals of Mandela,

Tambo and Sisulu and for having inflicted untold damage on the economy, ethics and people of his country.

In the end, history is made not just by historical forces, but by individuals, for ill in the cases of Zuma and Mugabe, for good in those of Mandela, De Klerk and those who distinguished themselves in South Africa's recent travails – Thuli Madonsela, Pravin Gordhan and a host of others. So over to you, Cyril, my friend from apartheid days and South African Breweries. We all would like to see you help to turn your magnificent country back into a more hopeful one.

ACKNOWLEDGEMENTS

This account is based partly on my own experience of dealing with successive South African governments since majority rule in 1994 and conversations with many of the principal actors in this drama. But no one writing about the current state of affairs in South Africa can fail to pay tribute to the meticulously researched study by the Public Affairs Research Institute under Professor Ivor Chipkin, *Betrayal of the Promise*, published in May 2017.

As set out in Chapter XX, the South African media have distinguished themselves in their reporting and analysis of these events. I am indebted especially to the *Daily Maverick*, the *Mail and Guardian*, *Business Day*, *News24* the Johannesburg *Sunday Times* and the *Financial Mail* and to the remarkable group of investigative journalists associated with the amaBhungane Centre for Investigative Journalism.

Self-evidently, I am indebted also to the authors listed in the footnotes, and especially to the authors and works mentioned in Chapter XX, all of which have made an important contribution to the present-day history of South Africa.

I am very grateful to Pravin Gordhan for his comments on the chapters about state capture, to John Battersby for his help with Chapters XX and XXI and to Dario Milo and Professor Ivor Chipkin for their comments on the manuscript.

I am grateful, very especially, to Zapiro for allowing this account to be illustrated by his work, which contains within it an exceptionally accurate portrayal of the heroes, heroines and villains of this story.

My thanks are due to James Stephens, Olivia Beattie, Laurie de Decker and their colleagues at Biteback Publishing for their help and support, to Douglas Cooper for his assistance with the manuscript and to Marie-France Renwick for her help with the illustrations.

ENDNOTES

NOTES TO INTRODUCTION
1 Thandeka Gqubule, *No Longer Whispering to Power*, Jonathan Ball, 2017

NOTES TO CHAPTER I
2 Dikgang Moseneke, *My Own Liberator*, Picador Africa, 2016, p. 267
3 John Carlin, *Knowing Mandela*, Atlantic Books, 2013
4 Tony Leon, *On the Contrary*, Jonathan Ball, 2008, p. 94
5 Robin Renwick, *Helen Suzman*, Biteback and Jonathan Ball, 2014, p. 192
6 Andrew Feinstein, *After the Party*, Jonathan Ball, 2007

NOTES TO CHAPTER II
7 James-Brent Styan, *Blackout: The Eskom Crisis*, Jonathan Ball, 2015

NOTES TO CHAPTER III
8 Mark Gevisser, *Thabo Mbeki: The Dream Deferred*, Jonathan Ball, 2007, p. xli
9 Ronnie Kasrils, *A Simple Man*, Jacana, 2017, pp. 105–6

NOTES TO CHAPTER IV
10 *Mail and Guardian*, 13 December 2012
11 *Betrayal of the Promise: How South Africa is Being Stolen*, The Public Affairs Research Institute (PARI), May 2017
12 Helen Zille, *Not Without a Fight*, Penguin Books, 2016, pp. 324–5

NOTES TO CHAPTER V
13 On the Zuma first term, see Richard Calland, *The Zuma Years*, Zebra Press, 2013

NOTES TO CHAPTER VI
14 *Betrayal of the Promise*, op. cit.
15 For this and other useful background on the Guptas, see Pieter-Louis Myburgh, *The Republic of Gupta*, Penguin, 2017
16 *News24*, 1 November 2017

17 *State of Capture* report and *City Press*, 9 October 2016

NOTES TO CHAPTER VII
18 Affidavit by Mentor to the South African Police Service, 9 May 2016; Vytjie Mentor, *No Holy Cows*, 2017
19 *Business Day*, 9 June 2011
20 *Betrayal of the Promise*, op. cit.
21 amaBhungane, 19 June 2016
22 Jacques Pauw, *The President's Keepers*, Tafelberg, 2017
23 *Daily Maverick*, 1 June 2017
24 *Betrayal of the Promise*, p. 13; *News24*, 14 November 2017

NOTES TO CHAPTER VIII
25 Adriaan Basson and Pieter du Toit, *Enemy of the People*, Jonathan Ball, 2017, p. 88. Dramat letter to the Minister of Police, 24 December 2014. Jacques Pauw, op. cit., pp. 252–4
26 Vusi Pikhole and Mandy Weiner, *My Second Initiation*, Picador Africa, 2013. See also Glynnis Breytenbach, *Rule of Law*, Pan Macmillan, 2017. Jacques Pauw, op. cit., provides a comprehensive account of the neutering of all the main investigative agencies and the systematic smearing and ousting of the most effective investigators in Zuma's second term.
27 For General Booysen's side of the story, see Jessica Pitchford, *Blood on their Hands* Pan Macmillan, 2016
28 Adriaan Basson and Pieter du Toit, op. cit., p. x
29 Jacques Pauw, op. cit., p. 96
30 Johann van Loggerenberg with Adrian Lackay, *Rogue: The inside story of SARS's elite crime-busting unit*, Jonathan Ball, 2016
31 amaBunghane, 16 May 2017. Reuters, 13 July 2017

NOTES TO CHAPTER IX
32 Adriaan Basson and Pieter du Toit, op. cit., p. 160
33 *Business Day*, 21 November 2016

NOTES TO CHAPTER X
34 Crispian Olver, *How to Steal a City: The Battle for Nelson Mandela Bay*, Jonathan Ball, 2017

NOTES TO CHAPTER XI
35 *Business Day*, 25 August 2016
36 *Mail and Guardian*, 18 November 2016
37 *Mail and Guardian*, 25 November 2016

NOTES TO CHAPTER XIII
38 Crispian Olver, op. cit., p. 229

NOTES TO CHAPTER XIV
39 On the authenticity of the Guptaleaks, see Justice Malala in *Times Live*, 19 June 2017

40 Published by amaBhungane on 1 June 2017
41 amaBhungane, 1 June 2017
42 *City Press*, 30 July 2017
43 *Business Day*, 9 November 2017

NOTES TO CHAPTER XV
44 *The Times*, 23 September 2017
45 *Business Day*, 20 October 2017
46 Jacques Pauw, op. cit.
47 *New York Times*, 17 December 2012; Jacques Pauw, op. cit., pp. 107–8
48 *News24*, 20 February 2018

NOTES TO CHAPTER XVI
49 Helen Zille, op. cit.
50 Published by Jonathan Ball, 2017

NOTES TO CHAPTER XVII
51 *Mail and Guardian*, 19 September 2013

NOTES TO CHAPTER XVIII
52 Alec Russell, *After Mandela*, Windmill Books, 2010
53 Roger Southall, *Liberation Movements in Power*, James Currey, 2013
54 Stephen Ellis, *External Mission: The ANC in Exile*, Hurst, 2012
55 Padraig O'Malley, *Shades of Difference*, Viking, 2007, p. 11

NOTES TO CHAPTER XIX
56 Moeletsi Mbeki, *Architects of Poverty*, Central Books, 2009
57 *Financial Times*, 19 September 2017

NOTES TO CHAPTER XX
58 Thandeka Gqubule testifying in Parliament, 11 December 2016
59 *Mail and Guardian*, 4 September 2014
60 Jacques Pauw, op. cit.
61 *Mail and Guardian*, 28 November 2014
62 ANC statement on 21 March 2016
63 Alex Boraine, *What's Gone Wrong?*, Jonathan Ball, 2014; Justice Malala, *We Have Now Begun Our Descent*, Jonathan Ball, 2015
64 R. W. Johnson, *How Long Will South Africa Survive?*, Hurst and Company, 2015; Ferial Haffajee, *What If There Were No Whites in South Africa?*, Picador Africa, 2015; Pieter-Louis Myburgh, op. cit.; Adriaan Basson and Pieter du Toit, op. cit.
65 Moeletsi Mbeki, op. cit.

NOTES TO CHAPTER XXI
On the judiciary in post-apartheid South Africa, see Edwin Cameron, *Justice: A Personal Account*, Tafelberg, 2014; Dikgang Moseneke, *My Own Liberator*, Picador Africa, 2016; and Albie Sachs, *The Free Diary of Albie Sachs*, Random House, 2004.

NOTES TO CHAPTER XXII

66 Anthony Butler, *Cyril Ramaphosa*, Jacana, 2008; Ray Hartley *Ramaphosa: The Man who would be King*, Jonathan Ball, 2017

NOTES TO CHAPTER XXIII

67 Prepared remarks at the University of Pretoria Gordon Institute of Business Science 19 August 2017. See also Carien du Plessis, *Woman in the Wings*, Penguin, 2017
68 Sizwe sama Yende, *Eerie Assignment*, Lebedi House, 2017

NOTES TO CHAPTER XXIV

69 *Bloomberg*, 11 November 2017

INDEX